THE RAV
The World of
Rabbi Joseph B. Soloveitchik
VOLUME TWO

THE RAV

The World of
Rabbi Joseph B. Soloveitchik

VOLUME TWO

by

Aaron Rakeffet-Rothkoff

Edited by

Joseph Epstein

Photography Editor

Irwin Albert

KTAV Publishing House

By the Same Author

Bernard Revel: Builder of American Jewish Orthodoxy

The Silver Era: Rabbi Eliezer Silver and His Generation

Rakafot Aharon: A Collection of Published Scholarship in the Fields of Halakhah and Jewish History (2 vols.)

Rakeffet-Rothkoff, Aaron.
    The Rav: the world of Rabbi Joseph B. Soloveitchik / by Aaron
    Rakeffet-Rothkoff ; edited by Joseph Epstein ; photography editor,
    Irwin Albert.
    p.   cm.
    Includes bibliographical references and index.
    ISBN 978-088125-614-7 (v. 1). —ISBN 978-088125-615-4 (v.2)
1. Soloveitchik, Joseph Dov. 2. Rabbis—United States Biography.
3. Judaism. I. Epstein, Joseph. II. Title.
BM755.S593R35   1999
296.8'32'092—dc21
[B]   99-37285
                                                             CIP

KTAV PUBLISHING HOUSE
527 Empire Blvd.
Brooklyn, NY 11225

Website: www.ktav.com
Email: orders@ktav.com
Ph: (718)972-5449 / Fax: (718)972-6307

Printing year 2018

Contents

COLLEAGUES AND DISCIPLES

YESHIVA UNIVERSITY

Table of Photographs

YESHIVA UNIVERSITY

Family Impressions

11.01 A Child's Total Faith

Related by the Rav in his lecture on Parshat Hayei Sarah (Genesis 23:1–25:18) to the Yeshiva University Rabbinic Alumni, Yeshiva University, November 12, 1973.

In the English language the word "faith" is profaned when applied to man. For instance, it is improper to say "I have faith" in another human being. From a strictly philosophical and philological viewpoint, no one can have faith in another man. It is blasphemy to say "I have faith in man." Confidence, yes, but not faith. To have faith in people means the deification of man. It is sacrilegious.

Faith means an absolute act which results in complete reliance without any reservations, conditions, or qualifications. Faith means complete trust. The person in whom I have faith will not betray me—never, never, never!

Faith in God also requires something else of us. Faith in God requires that the faithful suspend judgment from time to time. It is not only the surrender of the body but of the mind. Emunah [faith] confronts man with the challenge to suspend his intuitive judgment and to act irrationally and illogically. At times man must act in a certain fashion even though he does not understand why he is required to conduct himself in such a manner.

Faith confronts man with the challenge to suspend his judgment and to deny the principle or norm he has been preaching all

1

his life. Only a man-child can surrender and suspend his judgment.

I remember observing a little boy who had almost unlimited faith in his mother. Whenever he was asked a question he would in turn inquire: "What did mama say?" Though he was a very capable and intelligent child, he would suspend his own judgment because of his unlimited trust in his mother. This is exactly the way that an adult should act in his relationship with God.

However, an adult is not capable of such behavior. Who can do it? Only a child. So the adult has to rise and wake up the child within him. He must have this child perform on his behalf an act of total faith. Then the adult must say to the child within him: "I will join you!"

11.02 A Mother's Memory

Related by the Rav in the first Tonya Soloveitchik Memorial Lecture, Yeshiva University, March 10, 1968.

There are two types of memories. There is an image memory where I recall the past but the recollection does not motivate me today. There is also an event memory where I not only recall the past but also relive it. Old pictures come to life and the past becomes tangible.

A father has an image memory. He recalls the past but does not relive it. A mother has an event memory. She not only recalls but relives the past. My wife used to show me pictures of our children when they were small. She could recall where and when the pictures were taken. She could recall all the circumstances and even the details about the clothes they were wearing. A father lives in the present with his children. A mother, however, dwells in both the present and the past.

11.03 Senior Citizens

Related by the Rav in a lecture on Shavuot, Yeshiva University, June 2, 1981.

Interesting is the sentence authored by King David: "The days of our years are seventy years, or by reason of special courage they are eighty years" [Psalms 90:10]. Not everyone lives to be seventy. Only some do. If one has the courage, he may attain the age of eighty.

The late Yaakov Herzog [1921–1972; Israel's minister plenipotentiary in Washington] told me the following story. When he was in Washington, he was once invited to dinner by John Foster Dulles [1888–1959; U.S. Secretary of State]. So Herzog went, and Dulles told him that the main reason for the invitation was not politics. It was rather that he wanted Herzog to explain to him a sentence in the Bible. Dulles was then in his seventies, and he wanted to know the meaning of "or by reason of special courage they are eighty years." What is the special courage that one must possess in order to live eighty years? This sentence disturbed him, and Dulles wanted to understand what man can do in order to live to be eighty.

What does this sentence actually mean? Never mind Dulles now. It means that in order to reach eighty and to live with dignity, you have to be a courageous person. How does this courage express itself? First of all, in admitting that you are eighty years old. Some people do not admit their age. They act as if they were still twenty. First of all, admitting one's age. Secondly, in having the courage to carry on, even though certain faculties are indeed affected by one's age. One must go on. It is even more than that; it is the courage not to get frightened whenever one feels a pain. Usually, an old man develops hypochondria. Any change that occurs in him frightens him. The same is true intellectually. An old man should not say that he cannot create anymore, that he cannot carry on; that he has to retire now. This is also cowardice.

There is a tendency on the part of our elderly or senior citizens to say that they are not responsible anymore. We cannot accept responsibility. I am eighty years old and have retired from business. What can I do at this age? The older person simply thinks that he has been relieved of the awareness of responsibility. But awareness of responsibility is intrinsic to our "I–human" awareness. It is part of the human ego, that I am here. The old man forgets about this. He is not responsible. He cannot give charity because he has willed his money to his children. He cannot go to a shiur at night because he had a pain in his leg the night before. Old age in modern life is basically cowardice and laziness.

That is why the psalmist tells us that if you have courage you will achieve a much more pleasant old age than the modern concept. Nowadays, the greatest problem for the aged is what to do with their time. Years ago, man also got old, but then there was no question about what to do with time. They used to go to shul and study a blat of Gemara. I knew people who were eighty-five or ninety. They used to come to the bet medrash where I studied. They came regularly every night. They used to take a Gemara out, light a candle, and study for a couple of hours. They had a feeling for time. Time was precious for them, as it is to everyone. There was no problem about what to do with time.

One old man recently told me that, thank God, he today has no financial problems. This had always been his main preoccupation, and now he does not know what to do with his time. This is his main problem. I told him that with your time you can do a lot. Just be careful that the Almighty does not take time away from you! [Laughter.]

11.04 The Torah Scroll Fell

Related by the Rav in his lecture on Parshat Beha'alotkha (Numbers 8:1–12:16) at an RCA Dinner honoring Rabbi Israel Klavan, June 10, 1974.

[Because of the complaints of the people in the wilderness, Moses intuitively knew that his generation would not enter the Holy Land]. The people were not worthy of entering the land. Suddenly the parshah [section] of "When the Ark would journey" [Numbers 10:35] found itself displaced, dislocated. The distance to the Holy Land suddenly became very long. Of course, there was no edict yet concerning the forty years that the people would have to spend in the desert. But Moses felt intuitively that the great march had come to an end. Hopes he had would be unfulfilled, visions he had would never be realized, and his prayers would be rejected. He knew all this. I will tell you frankly, I do not have to say Moses. Of course, Moses was a master of prophecy even when God did not reveal it to him. I remember from my own experiences during the illness of my wife. She was sick for four years. I am a realist, and it is very hard to fool me; not even doctors can fool me. Nevertheless, I was convinced that somehow she would manage to get out of it [her illness]. I lived with hope and tremendous unlimited faith.

However, I remember it was the last Yom Kippur before she died. It was Kol Nidrei, and I was holding a Sefer Torah for Kol Nidrei. Then the hazzan finished Kol Nidrei and the Shehehiyanu vikiyamanu vihegiyanu lazeman ha-zeh blessing ["granted us life and sustenance and permitted us to reach this season"]. I turned over the Sefer Torah to a talmid of mine and told him to put it into the aron ha-kodesh. He put it into the aron ha-kodesh. Apparently, he did not put it in properly. I don't know exactly what happened, but the Sefer Torah slipped and fell. It did not fall on the floor, but in the aron ha-kodesh.

At that moment I knew that my wife would not survive. It was sealed. Don't ask me how I guessed it. Don't ask me why. I felt it was sealed. Nothing would help. Indeed it was so.

When the people—"the people took to seeking complaints" [Numbers 11:1]—began to complain and weep, Moses knew. He knew he would never see the Land of Israel. Never, never!

11.05 Clairvoyance

Related by the Rav in the Tonya Soloveitchik Memorial Lecture on "Insights into Megillat Esther," Yeshiva University, March 14, 1973.

Mordecai, the teacher and educator, seized the initiative. His clairvoyant gaze taught him what was in store for his people. He foresaw the great tragedy. He was not struck suddenly by the disaster. Mordecai refused to leave the palace. He sat constantly in the king's gate: "And when the maidens were gathered together the second time, and Mordecai sat in the king's gate" [Esther 2:19]. Why was he sitting in the gate? What was he waiting for? Why could he not leave the gate, go to the bet ha-medrash, join his colleagues, and at least say a shiur ?

Do you know why he was afraid to leave the gate? I understand it, unfortunately, because I had a similar tragic experience. Mordecai refused to leave the gate because he feared that something horrible, something monstrous, might occur during his absence. It is a strange feeling, an absurd feeling—as if one's presence could prevent the disaster from striking. You know it is wrong.

I experienced a similar kind of foreboding during the illness of Mrs. Soloveitchik. I never left her sickbed. Why? It is not that she needed me. She did not need me. I knew instinctively that if I left her, death would snatch her from me before I had a chance to return. That is exactly what happened to me on Thursday, the Fast of Esther, six years ago!

11.06 The Need to Pray

Related by the Rav in his essay "Majesty and Humility," Tradition, [32:2], pp. 32–33.

With the arrival of the dark night of the soul, in moments of agony and black despair, when living becomes ugly and absurd, plainly nauseating, when man loses his sense of beauty and majesty, God addresses him, not from infinity but from the infinitesimal, not from the vast stretches of the universe but from a single spot in the darkness which surrounds suffering man, from within the black despair itself.

Eleven years ago my wife lay on her deathbed and I watched her dying, day by day, hour by hour. Medically, I could do very little for her. All I could do was to pray. However, I could not pray in the hospital; somehow I could not find God in the whitewashed, long corridors among the interns and the nurses. However, the need for prayer was great; I could not live without gratifying this need. The moment I returned home I would rush to my room, fall on my knees, and pray fervently. God, in those moments, appeared not as the exalted, majestic King, but rather as a humble, close friend, brother, father. In such moments of black despair, He was not far from me; He was right there in the dark room. I felt His warm hand, so to speak, on my shoulder; I hugged His knees, so to speak. He was with me in the narrow confines of a small room, taking up no space at all. God's abiding in a fenced-in finite locus manifests His humility and love for man. In such moments *humilitas Dei*, which resides in the humblest and tiniest of places, addresses itself to man.

11.07 Withdrawal and Self-Limitation

Related by the Rav in his lecture on "The Profundity of Jewish Folk Wisdom," at the RCA Annual Convention, June 20, 1977.

The Torah requires of the Jew that he emulate the concept of tzimtzum, or withdrawal and self-limitation. At times he must even be capable of withdrawing from himself. Let me give you some examples of this from my own experience.

My wife died on the Fast of Esther. It was a Thursday. She was buried on Friday. I was very attached to her, and part of myself went into the grave with her.

I came home, took off my shoes, and sat down on the floor. I began to observe the seven days of mourning. This observance was therapeutic for me. The fact that I could sit down on the floor and cry was redemptive and cathartic.

Suddenly it was Sunday and Purim had arrived. I had to get up from the shivah observance, put on my shoes, and celebrate Purim. Did I have the strength to do this? No. But the halakhah required it. This was tzimtzum.

I was witness to a similar event. Someone died on Erev Pesach [the day before Passover]. He was buried late in the afternoon. The mourners barely had a chance to rip keriah [tear their clothes], take off their shoes, and sit shivah for half an hour. Suddenly the festival began. The mourners were commanded to forget the person they had just buried. They had to dress up and rejoice at the Seder. They had to recite the blessings with great joy. Can a human being do this? The Torah believed that the Jew could. This is the concept of tzimtzum. At times, you must even withdraw from yourself.

I get many questions regarding birth control. I am generally stringent in these matters. I know that it requires inner strength on the part of the women to heed my decisions. Many had to discontinue their education as a result. Others had to give up their jobs. They gave up many things. They withdrew and surrendered to the halakhah.

There are many examples of this principle in our religious life. I hate schnapps. I cannot drink it. Yet on Purim I force myself to.

I will tell you a story about an esrog that will also illustrate the principle of tzimtzum, or withdrawal and self-limitation.

It was the first year my father came to Warsaw. I believe it was in 1921. There was a shortage of esrogim in Warsaw that year, and my father spent a small fortune to buy a *mehudar* [beautiful] esrog. We did not have too much at the time, and it was a real expense. My father treated the esrog like a firstborn child, with much tenderness and love. He placed it in a silver case.

This is a true story and not a legend. The first night, my sister Shulamith, who now lives in Boston, apparently inspected the esrog and dropped it. The pittum [tip] fell off and its beauty was impaired.

My father did not say a word. My sister became hysterical. My father calmed her down and said: "Do not be hysterical. You did not want to drop it. It was a mistake. An esrog without a pittim may also have value on Sukkot under certain circumstances."

Is this not tzimtzum? To spend the five or ten dollars at that time was one thing. But to contain oneself and not get angry was withdrawal par excellence and a perfect example of tzimtzum. This is not a hasidisher maaseh. This is a true story.

11.08 Mourning His Father

Related by the Rav in a personal letter to Rabbi Israel Rosenberg.[1] The original letter is located in the Rosenberg file at the Jewish Theological Seminary in New York. There is a copy in the archives of the Institute of Contemporary Jewry of the Hebrew University, Jerusalem. Dated erev Pesach 5701 [April 11, 1941], the letter was written in Hebrew.

[This letter was written as the first Passover approached after the death of Rabbi Moshe Soloveichik on 3 Shevat 5701 (January 31, 1941).]

Writing is difficult for me today. My soul is poured out within me [Job 30:16] when I recall erev Pesach in the past. I see the image of my saintly father, my teacher, the Gaon of Israel, making the preparations for the festival. I think of his radiant countenance as he conducted the Seder and discharged the mitzvot of the night in great joy. His soul would overflow with spiritual splendor in honor of the Almighty. This year the holy ark has been broken, the celestial beings have conquered the mortals, and my saintly father, my teacher, has been called to the heavenly yeshiva. His family remains in a state of loneliness, despair, and mourning. The joy of the festival is gone, and our holiday has turned into lamentation.

Perhaps I am transgressing the mishnaic ruling that "one should not stir up wailing for his dead nor hold a lamentation for him thirty days before a festival" [Moed Katan 1:5]. What can I do, though? My sorrow overwhelms me. I am in the status of one unavoidably prevented from doing what is proper. My heart compels me to weep. To whom can I pour out my pain and affliction if not to you, my dear friend!

1. Rabbi Israel Rosenberg (1875–1956) was a leader of the Yiddish-speaking Orthodox rabbinate and particularly active in the Union of Orthodox Rabbis. For some information about him, see Rakeffet-Rothkoff, *The Silver Era*, pp. 63, 104, and 67 fn. 23.

11.09 The Concept of Mourning

Related by the Rav in a lecture on Parshat Ve-Yechi (Genesis 47:28–50:26), Yeshiva University, December 23, 1980.

I have never understood what took place when Robert Kennedy was murdered. When his mother was informed, she went to a tailor to have a new dress prepared for the funeral service that would take place at the cathedral. This is what Maimonides meant when he declared that those who do not mourn properly "are cruel" [Hilkhot Avel 13:12]. If you want an example, this is the best example. How was it possible, at such a moment, for a mother who had already lost a daughter and two sons [President John F. Kennedy, and another son, Joseph, killed in action in World War II] to think in terms of fashion and about the dress she was to wear in the church? However, this is the modern morality.

Nevertheless, we cannot move totally in the opposite direction and do everything in an extreme contrary fashion. To exaggerate mourning and act in a crazed manner is also wrong. What the Laws of Mourning seek to accomplish is to guide us to act logically and within certain standards that the Torah has formulated. This concept applies both at times of distress and also in times of excitement and rapture, such as marriage. This is the concept behind the laws of the seven days of mourning and the seven days of rejoicing for the bride and groom.

11.10 Longing for the Departed

Related by the Rav in his Teshuvah Drashah, September 1968. Published in Al ha-Teshuvah *[8:5], pp. 180–181 and* Soloveitchik on Repentance *[37:6], pp. 259–260.*

The longing for one who has died and is gone forever is worse than the torment of the depths of the grave. The soul is overcome and shattered by fierce longing for the departed. Before this Rosh Hashanah, in my mind I saw my father, the Gaon [Reb Moshe Soloveichik] of blessed memory, standing before me. He was the only rebbe and teacher I ever had. I opened my heart to him and said: "My father, my master, I have so many new insights that I have developed on the laws of the Temple sacrifices on Yom ha-Kippurim, on the topic of *mitzvot lav lehenot nitnu* [mitzvot are not intended for personal enjoyment], and on the laws of blowing the shofar. I have ideas that would have pleased you and brought you enjoyment; some that you would not have accepted and would have refuted."

That is how I spoke to my father in my vision, although I knew that I would never receive a response to my words. Oh, how much I would give to exchange words of Torah with my father for only five minutes. But I know that this man who loved me so much and whom I was so close to is now so distant. My heart breaks with longing to speak with him for only five minutes, a period of time which we did not know how to properly value when he was still with us.

The same is true regarding my mother and my wife. A few days ago, I was writing this annual sermon on repentance [teshuvah drashah]. I always used to talk about it with my wife; she would help me develop and polish my ideas. Again this year, while I was writing this lecture, I wanted to ask her: "Could you please help me? Should I shorten this idea? Should I expand on this point? Should I stress this concept or another one?"

I asked my wife, but there was no response. If there was a reply it was lost in the rustling of the trees and did not reach me.

Educating American Jewry

12.01 Abaye and Rava

Related by the Rav in his keynote address at the annual convention of the American Mizrachi Organization, November 17, 1955 (Yiddish).

On Motzai Shabbos, I say a shiur in Boston. Over three hundred young people come to every shiur. When I came to Boston, there were not even five people there who knew that Abaye and Rava once lived.

12.02 Responsibility for the Future

Related by the Rav in a lecture to the Hevra Shas in Boston, Mass., March 19, 1972.

Abraham is important because he is willing to pass on his traditions to his children and grandchildren. Whatever Abraham has achieved, he wishes to transmit to his children. Abraham wants to pass on his way of life to his descendants. "For I have known him [Abraham] because he commands his children and his household after him, that they may keep the way of the Lord" [Genesis 18:19].

This is exactly what American Jewry was lacking thirty and forty years ago. American Jews did not understand this idea. They thought that one is only responsible for oneself. When I came to

Boston there were many Jews who were perfect as far as responsibility for their own lives is concerned. They observed the Torah and were very careful about their religious conduct. There were many scholars among them, and some were actually fine lamdanim. I used to deliver drashot which were much more complicated than those I now deliver. I got away from that style of preaching and homiletics.

These people did not understand one major aspect of Judaism. The individual is responsible, not only for himself, but for the future. Perhaps his main responsibility is to the future and the countless generations that will come after him. The motto of the Jew has always been the importance of the Mesorah, or tradition: pass on and transmit. You received from your father and must transmit these traditions to your children!

12.03 Appreciating Jewish Education

Related by the Rav in his annual Yahrzeit Shiur in memory of his father, Rabbi Moshe Soloveichik, Yeshiva University, January 17, 1945. (Yiddish).

I lived for many years in Europe in Jewish surroundings and in Jewish milieus. Yet I never truly felt the beauty of the Sabbath at that time. I resided in Warsaw and saw all the stores closed on the Sabbath. I observed the hasidim in Warsaw with shtreimels on their heads on the Sabbath. Nevertheless, it is only in America that I feel the true beauty of the Sabbath. Here all the stores are open on the Sabbath. Everything is like a weekday, and there is no Sabbath spirit. When I come into a home where the Sabbath candles are aglow and the table is set for the repast, then I appreciate the holiness of the Sabbath. The contrast makes the Sabbath all the more precious and dear, and its message all the more timely. Then I start to wonder how a Jew can live without the sanctity of the Sabbath in his life!

It is here in America that I first started to properly appreciate Jewish education. This morning, on my porch, I heard Jewish children speaking about the bacon and eggs they had for breakfast. When I come into a day school and see Jewish children reciting the Shema and making blessings before they eat, I truly value Torah education. It is the contrast which makes it so worthwhile!

12.04 Recreating the Destroyed World

Related by the Rav in his annual Yahrzeit Shiur in memory of his father, Rabbi Moshe Soloveichik, Yeshiva University, January 6, 1957. (Yiddish).

The Midrash relates that God created and destroyed many worlds before He allowed this world to remain in existence [Midrash Rabbah to Genesis 3:9]. Some of the earlier worlds were even more beautiful than the present one, but the Creator eliminated them. He then went ahead and created this world, which has endured.

What are the rabbis teaching us? What does it mean that God created and destroyed worlds? After all, He could have made this world to begin with, so why did God experiment with the earlier creations?

This Midrash conveys a very important concept to us. A person must know how to continue building and creating in life, even if his previous efforts are demolished. He cannot lose hope and must not give up. He must go ahead and build again. Perhaps the new world created will not be as beautiful as the earlier one; nevertheless, he must continue to rebuild. God was able to say about His final world: "Behold, it was very good" [Genesis 1:31]. That is, that the final, permanent world is very good, even though some of the earlier ones may have been even more beautiful. They are gone, and we must maximize what we have now.

Today, we must judge the Torah world we are reconstructing after the Holocaust as "very good," even though earlier ones may have been more beautiful. I am very proud of the Maimonides Day School in Boston. Many times I test the students on the Humash and Rashi that they are studying. I am impressed by their knowledge and inspired by their achievements. Then I ask myself why I am so excited by such small accomplishments. After all, I saw the giants of European Torah Jewry before the Holocaust. I discussed talmudic topics with my grandfather, Reb Chaim Soloveitchik of Brisk. I visited with Reb Chaim Ozer Grodzinski [1863–1940] in Vilna [Rabbi Grodzinski was the author of three volumes of responsa literature entitled *Ahiezer*]. I debated with Reb Shimon Shkop [1860–1940; Rabbi Shkop was the leading Lithuanian rosh ha-yeshiva in that period] concerning the explanation of certain talmudic passages. I spent entire nights with Reb Baruch Ber Leibowitz of Kaminetz [1866–1939; Rabbi Leibowitz was the closest student of Reb Chaim Soloveitchik] attempting to comprehend difficult rulings in the Code of Maimonides. Why am I so impressed that American youngsters can master a little Humash with Rashi, the rudiments of Torah study?

This is the message of the re-creation of destroyed worlds. A Jew has to know how to emulate God, and, like God, to continue to create even after his former world has been eradicated. True, what I have in Boston may not be as beautiful as the European Torah world before the Holocaust. Nevertheless, it is the world we now have. We have to continue to build it and not look back. We must not be cynical, and we should direct our attention and efforts to the future. We must look ahead!

12.05 Attitudes of the Modern Jew

Related by the Rav in an address published in Yemei Zikaron *[17:5], pp. 122–123. (Hebrew).*

I often reflect on the attitude of the modern Jew. On one hand, I am continually fascinated at the vast resources, ability, concentration, and intellect he invests in order to satiate his material desires. On the other hand, I am amazed at how this same Jew shuts out the spiritual values of Judaism through a selective dullness, insensitivity, and numbness to all things holy. I am continually reminded of the rabbinic saying: "Cursed are the wicked, for wherever they raise their eyes they see lewdness and unchaste behavior" [cf. Avot de-Rebbe Natan, version A, chap. 36]. A life of lewdness means a life devoid of inherent meaning, an existence bereft of spirituality and divine splendor. They lead a life totally dedicated to the satisfaction of their bodily urges and material desires.

I observe the modern Jew dedicate vast emotional resources, talent, and ingenuity to acquire material possessions. For these goals he knows full well how to maximize his creativity, to plan ahead and keep his ambitions vivid in his race to acquire material possessions. When it comes to acquiring our spiritual inheritance and matters of sanctity, however, his keen material senses suddenly become myopic, and his enterprising disposition turns insipid and uninterested. His analytical ability becomes critical and doubtful and does not allow him to take any chances.

When I consider these pronounced contradictory tendencies, I am always reminded of the teachings of the Tana de-Vei Eliyahu Zuta [chap. 14]:

> I was once walking from place to place, and I chanced upon a person who was not learned either in the Scriptures or in the Mishnah and was constantly mocking the traditions. I engaged him in conversation and asked him how he would justify his behavior before his Heavenly Father on Judgment Day. He declared that he would claim that heaven had not granted him the ability to comprehend the Scriptures and the Mishnah. I then asked him about the nature of his profession. He explained that he was a fisherman. I asked him how he knew how to prepare the nets and trap the fish. He responded that this type of knowledge had been granted to him. I then told him that if he had this ability, he could certainly master the words of the Torah, about which the Scriptures state: "But the word is very near unto you, in your mouth and in your heart, that you may observe it" [Deuteronomy 30:14].

One of the greatest irreverences of the modern Jew is the unworthy antithesis between the ability he devotes to his personal affairs and his indifferent, fidgety approach to Judaism.

12.06 The American Jew

Related by the Rav in his lecture on "The Abridged Havinenu Prayer," at the RCA Midwinter Conference, February 7, 1968.

The problem with the American Jew is that he is not sensitive to Torah values. He must understand that human happiness does not depend upon comfort. The American Jew follows a philosophy which equates religion with making Jewish life more comfortable and convenient. It enables the Jew to have more pleasure in life. This deemphasizes Judaism's spiritual values. What the rabbi should do is to somehow expose the Jew to proper Torah Judaism. This cannot be accomplished by preaching and sermonizing. Many times, as I know from my own experience, they accomplish precisely the opposite.

However, by exposing the American Jew to Torah Judaism you will touch his heart. Once he is sensitized, the American Jew is brave enough to respond to the moral challenge. The American Jew has heroic attributes and is much more courageous than the Lithuanian or Polish Jews were. The American Jew will have the courage to seek the proper alternative once he understands the demands of Torah and mitzvot. That is the meaning of the passage in the Amidah: "Restore us, our Father, to Thy Torah; draw us near, our King, to Thy service" [*Daily Prayer Book*, trans. Philip Birnbaum, p. 86].

Many times, an American Jew comes to me and says that he cannot close his business on the Sabbath but still wants to come to shul. Shall he go to shul, or is he acting hypocritically by going to shul and returning to his business? If we bar him from entering the shul, we are excluding him from the community, and he will become a hopeless case as far as Torah is concerned. On the contrary, the American Jew should be exposed to prayer, Torah, and mitzvot. He should not be condemned, reprimanded, or reproached. On the contrary, he should be invited, drawn closer and nearer to ourselves. Little by little you will see the heart of the

Jew blossom. In a short time, the American Jew will make the courageous decision to follow Torah and mitzvot.

12.07 The Courage to Change

Related by the Rav in his lecture on "The Profundity of Jewish Folk Wisdom," at the RCA Annual Convention, June 20, 1977.

When the righteous man falls he has the strength to rise again. However, there are those who do not have the strength and courage to stand up once more. They have no courage to rise. One of the main factors that prevent people from making amends and repenting is a lack of faith in themselves. They say it is too late. They state: "I am not capable of performing such a deed, of changing my life, of changing my identity and personality."

I remember a certain person, a very tragic person, who attended my shiur in Boston. He was very impressed. I am not bragging; I am just telling you the story. He was interested and moved by my teachings.

I once asked him: "Tell me. I see that you wish to cling to Yahadut [Judaism]. Why can't you take the final step and make your home kosher? Afterwards we will begin to think about the Sabbath laws."

So he said to me: "Rebbe. I would like to, but I can't do it."

"Why?" I asked.

He answered: "Because my family will declare me insane and I will be locked up. In addition, I do not belong in your society. I am far away. I do not belong in your community. I live a different life. I have no courage. I have to die a sinner."

12.08 Our Script Is Different

Related by the Rav in his lecture on "Covenants in the Book of Genesis," delivered to the Yeshiva University Rabbinic Alumni, Yeshiva University, ca. 1955 (Yiddish).

I was flying to New York from Boston to deliver my lecture to the Rabbinical Council of America before Yom Kippur. I had not finished preparing the lecture at home and continued to work on it on the plane. It was a coach plane with three seats to the row, and I was seated between two tall, blond gentiles. I was writing the final portion of my manuscript, which was in Hebrew and, of course, was written from right to left. I was so involved in my thoughts that I did not notice that the gentiles were staring at me in wonder. They were refined individuals and did not immediately ask what I was doing. Later, however, one of them inquired as to which language I was writing since I was going from right to left. I then realized how different we are from the other nations. Our script, our calendar, and our entire lifestyle are different. Our rejoicing, mourning, family life, and the entire structure of our external gestalt are different. The Jews lived in Poland for hundreds of years, yet they retained their uniqueness and did not become like the Poles.

12.09 Jewish Peoplehood

Related by the Rav to his Talmud class at Yeshiva University on Israel Independence Day, April 23, 1969.

Being part of the Jewish nation means participating in one destiny and experiencing the solidarity of the Jewish people. The American Jew is exposed to the danger of total assimilation on both the religious level and also in losing his feeling for Jewish peoplehood.

There is the danger in the United States that even if the American Jew remains observant, he still will not feel that he is part and parcel of the Jewish people. I saw this in Germany. I knew Jews in Germany who were observant to the last iota. One Orthodox rabbi in Germany told me about his relationship with Polish Jewry. At least with the religious Polish Jew he felt that he still had something in common. However, with the nonobservant Polish Jew there was little in common. The rabbi named a German politician and claimed that he had more in common with him than with the nonobservant Polish Jew. He and the German politician shared the same German culture and German national aspirations. This German politician later supported the Nazi party! The rabbi declared that vis-à-vis Rabbi Chaim Ozer Grodzinski [1863–1940; the last rabbi of Vilna]: "I still feel a relationship and have something in common; but with the nonobservant Polish Jew, what do I have in common?"

The feeling of being part of the Jewish nation and the awareness of the togetherness of all Jews was lacking. This man was a leading German rabbi, and I can testify that his observance of the Torah was meticulous. Nevertheless, these were his words, and I am apprehensive that a similar viewpoint will evolve in the United States.

Reflections of American Jewry

13.01 Un-American Activities

Related by the Rav in his lecture at Yeshiva University's Institute of Mental Health Project (undertaken jointly with Harvard and Loyola Universities to study religious attitudes to psychological problems), February 26, 1959.

I had the following case during the crazy period of Senator Joseph McCarthy [U.S. Senator from Wisconsin, 1947–57]. There was a teacher of French in a high school. In his youth he had been a student at Yeshiva University.[1]

He was called before a state committee which followed in the steps of the Senate Permanent Investigations Subcommittee which was investigating so called un-American activities. The teacher was called before the local committee when they discovered that he had been a Communist in the thirties. It seems that McCarthy did not appreciate the concept of teshuvah [repentance].

They wanted him to disclose the names of his associates. They [the associates] were also teachers in the public school system. So instead of quoting the Fifth Amendment, which was the usual procedure, the teacher cited Jewish law, claiming that it prohibits informing. He said that he was a Jew who was committed to a set of moral principles which he could not violate.

The American Jewish Committee got scared. I do not wish to tell you the name, but the attorney of the American Jewish Committee called me and said that this was a public scandal. "What is the public scandal?" I asked.

So he told me the story. "The whole Jewish community," he claimed, "is alarmed. It will appear that Judaism protects Communists."

So I said to him. "Mr. So-and-So, if you want me to give you an answer, then ask me the question in writing. I don't care whether you publish my answer in the press if you so desire. Just address your inquiry to the Law Commission of the Rabbinical Council of America, of which I am the chairman. Then it will be my duty to answer. If no official inquiry is sent to me, then I am not obligated to answer."

So a letter arrived from the chairman of the state committee. We had a fight in the Rabbinical Council. Most of the rabbis said that in the present climate of prejudice and bigotry we could not defend an individual who refused to disclose the names of his associates. It was easy to be a pseudo-patriot by claiming that they were a menace to society. That is to say that a French and a physics teacher who both quit the Communist party in the thirties were still a menace today! This was in 1950 or 1951, I do not remember exactly.

Finally I wrote a brief which was never published. I said that as chairman of the Law Commission of the Rabbinical Council of America, I prohibited the teacher of French from disclosing any names. Informing is prohibited. We are obligated to inform the authorities when the person in question is a public menace, but in this case I did not see any public menace. Even if his associates who taught physics or biochemistry had been members of the Communist party ten years earlier, they had since quit. They left because they did not like its policies, and today they had only contempt for this party. The trouble with all these inquiries is that we do not know a basic law of the Bible—the law of repentance. A man can come back to God. This is why I will not allow him to inform on his colleagues.

The committee accepted my letter, and the teacher of French was not cited for contempt. The letter was not published by anybody and is probably still in their files.

1. Cf. Louis Bernstein, *Challenge and Mission: The Emergence of the English-Speaking Rabbinate* (New York: Shengold Publishers, 1982), pp. 58–59.

13.02 Communist Russia

Related by the Rav in his lecture entitled "Rashi on Aseret Hadibrot" at the RCA Annual Convention, June 30, 1970.

If you want to know how indispensable faith is, you must pay attention to the last of the commandments that deal with the relationships between man and man and see whether they are implemented by society or not. Social inequity and immorality are precipitated by the denial of divine authority. In other words, the vehicle of social ethics is faith in a transcendental personal God who expects man to follow in His footsteps or to imitate Him.

Does history confirm this viewpoint? I believe that the best illustration is modern Communist Russia. I want you to understand that there may be some truth to the accusations that religion is bankrupt and about the failings of clergymen, the men of God. There may be a lot of truth to such accusations, but as a whole the accusations are false. When we observe the society which Communist Russia has constructed, we see how false and undeserved such an accusation is. I do not assert that the West has succeeded in creating a great moral society. Western society is far from being a perfect community. It is hypocritical to a great extent, sanctimonious and self-righteous. Quite often, as we know, it is indifferent to the woes and suffering of a downtrodden and weak people. We learned this in the 1940s.

However, the West is still somewhat sensitive to moral issues. You can argue with the government. At least you have the opportunity to argue. You may argue, and you may discuss issues of interest with our State Department officials. You may even engage [Georges] Pompidou [1911–1974; President of France, 1969–

1974] or Mrs. Pompidou in an argument. She is responsible for the recent commotion [between France and Israel]. The French President is like Manoah, who "went after his wife" [Judges 13:11]. When she was in Chicago recently, there was a demonstration against her [Jews protesting France's policy toward Israel]. Whether the demonstration was justified or wise politically is a different problem. In any case, the demonstration took place. The police cleared a path for her and she squeezed through the Jewish demonstrators. Then she complained to the police: "They touched me!"

I recalled that when I moved to the Cape, to Onset, my next-door neighbor was from an old Irish family that had come to America before the [American] Revolution. He was very aristocratic and would often mention that his family had come long before the Kennedy family. He was a perfect gentleman, a true aristocrat. He looked typically Irish, with blue eyes, a pug nose, and a smile in his eyes. He was already an old man, but he used to tell me that when he was a little boy his mother would take him to Jordan Marsh [an upscale department store] in Boston. This was about seventy years ago, and the clientele was from areas such as Beacon Hill and Commonwealth Avenue. These people considered themselves true bluebloods. He would come with his mother, and the ladies would become hysterical lest they brush against him. Due to his looks, they identified him as an Irish boy who was a recent arrival. That is exactly what Mrs. Pompidou said about the Jews: "They touched me!"

Nevertheless, at least you can argue with them. The West tries to justify its actions or inactions, to explain, or at least somehow to fool or to deceive us. It feels, many a time, embarrassed. From time to time, the West is ready, even if only feebly, to correct its mistakes.

What about Russia? About [Leonid] Brezhnev, [Aleksei] Kosygin, [Nikita] Khrushchev, and [Nikolai] Podgorny? Can one reproach these Communist leaders? Can one discuss an issue with them? Any rebuke will be scornfully rejected. They distort facts and falsify historical data. They accuse little Israel of imperialism and colonialism, while Russia itself is the most brutal colonial and imperialistic power, I would say, in human history! The Jews committed an international crime when they invaded Egypt [in 1967] in order to protect the lives of the Yishuv. This prevented Nasser from massacring two million Jews. Had Nasser won the war there would have been another Treblinka plus Buchenwald and several other extermination camps in the Land of Israel. And Russia, of course, acted in accordance with international morality, and was motivated by the purest considerations, when she occupied Czechoslovakia.

Russia is immoral to the very bone and marrow, cruel and brutal. Completely insensitive to morality. Why? This is a strange question. Marxism is fundamentally an ethical doctrine. It is far more an ethical than an economic doctrine. The underlying idea of Marxist econometrics is justice. Labor, according to Marx, creates the economic value system. Hence, the profit belongs to the laborer, and not to the investor or the capitalist. The fascination of Marx for the Oriental peoples, for African tribes, lies not in the economic sphere but is a result of the ethical motif. Do not forget that Marxism, at the turn of the century, was a gospel, a religion! People sacrificed their lives for it. And yet this ethical doctrine turned into a gospel of brutality and tyranny. Why? Because Marxism did not comprehend the insight of the rabbis that the Ten Commandments were uttered in one sentence (Mekhilta to Exodus 20:1]. They are indivisible and indestructible as a whole. When you "sin and commit treachery against God," then you will soon "defraud your comrade" (Leviticus 5:21; Tosefta to Shevuot 3:6].

13.03 The First Deviation

Related by the Rav in his address at the Chag ha-Semikhah, Yeshiva University, ca. 1953 (Yiddish).

You all know what was the first change the reformers made in Berlin. Initially, they abolished the first of the two Yekum Purkan prayers recited after the reading of the Torah on Sabbath mornings. After all, how can one recite the first Yekum Purkan if this Aramaic prayer refers to the "holy societies that are in the land of Babylon." Babylon does not exist today!

Then they abolished the second Yekum Purkan because there was no need for this prayer in Aramaic as a similar prayer was recited in Hebrew right afterwards [the Mi she-berakh].

When the two Yekum prayers were abrogated, R. Shmuel David Luzzatto [1800–1865; Italian rabbinical and biblical scholar], often referred to by the acronym Shadal, remarked: "We now have seen a fulfillment of the biblical words that `He blotted out every living substance'" [*yekum* is the Hebrew word for "living substance" in Genesis 7:23].[1]

1. This insight was related by the Rav on a number of occasions. It is cited in Hebrew translation in *Yemei Zikaron* [17.8], p. 178. The translation there is inexact. See the critique of the translation by Rabbi Hershel Schachter in *Beikvei ha-Tzohn*, (Jerusalem: Hoza'ot Bet ha-Medrash d'Flatbush, 1997), p. 30, fn. 10.

13.04 Ancient Parchment

Related by the Rav in his lecture on Parshat Hukat (Numbers 19:1–22:1), at the RCA Annual Convention, June 27, 1974.

Tumat ha-met [the defilement engendered by death] is something unique and singular. It is not to be classified with other defilements. That is the reason the Torah did not mention tumat ha-met when it spoke about other tumot. It is something singular and strange.

I will give you an example. A kohen is permitted to defile himself by contact with a sheretz [the contaminating carcass of a creeping animal], a zav [a person contaminated by a venereal discharge], or a mezorah [a person afflicted with leprosy]. The kohen has been enjoined from contracting tumat ha-met, that is all. The same is true of a nazir [a person who vows abstinence from wine; Numbers 6:1–6:21].

I remind myself, I had an encounter quite a number of years ago with a representative of the so-called Hokhmat Yisrael [Wissenschaft des Judentums]. He was a very outstanding scholar.[1] He told me that lately they had discovered a parchment, a megillah [scroll], in which it was stated unequivocally that a kohen is enjoined from defiling himself with a sheretz.

So I said to him: "Do you take it seriously?"

"Of course," he answered, "very seriously." You know, they [the devotees of Hokhmat Yisrael] have the answer right away. It is a different kabbalah, a different tradition. They operate with "traditions" in the plural.

So I mentioned a name to him. This name was known to him, and I knew that he did not like the person. I asked him: "Do you know him?"

"Yes," he answered.

"Is he a scholar?" I asked.

"No, he is a boor and an am ha-aretz mide-oraita [ignoramous from the Torah]," he answered.

I said to him: "So only we have a monopoly on boors and amei ha-artez mide-oraita? Fifteen hundred years ago there were also boors and amei ha-aretz. Since there was no paper, the boor had to write on parchment. So you found nice hiddushei Torah [rabbinic novellas], so what!"

This is a true story.

1. The scholar whom the Rav was referring to was Professor Saul Lieberman (1898–1983) of the Jewish Theological Seminary of America. The Rav and Professor Lieberman, who were related by marriage, met at a brit milah (circumcision repast). Professor Lieberman was married to Judith Berlin, the granddaughter of the Netziv.

Cf. Rabbi Hershel Schachter, *Nefesh ha-Rav* (Jerusalem: Reishet Yerushalayim, 1994), p. 248.

13.05 Birkhat Kohanim

Related by the Rav to his Talmud class when the author was a student at Yeshiva University. Cf. Rabbi Hershel Schachter, Nefesh ha-Rav *(Jerusalem: Reishet Yerushalayim, 1994), p. 132.*

A rabbi has to be intelligent enough to recognize which issues are important enough for him to bring to a crisis. The Rav related that when he was a young rabbi in Boston, a festival fell on the Sabbath. In the shul in which the Rav prayed on that day there was a custom that the kohanim did not recite the Birkhat Kohanim [Priestly Benediction] when a festival coincided with the Sabbath. The Rav related that because of his youth and inexperience he made a scene by screaming and insisting that the kohanim must dukhan [recite the Priestly Benediction]. The Rav succeeded in forcing his will upon the congregants that day, and the kohanim did dukhan. The Rav, however, lost the synagogue, since its officers declared that he would not be welcome if he returned to worship there.

The Rav exhorted us to encourage the kohanim to dukhan on a festival which falls on the Sabbath. Yet there was a custom in some of the European communities that the kohanim did not dukhan on the Sabbath. While such a practice did not make sense from a halakhic standpoint, it was nevertheless a custom. Many times a minhag [custom] becomes more deeply rooted than the halakhah itself.

The Rav felt that a more mature rabbi would have stressed that the correct practice was for the kohanim to dukhan. However, if the kohanim had insisted on not dukhaning on the Sabbath, then let it be. The rabbi should wait a few months and then explain in a shiur why it is more proper for the kohanim to dukhan when a festival corresponds with the Sabbath. This is the more correct custom. It will take some time, but perhaps by the next time a festival falls on the Sabbath the congregants will be convinced that the rabbi is correct.[1]

1. For some of the sources dealing with this halakhic problem, see the Remah to *Shulhan Arukh*, Orah Hayyim 128:44; *Magen Avraham* 70; *Taz* 38; *Mishnah Berurah* 165–167; and *Arukh ha-Shulhan* 128:63-64.

13.06 Kehunah in the United States

Related by the Rav in the Benjamin Gottesman Lecture in Jewish Thought and the Tonya Soloveitchik Memorial Lecture entitled "The Haftorot Between Pesach and Shevuot," Yeshiva University, May 22, 1979.

Throughout the generations, the priesthood has constantly suffered from disintegration. During the Babylonian Exile there was a widespread breakdown of its sanctity. As a result, all of Jewish sanctity suffered. To revitalize its holiness, Ezra and Nehemiah intensified their efforts to renew the sanctity of the Jewish people in general, and particularly the holiness of the priests.

The kehunah [priesthood] is a very fragile institution. I discovered this to be particularly so in the United States. When I became a rabbi in Boston, I soon performed my first wedding there. The hatan [groom] was all dressed up and also had a beautiful carnation in his lapel. He impressed me as being a nice boy.

When I began to fill in the ketuvah [marriage document], I told him that he had to identify himself as a kohen, a levi, or a yisrael.

I was met with a quizzical look, with astonishment. He did not understand what I was talking about.

It was now my turn to be astonished. But I recovered from my astonishment. Do you know why? Because the vast majority of Jews in America absolutely do not know what the kehunah is. I am referring to when you meet a Jew in the street or a student on a campus. I do not mean the ba'alei teshuvah [returnees to Judaism]. I am not speaking about ba'alei teshuvah now. I am speaking about the average Jew in the United States. I mean the youth on the campus. Ask them whether they are kohanim, levi'im, or yisraelim. They would not understand your question. They would not have an answer. They would not understand what you are talking about.

That is why I always tell the kohanim, whether or not they have reached maturity, to go up and dukhan [recite the Priestly Benediction on the festivals]. Even children should go up to dukhan. There is no time now to play around with Rashi versus Tosafot as to whether there is hinukh [education of minors] regarding Birkhat Kohanim [the Priestly Benediction].[1] Why? Because today the whole institution of the kehunah is about to disintegrate and collapse. This is a terrible problem! Therefore we must encourage them to recite the Priestly Benediction so that they will appreciate and understand that they are kohanim even at an early age.

1. Megillah 4:6, 24a, and Rashi and Tosafot ad loc.

13.07 A Dissatisfied Kohen

Related by Rabbi Hershel Schachter, Nefesh ha-Rav *(Jerusalem: Reshit Yerushalayim, 1994), p. 283.*

The Rav related that in one of the Boston synagogues there was a kohen who observed that the rabbis and the communal leaders were constantly honored with the third aliyah. This was the first aliyah that could be granted to them after the kohen and levi aliyot [*Shulhan Arukh*, Orah Hayyim 136:1]. This kohen demanded of the gabbaim that he be honored with the third aliyah, but they told him that he should be satisfied to receive the first aliyah as a kohen. They explained to him that the entire importance of the third aliyah was because it directly followed the kohen and levi aliyot. Nevertheless, the kohen remained jealous of those who received the third aliyah. He finally went to a Conservative temple where he made a large donation on the condition that they would honor him with shlishi [the third aliyah].

13.08 The Shul President

Related by the Rav in a Purim Shiur in memory of ha-Rabbanit Tonya Soloveitchik on her Yahrzeit, Yeshiva University, February 24, 1983.

There was a president of a leading shul in Boston who would hear the Megillah in the following fashion. He would come to shul on Purim and wait for the cantor to say the blessings on the Megillah. He would open his Megillah and listen to the blessings. When the cantor began to read the text the president would put away his Megillah. He would unfold his newspaper to the stock exchange section and carefully read it. It was the latest edition of stock prices. When the cantor reached the final blessings after the reading of the text, the president would once again hold the Megillah in his hands.

13.09 The Groom's Request

Related by Dr. Tovah Lichtenstein, February 18, 1994.

There was a Conservative rabbi in the Boston area who was very close to the Rav.[1] "He loved my father and my father loved him."

Once they were at a wedding together. The Rav officiated, and the Conservative rabbi was among the guests. The parents of the bride were devotees of my father, although the bride herself was not that observant. Out of friendship for her parents, the Rav agreed to be the mesader kiddushin [officiant at the wedding ceremony]. Under the chupah [canopy], the groom informed the Rav that he wanted a double-ring ceremony. When the Rav refused this request, the groom became more adamant in his demand. He let the Rav know that he was a consul in the Foreign Service of the United States government. The Rav told him that he would simply walk away from the chupah, since he could not be party to a ceremony that contradicted Jewish tradition. Upon hearing this threat, the groom backed down and the Rav was able to be the mesader kiddushin.

At the conclusion of the ceremony, after the bride and groom walked down the aisle away from the chupah, the Conservative rabbi noticed that the wineglass which is broken to recall the destruction of the Temple was still whole. The groom had not succeeded in shattering it. The Conservative rabbi called the Rav's attention to what had happened. The Rav dismissed the matter and simply broke the goblet by himself.

After observing all this, the Conservative rabbi turned to the Rav and exclaimed: "Rabbi Soloveitchik, I do not understand you. On certain matters you are so stringent, while on others you are overly lenient. A double-ring ceremony upsets you, and yet you do not mind when the glass is not broken!"[2]

1. The rabbi was Joseph S. Shubow (d. 1969). A former army chaplain during World War II, Shubow lived in Brookline and was the spiritual leader of Temple Bnai Moshe in Brighton, Mass. The Bostoner Rebbe, Rabbi Levi Yitzchak ha-Levi Horowitz, described him as "the rabbi of a Conservative synagogue who possessed a truly Jewish soul [Yiddishe neshamah]." The interview with the Bostoner Rebbe took place on April 29, 1993.

2. What the Conservative rabbi did not comprehend was that the double-ring ceremony contradicted the essence of the halakhic concept of marriage, which is that the husband takes the wife unto himself (see Kidushin 1:1). Breaking the wineglass under the chupah is only a custom, and therefore was not of comparable halakhic significance; it could not be put on a par with the halakhah that it is only the husband who takes unto himself his wife. Thus the Rav was stringent in the former situation but lenient in the latter.

13.10 The Siyyum Before Pesach

Related by the Rav during a Sheva Berakhot talk in honor of David and Karen Klavan at the home of Dr. and Mrs. Allen Goldstein, Queens, N.Y., February 20, 1974.

The siyyum [on the day before Pesach] is often not a proper siyyum. Ninety percent of the rabbis simply select the last mishnah and read it for the siyyum.

I once had the case of a Conservative rabbi who called me up on erev Pesach all excited.

"Rabbi Soloveitchik," he said. "Please help me. Disaster has struck!"

"What happened?" I asked.

"I have prepared a siyyum on Mesekhet Makkot," he told me. "I enjoyed it very much and I kept my Gemara on my desk. Before Pesach my wife was cleaning up my office and she put away my Gemara Makkot among the other volumes of the Talmud. Now I cannot find the volume with Makkot in it. Where can I find Makkot? It has disappeared!"

So I advised him. "You should take the tractate of Sanhedrin. Makkot usually goes with the Gemara Sanhedrin. You may also wish to try Avodah Zarah, since Makkot may also be bound with this volume." Each time the rabbi took ten minutes to look but could not find Makkot.

Then I reminded myself that once, when I went to my father's home in New York so many years ago, I chanced upon a set of the Talmud that had been distributed by the Joint Distribution Committee after World War I.[1] In this set I noticed that Makkot was bound with Baba Kama. I remembered it because this order was strange to me.

So I said to him: "Go and look it up in the Gemara marked Baba Kama, at the end."

So he went to look for it. Suddenly I heard his voice on the phone again: "Rabbi Soloveitchik, you are a genius. You are a scholar; you have prophecy. Now I see why people consider you a great scholar. How could you know where it was in my edition of the Shas!"

These are the siyyumim that you have today on erev Pesach.

1. This unique Shas was published in 1897 in Vilna. After World War II it was also reprinted in this order in 1948 in Munich and Heidelberg under the sponsorship of the Procurement Division, European Quartermaster Depot, United States Army and the Joint Distribution Comittee. It was supervised by the Rabbinical Organization of the U.S. Occupation Zone of Germany and its chairman, Rabbi Shmuel Abba Snieg, who was the chief rabbi of the U.S. Zone. The Conservative rabbi had been a military chaplain and evidently had a set of the U.S. Army Talmud.

13.11 Surrender to Halakhah

Related by the Rav in his address on Gerut (Conversion) to the Yeshiva University Rabbinic Alumni, Yeshiva University, June 19, 1975.

The Torah summons the Jew to live heroically. We cannot allow a married woman, no matter how tragic the case is, to remarry without a get [divorce document]. We cannot allow a kohen to marry a giyoret [convert]. Sometimes these cases are very tragic. I know this from my own experience.

I had a case in Rochester of a gentile girl who became a giyoret ha-zedek [righteous convert] before she met the boy. She did not join our nation because she wanted to marry somebody. Then she met a Jewish boy who came from an alienated background and had absolutely no knowledge of Yahadut [Judaism]. She brought him close to Yahadut and they became engaged. Since he was now close to Yahadut, the boy wanted to find out about his family, so he visited the cemetery where his grandfather was buried. He saw a strange symbol on the tombstone—ten fingers with thumbs and forefingers nearly forming a triangle. So he began to ask—he thought it was a mystical symbol—and he discovered that he was a kohen.

What can we do? This is the halakhah. A kohen may not marry a convert [*Shulhan Arukh*, Even ha-Ezer 6:8]. We surrender to the will of the Almighty. On the other hand, to say that the halakhah is not sensitive to problems and is not responsive to the needs of people is an outright falsehood. The halakhah is responsive to the needs of both the community and the individual. However, the halakhah has its own orbit, moves at a certain definitive speed, has its own pattern of responding to a challenge, and possesses its own criteria and principles.

I come from a rabbinical house—the bet ha-Rav. This is the house into which I was born. Believe me, Reb Chaim used to try his best to be meikil [lenient in his halakhic decisions]. But there were limits even to Reb Chaim's kulot [lenient rulings]. When you reach the boundary line, all you can say is: "I surrender to the will of the Almighty."

With sadness in my heart, I shared in the suffering of the poor woman or the poor girl. She was instrumental in bringing him back to the fold and then she had to lose him. She lost him. She walked away.

13.12 Women Saying Kaddish

Related by Dr. Joel B. Wolowelsky, "Modern Orthodoxy and Woman's Self-Perception," Tradition, vol. 22, no. 1 (Spring 1986), p. 80, n. 9.

About fifteen years ago, the issue [of permitting a woman to recite Kaddish] came up in an out-of-town chapter of Yavneh, and I asked a board member [who was one of Rabbi J. B. Soloveitchik's students] to put the question to the Rav. He wrote me: "I spoke with the Rav about the question you asked concerning a girl saying Kaddish. He told me he remembers being in Vilna at the Gaon's kloiz, which wasn't one of your modern Orthodox shuls, and a woman came into the back [there was no ezrat nashim] and said Kaddish after Ma'ariv. I asked him whether it would make a difference if someone was saying it along with her or not, and he replied that he could see no objection in either case." An advisory board member subsequently confirmed that this was the Rav's opinion. Recently, I have heard of a number of people who recalled similar incidents of women saying Kaddish in prewar Lithuania.[1]

1. Cf. Rabbi Aaron Soloveichik, *Od Yosef Yisrael Beni Hai* (Jerusalem: Yeshivas Brisk of Chicago, 1993), p. 100.

The American Rabbinate

14.01 What Is a Rabbi?

Related by the Rav in a lecture to the Hevra Shas in Boston, Mass., March 19, 1972.

Every Jew today is a rabbi. What is the task of the rabbi? To teach and to impart the message of Yahadut [Judaism] to Jews who are ignorant of its message. Nowadays this task is not restricted to the official rabbi of the community. Every member of the community faces many complex situations and is confronted with many challenges. In order to meet these challenges courageously, he has to simply spread the message of Judaism.

In what respect does the rabbi differ from the rest of the community? There is not a single norm which is applicable only to the rabbi and not applicable to the ba'alei batim or the laymen. As for the number of mitzvot that one is obligated to perform, there is no distinction between the rabbi and the layperson. There is not a single mitzvah which is applicable exclusively to the rabbi and has no application to the layman. I do not know of any such mitzvah.

As you all know, I am a descendant of a rabbinic family. Indeed, it is difficult to find a layman among my ancestors on either side for the last century and a half. On both the paternal and maternal sides, they were all rabbis. If you should ask me what the rabbinate stands for, I cannot give you an answer. In my opinion, the rabbinate is not an institution. If it becomes an institution it might have disastrous effects as far as the future is concerned. The best example is the official rabbinate in the State of Israel. There has been a tendency to institutionalize the chief rabbinate in Israel. When I refused to accept the position of chief rabbi, I explained that one of my reasons was that the rabbinate has been institutionalized there. Willy-nilly, such a rabbinate will disintegrate. I am sorry that my prophecy was correct. It is now in a stage of disintegration.

The rabbinate has never been an institution. The rabbi has never been called "his eminence," as they do today in Israel. The rabbi has never walked with a silk coat, a cane in one hand, and the Bible in his other hand. All these mores reflect the Christian concept of the clergy. Of course, for Christianity the clergy is an institution. For us, the rabbinate is not an institution. It has become an institution in the United States, mostly among the Reform and Conservative rabbis. An institution means that the rabbi can do things that the layman cannot. There is not a single religious duty under the sun which the rabbi is authorized to do and the layman is not. The difference between them is only a question of scholarship. If the scholarship of the rabbi is limited, then he must not discharge those tasks that require scholarship and erudition.

What is a rabbi? I do not know. The question comes up quite often since we ordain rabbis at the Yeshiva [University]. Every year thirty to forty boys receive semikhah [rabbinical ordination]. I sign these certificates of ordination. I have signed about fifteen hundred or sixteen hundred ordinations over the years. I only hope that I will not receive malkot [the punishment of lashes] for each ordination that I granted. Perhaps the only question will be whether I get one lash or forty lashes for each certificate. [Laughter.]

Of course you send off the rabbis and you try to give them a message. I am always in a dilemma about this. What kind of message can I give them? I do not know what a rabbi is. The more I think about my forefathers, the more I realize that the rabbinate is not something solid, rigid, and stable which imposes its rules upon the individual. It is, rather, a many-faceted, variegated, and fluid phenomenon. Basically, it is not an institution or an office which willy-nilly must obscure the view of the rabbi as a human being. It is a personal commitment by an individual to live for, to be concerned with, and to be dedicated to the community. This community has only survived because countless individuals have dedicated their lives to its survival throughout the generations. Basically, it is a personal commitment, or, I would say, it is a style of living. The style of living of the rabbi differs from that of the laymen. The way of living cannot differ.

I would like to show you four different styles. I would like to portray four rabbis who occupied the pulpit of Brisk. I have selected these four because I am acquainted with their biographies and personalities. Their Brisk sojourns covered the years from 1840 until about 1918. The first was the famous Rim, Reb Yaakov Meir Padua [rabbi in Brisk, 1840–1855], the author of the *Ketonet Pasim* on the *Nimukei Yosef*. He was succeeded by Reb Zevi Hirsch Orenstein [1865–1874], the nephew of the famous author of the *Yeshuot Yaakov*, Reb Yaakov Meshullem Orenstein. Then my great-grandfather, Reb Yosef Baer, for whom I am named, was rabbi in Brisk [1877–1892]. Then came my grandfather, Reb Chaim [1892–1918].

Reb Yaakov Meir Padua was an ascetic. He led not only a moderate life but an abstemious life. He submitted himself to very rigid discipline. He ate very little and spent many days in fasting and prayer. He renounced wordly goods and always walked with his eyes cast down. He literally fulfilled the advice of Reb Moshe Chaim Luzzatto [1707–1746] in his *Mesillat Yesharim* [chap. 14] that "a person should not look beyond his immediate four cubits." Whenever he walked to shul he was accompanied by two people who guided him, because he never looked ahead. He was a type of porush [one who separates from the world], a hasid among hasidim, or simply a nazir. He would hardly talk to people. He spent his days and nights in study and in prayer. The Brisk Jews revered him and adored him. They called him a kadosh [holy person] or a hasid. This was one style of conducting a rabbinate.

He was succeeded by Reb Hirsch Orenstein, who had spent his youth in Koenigsberg, which was in East Prussia. His language was German. How the Brisk Jews understood him is still a puzzle to me. There was really no need to understand him. It was like the Shaagat Aryeh [Reb Aryeh Leib Gunzberg; 1695–1785]. He was the rabbi of Volozhin and later became the spiritual leader of Metz. The latter was a French town. How they communicated with each other in Metz is still a riddle to me. I do not know. However, there was no need for communication. The communication was through silence. This is the best type of communication.[1] Rabbi Orenstein used to walk around in satin and silk. He smoked Havana cigars. He greeted everybody with a smile, Jews and gentiles alike. He even spoke a little Russian. He would extend greetings to the governor on behalf of the community when the latter visited Brisk. Rabbi Orenstein maintained a cordial relationship with the ispravnic [chief of police]. On Jewish holidays, the ispravnic would come to the rabbi's house to extend holiday greetings to him on behalf of the tsar. Of course, the ispravnic used to drink a toast. Not one, but many, and quite often policemen had to come to take their chief home. Reb Hirsch Orenstein was the exact opposite of Reb Yaakov Meir Padua. Nevertheless, the Brisk Jews said: "God bless him! What an outstanding person! He can represent us before kings and can converse with royalty." It was a different style, the exact opposite of his predecessor! Yet the Jews of Brisk accepted both.

Then Reb Yosef Baer came. His whole personality commanded respect and reverence. He was a spiritual aristocrat. Even when you see his picture today you are impressed by his sensitive, pale face and deep-set eyes. He was known for his disciplined movements and gestures. He stood as straight as a soldier. His precise, brief statements inspired awe. He was by nature an aristocrat. He was a loner. Once he accomplished his task he retreated. Again the Brisk Jews revered him. Whenever they met him they would whisper to each other that he represented malkhut, or kingship. He was completely different from both Reb Yaakov Meir Padua and Reb Hirsch Orenstein.

Finally Reb Chaim came. He was just the opposite of his father. He was a democrat from head to toe. A real plebeian. He was gregarious and fond of all people. It did not matter whether they were intelligent or dull, rich or poor, observant or nonobservant. Reb Chaim was particularly in love with children. The great Reb Chaim could communicate with children in a way that only a mother can. Brisk residents used to see Reb Chaim surrounded by little boys. He would play games with them. Once, it is a true story, Reb Chaim came out of his house and found a group of children waiting for him. "What do you want?" he asked the youngsters. "We would like to play horses," was the reply. "Nu, so why don't you play?" Reb Chaim asked. They responded that nobody wanted to be the horse. They all want to be the drivers or the passengers. Reb Chaim immediately volunteered to be the horse. He was roped, and the little children forced the horse to move on.

Once, Reb Chaim played horses with them and the children got tired and hungry. They told Reb Chaim that they would tie him to the tree while they went home to get a snack. Reb Chaim said all right. They tied him to the tree with a few good knots— sailors' knots. They went home and forgot about Reb Chaim and their horse tied to the tree. The gabbai of the shul came out and saw Reb Chaim tied to the tree. All this happened in front of the shul. The gabbai said he would take a knife and cut the ropes. Reb Chaim refused, because he did not want to disappoint the children. He insisted that the gabbai bring the children to untie him.

Brisk Jews liked this type of behavior. Reb Chaim was not fired from his post. On the contrary, they were impressed with this humility on the part of the greatest intellect among the rabbis of the nineteenth century. He revolutionized the method of studying the Talmud. Throughout all the yeshivot in the United States and Israel, Reb Chaim's method, the Brisker method, is nowadays the accepted method. He introduced into the study of the Talmud something which Aristotle [384-322 B.C.E.], [Gottfried Wilhelm] Leibniz [1646–1716], and [Immanuel] Kant [1724–1804] had introduced into secular philosophy. A new method of analysis, conceptualization, abstraction, and classification. He actually modernized the study of the Talmud in a way which was unprecedented. As a matter of fact, my father told me that if not for Reb Chaim it would be impossible to study Gemara with boys who simultaneously study science, mathematics, and physics. The Gemara would lag behind their other studies. Now the Gemara does not lag behind any philosophical approach, even the most modern analytical approach. I know a little about modern philosophical analysis. We can compete with the most profound and the most precise philosophical analysis of today.

The contrast between these four rabbis had nothing to do with their way of life. The way of life was the same. It was the style of living that was different. There is a democratic style, an aristocratic style, a joyous style, and a sad, ascetic style of living. Any style is welcome; but a man must have a style.

1. Cf. *Divre Hagut ve-ha-Arakhah* (12:8), pp. 201–206.

14.02 The Heart of Tradition

Related by the Rav in his lecture on "Covenants in the Book of Genesis" delivered to the Yeshiva University Rabbinic Alumni, Yeshiva University, ca. 1955. (Yiddish).

A true conception of the mesorah, the heart of our tradition, can only be attained by study. Unfortunately, the last few years have witnessed too much concern with political issues and internal political maneuvering within the RCA and the [YU] Rabbinical Alumni. They should depoliticize. Even if all of this has truly originated "for the sake of heaven," such activity still defiles the organization. We must intellectualize our gatherings. Above all, this means that we must constantly be involved in the study of our Torah texts and philosophical works. We must tackle intellectual problems, and they must constitute our focus. We should arrange symposia at which our members will present learned papers. We should have an organ in which to publish original research and scholarly insights. This must be the main goal of the RCA and the Rabbinic Alumni.

If the RCA must at times be involved in politics, then let it be as our sages declare regarding Greek wisdom, "at a time that is neither day nor night" [Menahot 99b]. The members of the RCA must discharge the command to study Torah "day and night" [Joshua 1:8].

I know from my own experience that this is the only practical approach. There was a period in my life, after I arrived in America, during which I was thrown into the political arena. I was young at the time, and I was in strange and new surroundings. This took place during my first four or five years in America. I lost my entire true identity as a result. Had this period lasted longer, I would have had to go to a psychiatrist to find myself. Even that might not have helped. Then the Yeshiva entered my life. I became entirely depoliticized as a result of my association with the Yeshiva. I am therefore deeply indebted to the school. Besides all the Yeshiva has accomplished for Torah in America, I am also obligated to it on a personal level. If not for the Yeshiva I would have totally lost my way on the American scene.

There are many aspects of the rabbinate which denigrate the individual. You enter a community and are caught up in its insignificant problems. You deal with many people who are petty, coarse, and superficial. All rabbis encounter these difficulties in their communities. We must join together to strengthen one another. However, our meetings should not just be to grant solace and comfort to one another. We must form a fellowship dedicated to mutual study. Ultimately, this is the only way we will truly influence the American Jewish community. We must enhance our own Torah knowledge and understanding. We must become personalities who instinctively command respect from our congregants.

Our joint study and fellowship will strengthen our ties to the past and our unique covenant with the Almighty. It will also enhance our relationship to our teachers. The relationship between the rebbe and his students is a metaphysical bond. I was raised with the idea that the rebbe is a lot more than simply a teacher. At times, the idea of a rebbe may not apply to an individual, but to a collective body such as the Yeshiva. It is similar to the concept of a corporation, where there is a collective venture. The Yeshiva itself is also our rebbe. My father implanted within me the understanding that the essence of my existence is my rebbe. If I cut myself off from my past, I impair my own being.

I feel this not only in regard to my father, but in a tangible fashion this feeling extends all the way back to Maimonides. I have stressed many times my feeling that Maimonides was present at our Seders; my father would constantly refer to Maimonides and his views when chanting the Kiddush, eating the bitter herbs, and reciting the Haggadah. For me the Rambam became a true-to-life companion. This is the basic concept of the Jewish covenant which roots us to the past. That is why the Torah stresses that Abraham "planted an orchard [eshel] in Beersheva" [Genesis 21:33]. The trees in the orchard symbolize the Jewish people, who are rooted in their past just as a tree is rooted in the ground. This relationship results in the Jews' "proclaiming the Name of God of the Universe" [ibid.]. The Jews retain their spirituality because they have roots which cannot be severed.

The study of Torah alone is not enough. Torah must have a rebbe and must be rooted in the past. An institution can collectively discharge the role of the rebbe. The Yeshiva's alumni must appreciate the institution and its unique role in uniting us with the past. I do not wish to imply that you cannot criticize the Yeshiva. At times, there are faults that you can discern, and you have every right to point out these shortcomings. However, in your basic relationship to the school you must properly evaluate its great contribution to your spiritual commitment. It is similar to the relationship between children and parents. In psychological terminology we refer to adolescent turmoil or rebellion when the child turns on his parents. However, if the roots are deep and healthy, the child will remain connected to the faith of his forebears. Do you know when I first truly appreciated my father and grandfather? When I lived alone among gentiles. Then I started to consider and compare my parents with others. Then I truly understood who my ancestors were, and my rebellion evaporated. When did the biblical Joseph recognize the true value of his father? It was only in the palace of Pharaoh that Joseph really comprehended his father's greatness. Then comparison was possible, and his eyes opened to Jacob's saintliness.

When we are students in the Yeshiva we somehow notice the faults and failures. We do not appreciate our being in the institution. It is only after we leave the Yeshiva and start to make comparisons with what we see in the outside world that we begin to truly value the school. Then we recognize how important it is for us to forge a fellowship between ourselves and our great rebbe, the Yeshiva. Only through such activities will we strengthen our covenant with the Almighty. This is the importance of the RCA and the Rabbinic Alumni of the Yeshiva.

Recently, on Erev Sukkot, I received a call from a student who was serving as a chaplain at a naval base. He told me that he and the entire crew of the ship would have to stand for inspection on the second day of Sukkot.[1] Of course, he was concerned that he would be unshaven because of the holiday prohibitions. I was sorely tempted to allow him to shave on the second day, when it is a rabbinical prohibition. Perhaps there were extenuating factors which would justify on halakhic grounds his shaving under these circumstances. Perhaps he could have been shaven by a non-Jew on the second day of Sukkot. However, once I thought about Abraham's covenant with the Almighty, I could not approach this question on a purely dry, halakhic level. "I will ratify My covenant between Me and you and between your offspring after you, throughout their generations, as an everlasting covenant to be a God to you and to your offspring after you" [Genesis 17:7]. "This is My covenant which you shall keep between Me and you and your descendants after you: every male among you shall be circumcised" [Genesis 17:10].

Once I thought about this covenant I realized that a Jew must be ready to sacrifice for his religion. We subject a child of eight days to circumcision, and likewise a chaplain who is a rabbinic graduate of the Yeshiva must be ready to suffer for his spiritual commitment.

The chaplain followed my guidance and did not suffer as a result. Perhaps it is good that it was only with gentiles that the chaplain had this problem. He explained why he could not shave, and they understood! However, with Jews, at times, it is more difficult. They refuse to understand! [Laughter.] Some of our ignorant Jewish laypeople are arrogant and are convinced that they know it all. Our rabbis endure endless difficulty at their hands. That is why I have the highest regard for the rabbinical graduates of our Yeshiva and the other yeshivot. These men serve as rabbis in farflung places. They somehow tolerate the ignorance and boorishness of many of their congregants. These rabbis succeed in retaining some semblance of Torah Judaism throughout the United States. Without their heroic efforts, Judaism would be entirely swept away in America.

Nevertheless, while in their communities, these rabbis lose some of their spirituality. They are partially detached from their roots. That is why the Yeshiva and its Rabbinic Alumni must aid the rabbis in recharging their spirituality. That is exactly the idea of the pilgrimage to the Temple in Jerusalem on each festival. "Three times during the year shall all your menfolk appear before the Lord" [Exodus 23:17]. The farmer in the Galil can gradually forget his roots. It is important for him to go to the Temple and be imbued with its spiritual atmosphere. In the same way, the rabbi must leave his difficulties with the sisterhood and the synagogue. He must return to the Yeshiva, where he will be once again exposed to a world of spiritual aspirations and intellectual inspiration. The rabbi will return to his community with new commit-

ment and understanding of the eternal covenant between the
Almighty and the Jewish people.

1. The chaplain who asked this question was Rabbi Nisson Shulman. While serving
as spiritual leader of St. John's Wood Synagogue in London, Rabbi Shulman detailed this
incident in his eulogy for the Rav. Rabbi Milton Nordlicht provided the author with a
cassette copy of the June 3, 1993 hespedim for the Rav in London.

14.03 Social Justice

*Related by the Rav in his lecture on "The Role of the Rabbi" to the
Yeshiva University Rabbinic Alumni, May 18, 1955. (Yiddish).*

It is not sufficient for the Rabbi to know Torah and possess the
competence to issue halakhic decisions. The religious leader must
not only be a scholar and teacher, but he also must be a hero who
has a firm hold on spiritual strength and courage. Maimonides
stresses the latter traits when he delineates the mission of the king:
"His goals and intentions must be to enhance the true faith, fill the
world with righteousness, break the arms of the wicked, and fight
the battles of the Lord" [Hilkhot Melakhim 4:10]. The king must
be the symbol of righteousness and the enemy of viciousness.
Every rabbi is a king in miniature. The sages of the Talmud already
declared that rabbis are called "kings" [Gittin 62a]. The Torah has
therefore also given the rabbi the task of personifying absolute
righteousness and justice.

This is one of the most difficult tests the rabbi constantly
faces. It is an ongoing trial for him. I am speaking to myself about
the need for proper deportment in this area. This is a monologue.
You all know what I told you about Reb Chaim and his drashot on
the Sabbath of Repentance. Reb Chaim felt that he was not worthy of reprimanding his audience. He was only comfortable rebuk-
ing himself. So he told the assembled congregation that Chaim
was speaking to Chaim, but that they could eavesdrop if they so
desired. Similarly, I am now addressing myself. If you wish to listen you are welcome.

To personify absolute righteousness is the greatest challenge
facing the rabbi. The laws of proper behavior between man and his

fellow man create the greatest tests that a rabbi must pass. The leading rabbis throughout the generations succeeded magnificently in these areas. They were totally honest in their decisions in monetary litigation. When the halakhah so indicated, they ruled in favor of the poor; they were not overwhelmed by the wealthy. The community's water-carriers were treated exactly like its affluent lay leaders when they appeared before the rabbi together.

The greatest rabbis throughout the millennia displayed their greatness in the sphere of social justice. These great Torah scholars would certainly pray thrice daily and don Rabbenu Tam tefillin. They taught much Torah and fasted frequently. Yet, in the stories and the anecdotes about these leading rabbis, you do not read about their fasting; you read about their humility, modesty, and skill in conducting dinei torah [rabbinic litigations]. A pompous rich man was not treated any better than a simple tailor who came from the backstreets of the slums. Often it happened that the downtrodden Jew would be vindicated and the wealthy man would come off second best.

We do not know everything that happened in the past. When we read history we learn about culture and economic progress. We read about decrees and pogroms. However, we do not study how the spiritual leaders of the Jewish community functioned in their daily routine. Do you know, for instance, about Rabbi Yom Tov Lipmann Heller [1579–1654], the author of the *Tosefot Yom Tov* [a commentary on the Mishnah]. In his city he was assigned the responsibility of deciding on the distribution of liability for taxes within the Jewish community and for turning over the money to the civil authorities. He instituted a system of progressive taxation so that the wealthy paid more and the poor less. For this supposed inequity he was jailed and was in danger of losing his life. His slanderers claimed that the title of his volume on the Rosh [R. Asher ben Yehiel, 1250–1328], *Maadanai Melekh* ["Delights of the King"], indicated that he was conspiring against the throne!

Yes, I must tell you the truth. I cannot describe all the great rabbis [gedolei yisroel] to you, but I do know of some of my family's involvement with social justice. I am not saying that we were particularly distinguished; there were many great rabbis. However, I can only talk about that which I know. For instance, I can tell you about my grandfather Reb Chaim. He was a great intellectual and revolutionized talmudic study by introducing the abstract method of analysis. This mode of study has enabled talmudic learning to thrive in the modern world. If Reb Chaim had not lived, it would be impossible to study Torah today with the serious American Jewish student. Reb Chaim's method can equal or even surpass any contemporary mode of secular philosophical epistemology and logistic doctrine of terms. This was Reb Chaim's life work. In my eyes, he was a hero not only because of his intellectual stature but especially because of his resolute stand for justice. He was absolutely trustworthy in mundane matters. I remember when my father was consulted regarding the inscription on Reb Chaim's monument. He insisted that the main title should be: Rav ha-Hesed ["Master of charitable deeds"]. He totally fulfilled the admonition of the prophet Ezekiel that "in a controversy they shall stand to judge; according to My ordinances shall they judge it" [Ezekiel 44:24].

Let me relate one incident about Reb Chaim. Once upon a time in Brisk, a poor tailor died in the morning. Two hours later the richest man in town also passed away. The wealthy person was an outstanding Torah scholar. He had been responsible for the selection of Reb Chaim as the rabbi of Brisk. The committee that originally met with Reb Chaim had claimed that he was not sufficiently learned to be the Brisker Rav. This wealthy layman then met with the candidate and soon made known the greatness and uniqueness of Reb Chaim's approach to talmudic study.

These two deaths took place during the winter month of Tevet when the days were very short. The burial society [hevra kadisha] could only handle one funeral at a time. The members of the hevra kadisha reasoned that the tailor's funeral would be attended by only three other tailors. The funeral of the wealthy man, on the other hand, would be attended by a large crowd. The discussion revolved around the question of which burial should be held first. Actually, Jewish law declares that the one who died first should be buried first [*Shulhan Arukh*, Yoreh Deah 354:1]. Nevertheless, the burial society decided to bury the wealthy man first, and they set about preparing the body.

When Reb Chaim heard what was happening, he sent messengers requesting that the tailor be buried first. The hevra kadisha ignored his directions and continued their preparations for the wealthy man's funeral. When Reb Chaim realized that his instructions were being ignored, he set out with his cane, accompanied by the Brisker dayyan, Reb Simhah Selig Reguer. Reb Chaim insisted that the tailor be buried first, and the burial society was forced to submit to his authority. As a result, many people attended the funeral of the tailor. However, only a sparse crowd was present at the interment of the prominent communal leader, since it was finally held after nightfall. The wealthy man's family became Reb Chaim's opponents as a result of this incident. This story means more to me than all of my grandfather's innovative insights on Torah topics.

Let me tell you about another incident concerning Reb Chaim. In 1905, a young Jewish man from Brisk who was a Bundist [a member of the Bund, the Jewish socialist party] threw a bomb at a Russian general in Warsaw. There were winds of revolution in the air, and the young man had been influenced by the socialistic Bundist propaganda.

The wrongdoer was apprehended and speedily brought to trial. He was found guilty and the verdict was death by the firing squad within twenty-four hours. Reb Chaim heard the news during the Kol Nidrei prayer. He immediately stopped the prayers and demanded that the people go home and return with money for the young man's ransom. Reb Chaim sent his sexton to every synagogue in Brisk to interrupt the prayers and collect money. His dayyan, Reb Simhah Selig, stood beside Reb Chaim and supported him in these endeavors. I believe that three thousand rubles were collected. Reb Chaim and Reb Simhah Selig went with the money to the home of the police commissioner of Brisk. At first he refused to accept the money, but after some gentle persuasion the police commissioner acquiesced.

The next day, on Yom Kippur, the rabbis accompanied him on the train to Warsaw. On Yom Kippur morning the police commissioner testified and swore that the young man had been with him when the attempted assassination took place. There was now an alibi, and the young man from Brisk was released. This is what our rabbis did. This was Reb Chaim.

We rabbis were frightened to say a word a few years ago when Senator Joseph McCarthy [Republican of Wisconsin; 1908–1957] caused us so many problems. Reb Chaim was not afraid to speak up in tsarist Russia in 1905. He did everything to save a Bundist who was charged with killing a general who was the nephew of the tsar!

So, my rabbis, what is the moral to be learned? How does this affect us? We generally are not involved with monetary litigation, and we do not sit on dinei torah. Once, we were the spokesmen for our synagogues; today, we do not even qualify as members. Nevertheless, these stories I have told you are not irrelevant. This is at the heart of the problem: How can the rabbi make this message applicable? He must understand that he is the leader. He must set the proper example. The rabbi should neither fear nor favor any of his congregants. He should well understand the prohibition that "You shall not be afraid of any man" [Deuteronomy 1:17]. The rabbis must treat his congregants evenhandedly. He cannot give a wealthy person his whole hand and extend only three fingers to a poor man. That is the meaning of "You shall hear the small and the great alike" [ibid.].

Reforms in the synagogue do not start with demands from the majority. They start with the rigidity and aggressiveness of one person. He soon becomes a leader in the synagogue and finally gets his way. If the rabbi will only display his courage from the outset, the other congregants will stand behind the spiritual leader. If, however, the congregants see that the rabbi is afraid of him, cliques form in the synagogue and the rabbi loses. This, too, is the message of Ezekiel that "in a controversy they shall stand to judge; according to My ordinances shall they judge it."

Even in the area of deciding questions of Jewish law, the rabbi needs courage today. Once upon a time, you did not need any courage to issue a halakhic ruling. When you deal with a monetary question in a din torah, however, you do need courage. Rabbi Jonathan Eybeschuetz [1690/95–1764], who served in rabbinical posts in Prague, Metz, and Altona, related that when he declared an animal treif it never led to enmity. Once a poor butcher brought a cow to Rabbi Eybeschuetz and he declared it treif. The butcher was satisfied even though he lost fifty thaler as a result. He complimented the rabbi for having decided in accordance with the halakhah. However, when two congregants came before Rabbi Eybeshuetz in a dispute over a dish, the loser became a sworn enemy of the rabbi. Here it was exclusively a monetary issue.

Nowadays, with some of our vulgar congregants, even to decide ritual questions you need courage. Sometimes, laymen insist that the questions must be decided in accordance with their wishes. Here, too, the rabbi must stand firm. "You shall not be afraid of any man" applies not only to issues between man and man but also to those between man and God. The rabbi needs courage to decide what is kosher and what is treif, what can be part of the synagogue and what cannot; what is the halakhah and what does not qualify. The rabbi must be the symbol of fearlessness.

14.04 Rabbinic Responsibility

Related by the Rav in his lecture entitled "Rashi on Aseret Hadibrot" at the RCA Annual Convention, June 30, 1970.

Moral schizophrenia is alien to Judaism. The integrity and the unity of the Decalogue challenge us not to separate the theological faith premise from the moral normative system, either way. One cannot practice morality without serving God at the same time.

Nor should one try to serve God without an unconditional commitment to morality.

I am stressing this point because there is a danger that American piety is oblivious of the moral norm in many respects. This is very true of the piety developed in the elementary yeshiva day schools. I will tell you why, and please do not call me a socialist. I am not. Something strange has happened in America. The so-called modern Orthodox Jews in America are almost identical with the upper middle class. The proletariat is not committed. The aristocracy, the Jewish aristocracy, is assimilated. There is a certain middle class of professionals who have come back to Judaism. And please, forgive me, the middle class has a patent on self-righteousness and hypocrisy.

We are engaged in a mortal struggle with the dissident community. You can call them Reformers or Conservatives. I do not care about the name. We are even contending with secularists. The danger of secularism is very great today. American secularism is such a powerful tide that hundreds of thousands of our youth on the college campuses are floating with the tides of secularism. We will not win the battle or lose the battle by excommunications, prohibitions, fist fights, or throwing stones. We are engaged in a battle on two fronts, on the front of religious dissidence and on the front of secularism. We will only win if we understand two concepts. First, we must be capable of interpreting Judaism profoundly. We must show the world the sweep and thrust of Judaism, and that it is a value system and a hierarchy of ideas. These ideas embrace the universe no matter what kind of social order prevails. The Torah can thrive in a capitalist, socialist, hedonic, or moralistic society. Judaism is ready to accept the challenge at any time.

A profound understanding and explanation of Judaism might give us victory. However, we must also understand the second principle. We will only emerge victorious if the people feel that the Orthodox Jew is morally superior. If the skeptics, agnostics, and dissidents admit that the Orthodox Jew is morally superior to them. If this admission is forthcoming, then we will be the winners. If Reform, Conservative, or secular Jews should conclude that the Orthodox rabbi is not superior to a Reform rabbi, then we will lose. If the people feel that the Orthodox rabbi has the same quest for publicity, the same urge for money, the same vainglory, and the same involvement in secular, political, and institutional activities, then we will be the losers.

The integrity of the Decalogue is the only instrument that can give us victory. Morality cannot be separated from faith, and the worship of the Holy One cannot be separated from morality.

14.05 The Rabbi-Teacher

Related by the Rav in his lecture on "The Role of the Rabbi" to the Yeshiva University Rabbinic Alumni, May 18, 1955. (Yiddish).

Judaism must be explained and expounded on a proper level. I have read many pamphlets that have been published in the United States with the intention of bringing people closer to Judaism. There is much foolishness and narrishkeit in some of these publications. For instance, a recent booklet on the Sabbath stressed the importance of a white tablecloth. A woman recently told me that the Sabbath is wonderful, and that it enhances her spiritual joy when she places a snow-white tablecloth on her table. Such pamphlets also speak about a sparkling candlelabra. Is this true Judaism? You cannot imbue real and basic Judaism by utilizing cheap sentimentalism and stressing empty ceremonies. Whoever attempts such an approach underestimates the intelligence of the American Jew. If you reduce Judaism to religious sentiments and ceremonies, then there is no role for rabbis to discharge. Religious sentiments and ceremonies are not solely possessed by Orthodox Jewry. All the branches of Judaism have ceremonies and emotions.

This is not the only reason why we must negate such a superficial approach. Today in the United States, American Jewish laymen are achieving intellectual and metaphysical maturity. They wish to discover their roots in depth. We will soon reach a point in time when the majority of our congregants will have academic degrees. Through the mediums of white tablecloths and polished candlelabras, you will not bring these people back to Judaism. It is forbidden to publish pamphlets of this nature, which emphasize the emotional and ceremonial approaches.

There is another reason why ceremony will not influence the American Jew. In the United Sates today, the greatest master of ceremony is Hollywood. If a Jew wants ceremony, all he has to do is turn on his television set. If our approach stresses the ceremonial side of Judaism rather than its moral, ethical, and religious teachings, then our viewpoint will soon become bankrupt.

The only proper course is that of Ezekiel's program for the priests: "And they shall teach My people the difference between the holy and the common, and cause them to discern between the unclean and the clean" [Ezekiel 44:23]. The rabbi must teach his congregants. He must deepen their appreciation of Judaism and not water it down. If we neutralize and compromise our teachings, then we are no different than the other branches of Judaism.

How do we teach Torah? First of all, we should not underestimate our congregants. If five hundred people come to hear my drashah, which will last for one hour, then I should work on preparing this talk for two whole days. It must have real content.

Secondly, we should teach by utilizing texts. For instance, we should study Humash with the commentary of Rashi [1040–1105]. We should analyze that which is implied between the lines of Rashi. If we are content simply to explain words, then the listeners do not need the rabbis. There are already English translations of Humash and Rashi. Through detailed study of Rashi, teachers can uncover the basics of Judaism. These are the topics which we must convey to our congregants.

In general knowledge, methods have been developed to popularize mathematics and science for nonspecialists. And this is not limited to the social sciences; even the exact sciences can be made popular. We can certainly do this with the teachings of Judaism. We do not do so now. Nowadays we either discusss our studies in a profound Yeshiva fashion or we oversimplify them. We must master the technique of presenting Judaism on a popular but deep level.

For example, we must explain prayer as a lot more than ceremony. We must analyze the concepts and the structure of the Amidah [the "Standing Prayer," consisting of nineteen blessings, said on weekdays]. One must explain the status of the first three, middle, and last three blessings. If our congregants understood the depth of prayer and worship, they would not request reforms and innovations in the synagogue. If we were to document and explain the differences between the unclean and the clean, then our congregants would realize that Jewish prayer is unique. They would understand why we cannot agree to a joint service with Christian churches.

A rabbinical graduate of Yeshiva University told me that in the past he always had trouble in his synagogue on Saturday nights. The congregants always wanted to start the evening prayers before the appropriate time. Finally, the rabbi explained to them in detail the laws of sunset and the appearance of the stars and their implications regarding the length of the Sabbath. From that time on, there was no longer any pressure on the rabbi to permit early worship on Saturday night. Once the congregants understand the halakhic principles, they will no longer protest. The prime responsibility of the Yeshiva should be to produce rabbinical graduates who can popularize halakhah.

This stance is the uniqueness of our position. The Reform and the Conservatives also make claims to Jewish philosophy. If we stress the halakhah, then our Jewish philosophy will be correct and unique. Otherwise, it simply becomes universal teaching. Our central theme must be the principles of the halakhah. If every synagogue had among its members ten congregants who understood the halakhah, these ten would become the bedrock of support for the rabbi. I know from my own experience that this is possible, and that we can popularize the halakhah in addition to Jewish philosophy and aggadah.

14.06 American Orthodoxy

Related by the Rav in his lecture on "The Duties of the King," at the RCA Midwinter Conference, January 18, 1971.

It is an obligation to enhance and elevate the prestige of Judaism. "To show off to the people and the officials her beauty, for she was beautiful to look upon" [Esther 1:11]. How do you display the beauty of the Torah? The most basic method is by setting a proper example. This does not mean only an example of piety in the strict sense of the word, but also by moral and ethical behavior. In my opinion, the Orthodox Jew is also defined by his ethical and moral behavior. Ethics and morality are an integral part of the Torah. The concept of piety is not restricted to the ritual. The Torah never separates rituals and ethics. These laws are interconnected in the Torah. For example, "Every man: Your father and mother shall you revere, and My sabbaths shall you observe" [Leviticus 19:3]. "You shall not steal, you shall not deny falsely, and you shall not lie to one another. You shall not swear falsely by My Name, thereby desecrating the Name of your God, I am the Lord" [Leviticus 19:11–12]. When the Torah speaks about a ritual commandment, the next moment the Torah introduces an ethical law, an ethical norm. There is no difference; there is no distinction. The Torah in its entirety has never distinguished or discriminated between ethics and ritual or between piety and morality. It is one unit, one entity. This concept is important for American Jews and particularly for American rabbis.

I believe that we have made great advances in the last twenty-five, thirty years. Now we have religious Jews. I would have never dreamed, ten years ago, that one hundred and thirty boys would sit with such a meshuganer as I am for five hours to study mishnayot on a Sunday, from 10:00 A.M. to 3:00 P.M. It happened yesterday. It was the yahrzeit for my mother. When I study mishnayot, time is no object at all. We sat for five hours and learned four chapters of mishnayot. Young boys sat with me for five straight hours and discussed these mishnayot with me. They were young boys from various universities. They were not rabbis but simple boys. They come from educated homes, more or less. And somehow they found Judaism. I do not know where, on the street or on campus, but not in their parents' homes. Definitely not.

They listen to every word of my shiur. I start the shiur on time. When I will end, I never know. I started here tonight at 8:00 P.M. When I will end, I do not know. You will have to stay with me the whole night. [Laughter.] Yes, we have accomplished a great deal, particularly through our day schools. However, the final word has not been spoken yet. Who will win the battle in America between Orthodoxy and the dissident groups, such as the Conservative and the Reform? There is no prophet who can foresee the outcome. In my opinion, the battle will be won by the party that understands two things.

Number one, it will be the one that excels not only in piety but in morality. The Orthodox rabbi will be accepted by the whole Jewish community only when he shows the entire community that he not only wears a yarmulka but is a moral person, head and shoulders above the Reform and Conservative rabbis. The Orthodox rabbi must show that he is not a publicity hound; that he is not a lover of money. I do not say that money is bad, but there is a difference between earning a dollar and loving a dollar. The Orthodox rabbi must show that he is more sincere, more committed, and more consistent with himself than the Conservative and Reform rabbis. That is what will decide the battle: higher morality, superior morality.

And I want to tell you, the American Jew is very intelligent. He is intelligent, discriminating, and understanding. I have great faith in the American Jew.

Number two, the outcome of the battle will be decided by the intellectual achievements of the rabbi. For instance, the Orthodox rabbi should be head and shoulders above the Conservative and Reform rabbis as far as knowledge is concerned. I mean knowledge in the widest sense of the word. The Orthodox rabbi should attain a profound understanding of Judaism. He should reach out for new horizons in his intellectual understanding of Judaism. Such achievements will make him the winner.

Morality and intellectuality, Torah knowledge in the widest sense of the word, will ultimately decide the outcome of the battle. In reality, the battle has not yet been won; we do not know the outcome.

14.07 Halakhic Guidance

Related by the Rav in his lecture on "The Role of the Rabbi" to the Yeshiva University Rabbinic Alumni, May 18, 1955. (Yiddish).

The rabbi must know how to properly decide questions of Jewish law. "And they shall teach My people the difference between the holy and the common" [Ezekiel 44:23]. This is the task of hora'ah, of providing halakhic guidance. There is a great difference between theoretical physics and practical physics. For a long time the theory of building an atom bomb was known. In practice, it required many years to achieve. Similarly, there are many talmudic scholars who can give excellent talmudic lectures, but they do not know how to issue decisions in Jewish law. To be expert in determining the halakhah, one must not only be learned but he must also possess the intuition to understand the circumstances surrounding the halakhah and the context in which the question is asked. In the oral exams which we administer to the rabbinical students at the Yeshiva, I have often found that they truly know the theoretical material. They are masters of the Shulhan Arukh Yoreh Deah with all the commentaries of the Shakh and the Taz. Nevertheless, when I ask them how they would proceed if a woman calls to ask a question about a milk pan and a meat spoon, they do not know how to begin to handle the inquiry.

Some believe that there is no need to teach the ability to decide Jewish law in the United States, since few questions are asked by our congregants. This is not so. There are more difficult questions in the United States than the rabbis generally received in Lithuania. We have, perhaps, fewer routine questions, such as those regarding mixtures of meat and milk or permitted and forbidden substances. However, we have the most difficult and unique questions in such areas as those forbidden to marry into the Jewish community or the status of the deserted wife [agunah]. In the past, in Europe, such difficult questions were referred to the leading posekim [experts in deciding Jewish law], such as Rabbi Isaac Elchanan Spektor of Kovno [1817–1896] or Rabbi Naftali Zvi Yehudah Berlin of Volozhin [1816–1893]. They would issue a definitive decision, at times with the stipulation that one or two other posekim agree with their conclusions. Thus these questions were resolved.

In America we have very difficult questions regarding conversion, mamzerut, women prohibited to kohanim, forbidden marriages, and even whether one is considered Jewish or not. Here in the United States I receive these complicated inquires over the phone! When a rabbi receives such questions, he is ashamed to say that he needs time to thoroughly research the problem. He is apprehensive lest his congregants say that the rabbi is not erudite. At times, these most difficult problems—which will have an effect on countless generations—are decided immediately over the phone.

The truth is that many rabbis are prone to the misconception that all questions must be answered immediately. I noticed in your Yeshiva University Rabbinic Alumni program for today that you scheduled a lecture on the halakhic ramifications of artificial insemination. I do not know what was said regarding this topic. You certainly can speak and lecture about it. But let me tell you, it is a bitter question. I do not know how to be posek [how to decide] in this area. When it is a problem of A.I.H. [artificial insemination from the husband], I can be lenient in my ruling. However, when it is A.I.D. [artificial insemination from a donor], I do not know how to decide the halakhah on a practical level. I know all the halakhic opinions regarding this issue, but I still have not reached a conclusion.

Let me tell you what happened to me. A few weeks ago on a Sunday morning, the phone rang at 7:15 a.m. A woman called from New York. The woman's husband could not father children. Five years earlier she bore a son as a result of artificial insemination. She now wants another child through artificial insemination. However, she was told that such a child could very well be a mamzer. The woman turned to her Conservative rabbi, and he tactfully explained to her that he could not decide such a difficult question. He suggested that she consult with me.

"What should I do, Rabbi," she asked me.

"I do not know," I answered.

"Rabbi, what do you mean you do not know? They say you are a great scholar," she exclaimed.

Pleading ignorance, I answered her: "I do not know if I am a great scholar or not, but I do not know the answer to your question."

"Shall I break the appointment with the doctor?" she asked.

"Break the appointment," I answered, "and call me back in four or five weeks. Perhaps I will have a definitive answer for you at that time."

This particular case is very difficult for me because the woman already has a son through A.I.D. If she cannot do it a second time, then the first child is a mamzer. No matter what I decide I will be in a difficult predicament under these circumstances. In such a situation, the Talmud already declared: "Woe is me because of my Creator, woe is me because of my evil inclination" [Berakhot 61a: "Woe if I follow my evil inclination, and woe if I combat it"].

I am not one of those rabbinical scholars who is afraid to issue a halakhic decision. When I see it clearly I am posek.

Some questions, however, simply do not lend themselves to any clear determination. If it is a question of whether one has to repeat Ya'aleh ve-Yavoh [the special appendum to the Amidah prayer on the New Moon] at the Minhah [afternoon] prayer, I will be lenient if I see it clearly. However, in instances of vexatious

questions of family status and pedigree, many times I am hesitant.
Did not Rabban Yohanan ben Zakkai already declare that "there
are two ways before me, one leading to Paradise and the other
leading to Gehinnom, and I do not know by which I shall be taken;
shall I not weep?" [Berakhot 28b]. Certainly, Rabban Yohanan ben
Zakkai knew how to decide questions of Jewish law better than the
Halakhah Committee of the Rabbinical Council of America and
its chairman [i.e., Rabbi Joseph B. Soloveitchik]. Nevertheless,
Rabban Yohanan ben Zakkai was frightened by this responsibility.
We certainly should be. We cannot answer these questions superfi-
cially.

I remember that once I was studying Talmud with my father. I
asked him why the Talmud did not resolve the problem under discussion in so many cases. Instead the Talmud concludes with the
phrase *teiku* ["stalemate"]. Why was no conclusion reached by the
talmudic sages? My father explained to me that a Jew must appre-
hend that he cannot understand and comprehend everything.
When a Jew learns that there are halakhot which are ambiguous,
then he will also come to the realization that there are other areas
that are also not clear-cut. In matters of faith, teiku will also be
encountered. The greatness of Abraham, our forefather, was that
he knew how to say "Here I am" [Genesis 22:1] even though he
did not understand the request that God made of him. The basis
of faith is teiku. If a Jew does not master the concept of teiku, then
he cannot be a true believer. It would not hurt if the rabbi possessed the courage and resoluteness to admit to teiku. The rabbi
must not be ashamed to declare that he must refer the question to
greater experts on the topic.

Excuse me, please, if I ask you a question which is close to my
heart. I receive many inquiries from the rabbinical graduates of the
Yeshiva. Sometimes I want to disconnect my telephone and tear
the wires out of the wall. For some rabbis it has become a mania to
call me and confer with me about all the questions that they
receive. With all this, I do not receive enough of the difficult questions that I know exist in the United States. I am certain that the

hundreds of Yeshiva-ordained rabbis receive many such inquiries. Whom do they consult with? Whom do they ask? I checked with my colleague Rabbi Moshe Shatzkes [1881–1958; Yeshiva University rosh yeshiva and former rabbi of Lomza], and he too does not receive many questions of this nature. The Halakhah Committee of the Rabbinical Council and I should be receiving many such inquiries. Where are these American sheilahs [halakhic questions]? To whom are they being referred? The rabbi should know how to pass these problems on to the proper authority. I do not know all the answers, but let me stress once again that it does not hurt to admit this. A rabbi will not lose his rabbinic crown if he declares that he cannot answer a particular question on the spot.

14.08 The Monsignor's Funeral

Related by the Rav in his lecture on "The Role of the Rabbi" to the Yeshiva University Rabbinic Alumni, May 18, 1955. (Yiddish).

There are questions that only a true scholar [lamdan] will recognize and delineate. These exist mainly in areas of public relations. There are great pressures upon the rabbi in the areas of relations with non-Jews and similar issues.

I would like to share with you an experience that occurred a few weeks ago. I was awakened out of a sound sleep at 6:00 a.m. on a Sunday morning. I have a phone by my bed, and sleepily I lifted the receiver and asked who it was. The man identified himself. He was a sincere, honest, and responsible rabbi who lives in one of the suburbs of Boston. In a tremulous voice, he said to me: "Rebbe. Do you know what happened yesterday? The monsignor of our hometown died!"

I said to myself: "Nu, baruch dayan ha-emet [Blessed be the True Judge, the benediction on hearing news of a death]. May he have a prominent place in heaven!"

The rabbi continued: "I have received a telegram from the Catholic hierarchy asking me to be present in the church for the funeral ceremonies. If I don't go, the president of my synagogue told me that we will have a pogrom!"

The rabbi informed me that people were saying that the Catholic monsignor was one of the truly pious non-Jews. I thought to myself that the monsignor was suddenly growing in stature to great proportions; he was becoming the savior of all mankind. I was still half-asleep. The rabbi at the other end of the telephone was half-hysterical and I could sense fear in his voice. I knew that my decision should not be based solely upon the *Shulhan Arukh*. There are many decisions that must be made not necessarily based only on the *Shulhan Arukh*. You must also consider Jewish history. There are problems that can be best dealt with by basing yourself on Jewish history, that is, what Jews have done in similar situations in previous generations. "Go forth and see how the public are accustomed to act" [Berakhot 45a] is an important principle. At times it is an alternative to the decisions of the Rambam, the Rabad, Rabbenu Tam, and all the other opinions that are analyzed in the various classes of the Yeshiva.

Nevertheless, I told him to call me toward evening; in the meantime I would have to research the issue. After all, I said to him, the funeral was not scheduled to be held immediately.

He called again toward evening and was still very tense. I told him that since the funeral would take place on Tuesday and it still was two days away, perhaps we should meet personally. This calmed him down.

We finally met on Monday, because I was flying to New York on Tuesday. I said to him: "How relevant are the decisions of the *Shulhan Arukh*, *Shakh*, *Taz*, and *Bet Yosef* to you? Throughout our history, if the Jews had gone to the funerals of monsignors and participated in High Mass in the Catholic Church, we would not be here today. You would not be getting a salary from your synagogue, and I would not be a rosh yeshiva in Yeshivat Rabbenu Yitzhak Elchanan. There would be no Jewish communities in the world. Jews have always made sacrifices. If during the Crusades [1040–1215] or the Chmielnicki massacres [1648–1655], Jews had gone to High Mass, even without believing in the Christian doctrines, we would not be here today. We would not have sacrificed the lives of over a half million Jews for the Santification of God's Name [Al Kiddush Hashem] in the Ukraine and in the communities of Mayence and Magence in Germany. We can derive this ruling from the martyrdom of Hannah and her seven sons at the times of the Macabees."

I then showed him the sources in the *Shulhan Arukh*. The rabbi did not go to the funeral, and there was no pogrom.

14.09 Rabbi Eliezer Silver

Related by the Rav in his memorial address for Rabbi Eliezer Silver (1881–1968), Yeshiva University, March 27, 1968. (Yiddish).

I remember that during the first year that I was in the United States, I deliverd a shiur on the Avodah [sacrificial ritual of the high priest in the Temple on Yom Kippur] before the members of the Agudat Harabanim during their kinus teshuvah [repentance lecture]. Before my lecture, my father told me not to be apprehensive because of the august rabbinical garb of the participants. The only one I should be anxious about, he said, was Rabbi Eliezer Silver, because he knew all the tosafot to the talmudic tractate of Yoma by heart, word by word. During my shiur, Rabbi Silver seemed to be taking notes. Afterwards, he handed me his memorandum. It consisted of five or six difficult questions on my lecture. He was truly a great scholar!

14.10 Rabbi Joseph Lookstein

Related by the Rav in his lecture on "The Synagogue as an Institution and as an Idea," delivered at New York's Congregation Kehilath Jeshurun, December 6, 1972. Later edited and published in Rabbi Joseph H. Lookstein Memorial Volume *[34], pp. 338–339.*

I have a liking for pioneers, for experimenters, for people who do not follow the crowd. I always admired the first ones, the early ones, the beginners, the originators. Even in my derashot, I prefer to speak about Abraham, Joseph, or Moses. They were the early ones, the biblical figures who defied public opinion. They disregarded mockery and ridicule, and blazed new trails in the historical jungle of pagan antiquity.

My presence here tonight to deliver this address is only due to my profound respect and sincere friendship for your rabbi, Joseph Lookstein [1902–1979]. . . . Your rabbi was a courageous pioneer. He performed an almost superhuman task in representing the Orthodox Jewish community vis-à-vis the outside world, both the non-Orthodox Jewish community and the gentile world. He did this with tact, dignity, and wisdom. In so doing he greatly enhanced the image of Orthodoxy.

When I came to the United States so many years ago, Orthodoxy was at a low ebb. People, including Orthodox Jews themselves, laughed at Orthodoxy. They treated the Orthodox rabbi and the so-called Orthodox shul with disdain and contempt. As a matter of fact, twenty-five or thirty years ago, we were not confronted by opponents and enemies. We meant nothing. We could not arouse enmity or protest; no one fought us. We simply did not exist. We were met with laughter and ridicule, not with opposition. The situation today is quite different. The change is due not to many people but to a few, among whom Rabbi Lookstein was the most outstanding pioneer. He showed the American Jew that it was possible to have a synagogue conform to the *Shulhan Arukh*, both architecturally and ritually. I must say that this type of bimah [the platform in the center of the synagogue] reminds me of my youth, of my childhood years. I feel kind of nostalgic about it. It conforms to the *Shulhan Arukh*, and at the same time, this shul excels as far as good behavior, cultivated manners, and beautiful sermons are concerned. Rabbi Lookstein contradicted the accusation hurled at us—and I heard this accusation many times—that Orthodoxy is synonymous with slovenliness, vulgarity, ignorance, lack of culture, lack of refinement, and lack of artistic taste. I believe that we owe Rabbi Lookstein a yasher koach ["thanks, well done!"] for it.

He was not satisfied with a house of worship. He built the Ramaz School. It is a pretty good school, even though some say it is not pious enough. In order to offer solace and encouragement to Rabbi Lookstein, I can let him in on a secret. It is confidential. They say the same thing about the Maimonides School, which I founded in Boston! Organizing a day school—and a good day school—in New York forty years ago was an heroic gesture. I want to tell you: Many children who would have never attended a Yeshiva went to Ramaz. You know that I say a shiur in Humash every Saturday night in Boston. A big crowd, a young crowd, attends. Many times a young boy or a young girl comes over to me after the shiur. I ask them about their background and where they learned, and many times the answer is Ramaz. Rabbi Lookstein was also a pioneer in the field of Jewish education. He was responsible for the survival, growth, and development of Bar-Ilan University. One may like Bar-Ilan and another may disagree with it, but everyone must agree that no one else but Rabbi Lookstein could have accomplished the impossible. I believe that even for this he deserves a yasher koach.

I can only pray that your illustrious rabbi shall continue for many, many years to build and to be able to quest for greater and greater things and to reach out for the impossible. However, as far as Rabbi Lookstein is concerned, I do not know if "impossible" is the proper word.

14.11 Rabbi Israel Klavan

Related by the Rav in response to Rabbi Israel Klavan's introduction at the RCA Annual Convention, June 20, 1979.

Thank you, Rabbi Klavan, for your introductory remarks. I feel about you as you feel about me. I was not the one who exerted the influence. I was not always the *mashpiah* [influencer], and you were not always the *mekabbel* [recipient]. I do not know who influenced whom. There is no doubt about it that there are certain things that I have learned from Rabbi Klavan.

It is hard for me to portray my emotions. I was trained in my home as a child not to display emotions. If you love somebody, love him or her with your heart and soul, but do not tell anybody about it. Do not tell anybody about it, not even the person you love. If you are angry with somebody, you may be angry. No doubt about it. But do not tell it to him or to others. Be angry within yourself.

I have told people many times, I never received a kiss from my father, never! Even at the time when I departed [from Warsaw] and left him [for Berlin], and no one knew whether I would see him again or not, my father did not kiss me. He just shook my hand and said: "Lekh le-shalom, Ha-Kadosh Barukhu zul dir mazliakh zein" ["Go in peace, and may the Almighty enable you to be successful"]. No doubt about it, people were standing on the [train] platform and they saw this strange behavior. They thought, "This is Brisk, which has no concern for the heart, only the mind." The mind is cold, whereas the heart is so warm and overflowing. That is why Reb Moshe could not give a kiss to his son. It is not so. I know that my father loved me very much, very much. In actuality, whatever I possess belongs to my father. "Sheli ve-shelahem shelo hu" ["Mine and yours are his"; cf. Ketuvot 63a]. He loved me very much, but he did not express his love.[1]

I am a friend of Rabbi Klavan, yet I cannot portray my friendship for him. I have a great deal of respect for him, a great deal. As a matter of fact, let me just add that the Rambam [Maimonides] to Pirkei Avot [1:6] explains that friendship is a threefold experience. As a matter of fact, friendship imposes a triple duty on the friends.

First of all, a friend must be a haver le-ezra ["a friend for help"]. When your friend is in trouble, he has the right to knock on the door of the person who has been his friend and ask for help.

Then Maimonides speaks of friendship in the sense of haver le-davar ["a friend for conversation"]. This is friendship which one experiences while confiding in another. Friendship is achieved if I have faith in somebody and do not hide anything from him. I confide in him, or to him, both good news and bad news. It means that man must unburden himself of all his worries, fears, and doubts. He can unburden himself only to a person in whom he has absolute unlimited faith and confidence. As a matter of fact, I confided in Rabbi Klavan quite often. We used to speak not only about the RCA. The RCA took up very little time. Then I would confide in him, and he would reciprocate and confide in me. We would discuss our personal worries. There is no man without such problems. Man is burdened with worries and doubts.

Thirdly, Maimonides requires that a friend be a haver le-deah ["a friend in outlook"]. There should be a united effort to achieve something great. There should be the same ultimate end, purpose, and goal. The same vision should attract both friends. Their world perspectives should merge into one great perspective. I have had differences with Rabbi Klavan. At times I had and perhaps I still have. However, basically we are haverim le-deah. We march and move toward one destination. Our outlook on Yahadut [Judaism] is the same.

Therefore, I just want to convey to Rabbi Klavan, on behalf of all the rabbanim here, our good wishes for a complete recovery and a refuah shlemah min ha-shamayim. May you be at the head of the RCA and lead us all to greater achievements and victories.

1. Cf. The Rav's description of his relationship with his father in his eulogy for Rabbi Zev Gold, published in *Tzion min ha-Torah* (New York: Jewish Agency, Department for Torah Education and Culture, 1963), pp. 28–29.

BOSTON

David Leif, an early volunteer fund-raiser for Maimonides School, and the Rav in the school bus purchased for Maimonides School in 1945. Courtesy of Maimonides School.

Planning the new Maimonides campus at the home of Samuel Feuerstein, ca. 1959. Sitting on the couch (l. to r.) Rabbi Levi Yitchak Horowitz (The Bostoner Rebbe), the Rav, Morris Borkum, and Samuel Feuerstein. Standing (l. to r.) Sam Black, Larry Lasky, Edward Gerber, unidentified, Max Kabatznick, unidentified, Penneth Cline, and Rabbi Charles Weinberg. Courtesy of Maimonides School.

Formal groundbreaking ceremonies for Maimonides School's new Brookline facilities, June 26, 1960. (l. to r.) Morris Borkum, Rubin Epstein, Rabbi Joseph Soloveitchik, Maurice Saval, and Samuel Feuerstein. Courtesy of Maimonides School.

Placing the cornerstone in the new Maimonides School building in Brookline, ca. early 1960s. (l. to r.) Rubin Epstein, Rabbi Joseph Soloveitchik, Maurice Saval, Samuel Feuerstein. Courtesy of Maimonides School.

The Rav affixes the mezuzah *at the completion of Maimonides School's new campus in Brookline, ca. early 1960s. Courtesy of Maimonides School.*

Dr. Tonya Soloveitchik and the Rav on the way to the Maimonides School Banquet, December 1965.

A public shiur at Maimonides School, ca. mid 1970s. Photo: Joel Orent.

Maimonides School Graduation, ca. mid 1970s. The speaker is Rabbi David Shapiro (Maimonides School administration). (l. to r.) Rabbi Moses J. Cohn (Maimonides School administration), Robert Sperber (Superintendent of Schools, Brookline), Samuel Feuerstein, Rabbi Joseph Soloveitchik, Maurice Saval, and Dr. Kalman Stein (Maimonides Administration). Courtesy of Maimonides School.

Maimonides School's 1979 Annual Scholarship Banquet. (l. to r.) Chancellor Abram Sachar of Brandeis University, Rabbi Joseph Soloveitchik, and Sam Feuerstein. Courtesy of Maimonides School.

The Rav and his daughter, Dr. Atarah Twersky, greet entertainer Theodore Bikel. The singer performed at Maimonides School's 1979 Annual Scholarship Banquet. Courtesy of Maimonides School.

Dedication of a Sefer Torah. *The Rav with Maurice Saval, ca. 1979. Courtesy of*
Maimonides School.

Jewish Laymen

15.01 The Jewish Baal ha-Bayit

Related by the Rav in a talk delivered at the dedication of the renovated Bet Hamedrash (Rabbinic Study Hall) in the Main Academic Center of Yeshiva University in honor of Mr. Joseph Gruss, May 17, 1979.

We all know what kabbalah (tradition) and mesorah mean in the area of Jewish scholarship. Saturday afternoon during the summer, following the recitation of the Minhah (afternoon) prayer, we pronounce the famous dictum of Pirkei Avot [1:1] that "Moses received the Torah on Sinai and handed it down to Joshua." Torah knowledge originated in Sinai and has subsequently been passed down from generation to generation, from scholar to scholar, from individual to individual, throughout the centuries and the millennia.

If you ask what is the quintessence of Jewish history, I will tell you that Jewish history revolves around one basic relationship: rebbe and talmid, teacher and disciple. Moshe himself is not known to us as a liberator, redeemer, king, or priest, but rather as our teacher. He is called Moshe Rabbenu, Moses our teacher. One generation teaches; the other generation listens.

What does the earlier generation teach? A variety of things. Truth, morality, norms and laws. Moreover, an outlook is passed on. It is a method of understanding the world; a method of a lifestyle—how to live and interact with the world. In a word, there is a continuity of thoughts and concepts. One generation is responsible as the teacher, and the other generation as the disciple. In a word, it is a scholastic-rabbinic mesorah. The stress is on rebbe and talmid, teacher and disciple.

However, I believe, and I firmly believe in this, that there is another mesorah of great significance and of unlimited relevance. Namely, the mesorah of the practical tradition, or the lifestyle of the Jewish layman. Let me not play around with the word "layman," as I do not truly comprehend its significance. Let me substitute for layman the words baal ha-bayit. It is a strange word, both philologically and semantically. The history of the word is unknown. What does "baal ha-bayit" mean? What does it mean that "one owns a house"? As a type or representative of the layperson, what does the word "baal ha-bayit" mean? I do not know. I am not a philologist, and even trained philologists do not know. But let me speak about this concept without knowing the origin of the word. Let us speak of the baal ha-bayit as a person or personality.

In contrast with the scholastic tradition, the practical tradition is not one of concepts, abstractions, thoughts, methods, laws, and norms. The practical tradition is one of images; the continuity of things that are observed, something I feel and can reach out to. It is a tradition of a lifestyle, of action.

This practical tradition can be traced back to antiquity. If you ask me who was the first Jewish baal ha-bayit in history, in the Bible, I will tell you: Joseph. He was the prime minister of Egypt and at the same time the head of the House of Jacob that arrived in Egypt. This tradition also goes back to the so-called yakirei yerushalayim, or the aristocratic noblemen of Jerusalem before the destruction of the Temple. The Talmud tells many stories about their deportment. On Yom Kippur night they did not go to sleep, so that they could keep the high priest awake. The high priest was alone, and they wanted him to know that there were people who had compassion for him and were willing to help him. Yom Kippur was a great day for the high priest, and his grave responsibilities could make him feel overwhelmed. These noblemen gave him the courage to carry out the rituals of the Avodah [the Yom Kippur service] the next day. The Talmud states: "Some of the worthiest of Jerusalem did not go to sleep all the night in order that the high priest might hear the reverberating noise so that sleep should not overcome him suddenly" [Yoma 19b].

We tell stories, and the truth is that the Jewish people are experts in the art of storytelling. It has been developed to its greatest extent by the hasidim. It is a unique talent of the Jew. We tell stories not only about great rabbinic scholars but also about outstanding baalei batim, particulaly baalei zedakah, or Jewish philanthropists. For instance, we know many stories about the Gaon of Vilna [1720–1797], the greatest Jewish scholar of the eighteenth century. We also know, however, of a baal ha-bayit of that period whose name was Reb Berel Beres [d. 1830].[1] We have very nice stories about him, his lifestyle, personality, finesse, and generosity. Reb Berel Beres was a merchant and a contemporary of the Vilna Gaon.

As a matter of fact, it is not easy to become a genuine baal ha-bayit. True it is also not easy to become a scholar. It is even more difficult to become a genuine baal ha-bayit. He is exposed to more temptations than the scholar. The baal ha-bayit needs a lot of courage. I would say he needs to make an heroic effort in order to retain the title of baal ha-bayit. I am inclined to believe that our miraculous survival throughout the millennia and, in particular, the lonely nights of the galut is due not only to the rabbinic scholars but also because of the Jewish baal ha-bayit. The rabbis guided us and told us what to do and how to act. The baal ha-bayit enabled us to survive because of his discipline, intelligence, and readiness to suffer. Without this unique type of baal ha-bayit, I doubt whether we would have survived. "And he lodged there that night" [Genesis 32:14]. It was a lonely night. The rabbi, the scholar, and the baal ha-bayit were responsible for our successful survival.

You may ask me what these baalei-batim possessed? We have many books about our scholars, such as Maimonides, Nahmanides, R. Yosef Karo, the Remah, the Gaon of Vilna, and Reb Chaim of Volozhin. However, very little has been written about the Jewish baal ha-bayit. Historians have not been interested in this topic. But if somebody were to ask me what the baal ha-bayit possessed, what characteristics were responsible for the important role he discharged in Jewish history, what was unique about him, I would have an answer.

I believe that the Jewish baal ha-bayit distinguished himself with three characteristic traits or capabilities.

First, the baal ha-bayit possessed a sense of unlimited responsibility. He had a clear awareness of what the Talmud states as "all of Israel are sureties one for another" [Shevuot 39a]. He had a deep feeling not only for himself and his family but also for the Jewish community. And not only for the Jewish community in his town but for the entire Jewish community throughout the world. He not only had this sense of responsibility but he discharged its demands in dignity.

Second, the baal ha-bayit possessed a tough and pragmatic mind. He thought in strictly utilitarian and practical categories. He also had a capability for decision making and an unlimited capacity for implementing his decisions. Without these traits the baalei batim would not have achieved prominence.

Third, and this may sound nonsensical and absurd, they possessed not only a tough mind but a sensitive heart. Can a person be both at the same time? It seems illogical. Psychologically, I do not know if it is possible or not. It is difficult to be a dreamer. Yet the baal ha-bayit succeeded in having a utilitarian mind and a practical approach to the world and at the same time was a visionary, looking up to the stars. They combined the thesis and the antithesis. Somehow this thesis and antithesis forged a synthesis in their personality. It was a dialectical personality, opposites combined into one. On a practical level it was very hard to cheat the Jewish baal ha-bayit. Even our enemies knew this. The baal ha-bayit had a tough mind and was very consistent. He was influenced by the talmudic method of analysis, which had trained him to analyze everything in depth. At the same time he was a dreamer and a visionary who looked beyond the reality. "I will lift up My eyes unto the mountains" [Psalms 121:1]. In addition to this sensitivity of the heart and the dream which twinkled in the eyes of the baal ha-bayit, he also had unshakable faith in the redemption and the salvation of the Jewish people.

You will ask me, From whom did the baal ha-bayit inherit these basic characteristics? Where did he learn to be tough and to be a dreamer at the same time? As I have already mentioned, the baal ha-bayit inherited these traits from the first such Jew: the biblical Joseph. How does the Bible portray Joseph? What type of person was he? He was an unusual person. He would dream about sheaves of corn—"For, behold, we are binding sheaves in the field" [Genesis 37:7]. This was a very prosaic and practical dream! And at the same time he dreamed about stars in the sky. Somehow he was also able to dream about the uncharted lanes of the universe. Apparently, the two types of dreams were not mutually exclusive, and they found their synthesis in the personality of Joseph.

Now let me tell you something that happened about fourteen years ago. The late Mrs. Soloveitchik and I met Mr. Joseph Gruss. It was about fourteen or fifteen years ago, I do not remember exactly. I asked him for an appointment, but he came himself. I was ready to go up and see him, but instead he came to me. He did not spend a long time with us. Mr. Gruss is not a bore. He is a businessman. In a short time, perhaps after a half-hour, Mr. Gruss left. After he departed, Mrs. Soloveitchik said to me: "For the first time I have met in the United States a Jewish baal ha-bayit. He walked into our house from the pages of Jewish history." Indeed, Jewish history is the story of the Jewish baal ha-bayit.

My wife was right in her characterization of Mr. Gruss. Whenever I met him I was reminded willy-nilly, spontaneously, of the outstanding baalei batim of Jewish history. The name of Moses

Montefiore [1784–1885] comes to my mind when I see Mr. Gruss. I also think of Amschel Mayer Rothschild [1773–1855], whom the Jews in the ghettos of Eastern Europe called "the frumer [pious] Rothschild." I will tell you frankly, in my opinion, Mr. Gruss has given more to Jewish causes than Montefiore and Rothschild did together. This is not an exaggeration. The amount that Mr. Gruss distributes to charity and his motives in helping Jewish education are far superior to all the philanthrophic work which Montefiore or Rothschild did. Mr. Gruss continues and excels in their traditions.

1. For more on Reb Berel Beres, see Yisrael Klausner, *Korot Bet ha-Almin ha-Yashan be-Vilna* (Vilna, 1935), p. 58.

15.02 Man as an Individual

Related by the Rav in his lecture on "Holy Days and Weekdays," delivered to Social Workers, December 24, 1973.

Judaism understands the greatness of the existential experience of man alone. It is important to be an individual. Man is creative because he is an individual and is different. He can be alone and live in the recesses of his personality, unknown to others. On the other hand, Judaism also understands the greatness of the community, of the existential experience of living in the community. According to Judaism, both the thesis and the antithesis are correct. Jews must be capable of being alone and at the same time of being together. The Jew must be capable of withdrawing and escaping from society and the noise of the street. He must be able to leave behind the vulgarity, coarseness, and artificiality of society. However, he must also be capable of coming back, joining, merging, and once again being one with society.

The Jew should experience existence as a "together" affair as well as only an "I" affair. He should be concerned only with himself and at the same time with everyone else, with the community. The individual is both. He is a separate existential entity who cannot imagine existence outside of himself. As you know, as man gets older he begins to think in very strange and peculiar terms. I can imagine many things. I cannot imagine one thing because I am an individual. I cannot imagine how it is possible for the world to go on existing after I have left it.

There is a short story written by a master writer, Peter Altenberg [pseudonym of Richard Englaender, 1859–1919]. He was an assimilated Jew who lived in Vienna at the turn of the century. Altenberg opposed Theodor Herzl, the founder of the Zionist movement, who also lived in Vienna at that time. Altenberg wrote a short story which I believe was called "New Year's Eve, 1951." In it he describes the New Year when the streets are blanketed with snow, everybody is rushing, and the music plays in the cafés. He was a sensitive person, and he gives a portrayal of New Year's Eve in Vienna. You have to be Viennese to truly understand his portrait of the New Year's dances and the affection of the people for one other.

And then there is the last line. "The same New Year's Eve as I celebrated in 1903 will be celebrated in 1951. There will be only one difference. Peter Altenburg will not be around on New Year's Eve in 1951." In other words, he could not imagine how New Year's Eve could take place without him.

This is typical of many individuals. We do not generally think in these terms, but from time to time such thoughts converge upon us. And I, of course, do not think in terms of New Year's Eve. New Year's Eve is, let us say, not part of my fond memories. [Laughter.] I was once beaten up on New Year's Eve in Germany. A fat "beer" German met me and beat me up. I believe this happened in 1932.

But I think such thoughts in relation to Rosh Hashanah and Yom Kippur. I think of another Rosh Hashanah in the future. I see the same bet ha-medrash. I see the same routine, the chanting of the hazzan and the familiar melodies of the prayers. Everything is as it was. But there is only one difference. I will not be there! This is a tragic experience. The individual cannot imagine a world that he is not part of. This is basically a tragic experience, but it is also a creative experience. It is an inspiring experience. I cannot explain this to you. But it is inspiring, and it is rooted in the individuality and the exclusiveness of the human being. . . .

We are part of humanity and at the same time we are alone by ourselves.

15.03 Sacrifice and Anonymity

Related by the Rav in the Tonya Soloveitchik Memorial Lecture on "The Anonymous Man and the Covenantal Community," Yeshiva University, March 18, 1970.

A courageous life, an existence dedicated to service, creates a heroic life. A heroic life means a life of sacrifice. The highest level of sacrifice for a human being is not when he gives his life for his ideals. The highest form of sacrifice, as viewed by Judaism, is the readiness of man to leave the stage after discharging his role and vanish into anonymity and oblivion. More than a person wants to continue living, he wishes to be remembered. He wants to be recalled by individuals and by society at large. He wants to feel that he has accomplished something with his life.

This quest to be remembered and to not be forgotten is intensely powerful. I remember that many years ago in Boston an old woman would bring me some quarters every week in order to pay for a hundred-dollar memorial tablet in the shul. She would count the money with trembling hands: one quarter and another quarter, a third quarter and a fourth quarter. It was during the difficult years of the Depression. I finally asked her: "Tell me, my dear lady. Do you have savings in the bank?"

She answered that she had none.

"So why do you give the money to the shul? You cannot afford to do so," I stated.

She replied: "Rebbe, I want to be remembered. Once I die I know that my children will not think about me. They will never come to shul to say the Yizkor memorial prayer. This way the shul will remember me at Yizkor."

This is not just the mentality of an unlettered or perhaps a primitive old lady. She was an honest woman who was expressing the mentality of Western man. When [Lyndon] Johnson accepted [John F.] Kennedy's invitation in 1960 to run as his candidate for Vice-President, many felt it was a comedown for Johnson. A journalist asked him: "Why did you accept it? After all, as the majority leader of the [U.S.] Senate you wielded so much more power and influence. You commanded the respect of the White House, and now as the Vice-President you will be little more than an errand boy for the President."

Johnson answered the reporter: "Yes, you are right. But history textbooks will accord two more lines to the Vice-President than to the majority leader of the Senate."

To this way of thinking, power in the present means little if the individual will not be remembered in the future. This is in contradistinction to Judaism, where the stress is on anonymity. Let me give you an example.

There are many men here who study gemara. Many times in the Mishnah the anonymous opinion of the tanna [mishnaic sage] is quoted. He is known as the tanna kamah [the first tanna]. Who is he? What is his name? Who is the tanna bathra [the last tanna]? They are part of the majority of Jewish scholars who remain anonymous, men without names. In the Talmud we often come across the introductory phrase *tanu rabbanan* ["the rabbis taught"]. Who were these rabbis? What were their names? Why were the sages so tight-lipped about these rabbis? It is not just a coincidence or neglect on the part of the talmudic scholars. The names were purposely not recorded, to teach us that we must remain anonymous. The greatest of all sacrifices that a Jew must bring is his readiness to sink into oblivion and remain in the shadows of anonymity.

It is very strange, but we know much more about the lives of Aristotle, Socrates, and Plato than we know about the Vilna Gaon. What do I know about my father? Very little. He never spoke about himself and did not write an autobiography. What do I know about the life of my grandfather Reb Chaim? Only isolated episodes. He never confided his private experiences or clandestine emotions to anyone. Whatever happened, happened between them and God.

God requires of man the greatest of all sacrifices—anonymity. He hates vainglory but loves the actor or the actress who appears on the stage for a short while and humbly discharges his or her role, disappearing afterwards without receiving applause. Man stands in the limelight as long as he consecrates himself to the covenantal community. The very moment he finishes his job, the lights are dimmed or, rather, extinguished, and man steps off the stage.

What does the Megillah tell us about Mordecai and Esther after the Haman episode? Did she remain the queen of Persia? After all, she was a young girl and must have lived for many more years. Nevertheless, the Megillah does not mention one word about this part of her life. "Then Esther the Queen, the daughter of Abihail, and Mordecai the Jew, wrote down all the acts of power to confirm this second letter of Purim" [Esther 9:29]. The story was finished, and Esther removed herself from the stage.

What do we know about Mordecai the Jew? "And all the acts of his power and his might and the full account of the greatness of Mordecai, how the king advanced him, are they not written in the Book of Chronicles of the kings of Media and Persia?" [Esther 10:2]. Go ahead and find this volume! Yes, one episode of their lives, and a short one at that, was recorded. The rest was anonymous. That is exactly what the prophet Micah said: "He has told you, O man, what is good, and what the Lord seeks from you: only the performance of justice, the love of kindness, and walking humbly with your God." I would say: walking anonymously with your God.

15.04 Bontzye Schweig

Related by the Rav in his lecture at Yeshiva University's Institute of Mental Health Project (undertaken jointly with Harvard and Loyola

Universities to study religious attitudes to psychological problems), February 5, 1959.

Isaac Leib Peretz [1852–1915] wrote a short story which was later translated into many languages. The story is called "Bontzye Schweig." Bontzye is a name, and "Schweig" means "silent one" in Yiddish. One had to have lived in a shtetl in Lithuania in order to appreciate a person like Bontzye Schweig. In America I have not seen anyone like him, since such a child would be classified by the agencies as retarded and put away. There are no Bontzye Schweigs walking the streets of American cities.

In Europe, where the retarded child remained at home, he could not attend heder. If he did, the instruction was completely worthless and useless for him. So the retarded child grew up to become the town's idiot or half-wit. He became what we call in Yiddish a *shtat-meshuganer*. Sometimes such individuals were very noisy, and at times they were quiet and mute.

I knew such a man in the small Russian town that I lived in when I was about six years old. We used to call him *alte moron*, "the old moron." So what happened to him? He inherited a few hundred dollars from his father. Someone borrowed the money from him. Of course, he was to receive interest so that he would have a means of support. Yet it was forbidden for a Jew to receive interest for a loan. It was arranged that the retarded individual would do some daily work for the borrower. He would draw water and chop wood, and thus his interest became the payment for the services he rendered. Such individuals were an institution in the small towns in Europe. They were like Bontzye Schweig. Without knowing these people, it is hard to appreciate Peretz's story.

In his characteristic manner, Peretz portrayed the deep tragedy of Bontzye's anonymous life and all his sufferings. However, after his death, when Bontzye arrived in heaven, his status suddenly changed. There, Bontzye's arrival made a great stir. Throngs of angels preceded him and sang songs of welcome. The heavenly court recounted all that he had suffered during his lifetime. He was now the center of attention and eagerly welcomed into Paradise. Bontzye could choose any reward he wanted. Yet all he asked for was "a hot roll with fresh butter for breakfast every morning."

This is the true attitude of Judaism. The greatness and uniqueness of every individual must be stressed. Even a Bontzye Schweig discharges a prominent role in the Divine Creation.[1]

This was the greatness of the European rabbinical leaders. They were humble, and every Jew could approach them. My grandfather Reb Chaim Brisker was a prime example of such deportment. This was also the greatness of the hasidic movement. Any Jew could approach the hasidic rebbeim and feel at home in their courts. Both the great and the simple were welcome. Every individual is unique. This is a basic tenet of Judaism.

1. Cf. the Rav's *Halakhic Man*, trans. Lawrence Kaplan (Philadelphia: Jewish Publication Society, 1983), p. 157, fn. 114; and Meyer Waxman, *A History of Jewish Literature* (New York: Bloch Publishing Co., 1947), vol. 4, pp. 500–501.

15.05 Franz Rosenzweig

Related by the Rav in his Teshuvah Drashah, September 1972. (Yiddish). Summarized and published in Al ha-Teshuvah *[8:7], pp. 309–310, and* Soloveitchik on Repentance *[37:7], p. 318.*

Suddenly, life changes. Deep in your heart there is a sudden transition and the divine light is revealed. The person uncovers a new focus in his personality. From the depths of his soul he feels he has freed himself from his former convictions. Suddenly, all aspects of his personality and spiritual quest are united. He is now his own master and can exercise proper control over himself. All at once, the Almighty has freed him from his former lifestyle. "Then the Lord, your God, will bring back your captivity and have mercy upon you" [Deuteronomy 30:3].

I know stories of this kind about individuals who became ba'alei teshuvah [repentant returnees to Torah]. For instance, you have the example of the German Jewish philosopher Franz Rosenzweig [1886–1929]. He was a shomer mitzvot [observant Jew].

There were two friends, Rosenzweig and Martin Buber [1878–1965, also a German Jewish philosopher]. Buber was totally non-observant, but Rosenzweig was a shomer mitzvot and a true believer. Rosenzweig had previously reached such a level of assimilation that he had been desirous of converting away from Judaism. He debated with a priest, because he declared that he could not accept all of the concepts of Christianity. The priest insisted that he must accept all the tenets, and as a result his shemad [conversion] was impeded.

Imagine how distant and removed Rosenzweig was from Torah! Once, during World War I, he went into a small hasidisher shteibel on Yom Kippur. He saw how these Jews prayed, and he came out a completely different person. He totally reversed his former views. His feelings of estrangement, assimilation, and shmad vanished in a moment. He resolved to seek out his Jewishness and to master Judaism. Rosenzweig even desired to study Gemara.

Reb Yitzhak Breuer [1883–1946, practicing lawyer and leader of German Orthodoxy] related that when Rosenzweig completed his major work, *Der Stern der Erloesung* ["The Star of Redemption"], he sent a copy to Breuer. The two were friends and had studied together in the same school, so Rosenzweig sent him a copy of the manuscript. Breuer told me that it was during the summer and he was in the Bad Nauheim resort area outside of Frankfurt, where he read the book. Breuer did not write to Rosenzweig. Soon, a letter arrived in which Rosenzweig asked Breuer to evaluate the volume. Breuer responded that he must state the truth. "You wish to write about Jewish philosophy and not simply general religious philosophy. I do not see how you can publish a book on Jewish philosophy and yet not quote the Talmud even once."[1] Yitzhak Breuer told me that after Rosenzweig received his letter, he immediately came from Frankfurt to visit him in Bad Nauheim. Rosenzweig wept to him about his ignorance and resolved to study Gemara. He engaged a private tutor, but unfortunately Rosenzweig took ill and died at a young age.

This is an example of the spontaneous total reawakening within the individual which leads to complete and sudden teshuvah.

1. On the letter from Yitzhak Breuer to Franz Rosenzweig in which Breuer comments on the lack of talmudic sources in Rozenzweig's work, see Rivkah Horowitz, "Yitzhak Breuer, Franz Rosenzweig and Rabbi A. I. Kook," in *Torah im Derekh Eretz Movement*, ed. Mordechai Breuer (Ramat Gan: Bar-Ilan University, 1987), pp. 111–112.

The Land of Israel

16.01 The Loyalty of the Land

Related by the Rav in his lecture on the "Covenants in the Book of Genesis" to the Yeshiva University Rabbinic Alumni, Yeshiva University, ca. 1955. (Yiddish).

One of the miracles of God's covenant with Abraham is that the Land of Israel waited for the people of Israel. In this saga there is a momentous occurrence which is unintelligible when viewed in the perspective of general history. For instance, take the seventeenth, eighteenth, and nineteenth centuries. These were years of massive colonization throughout the world. The European nations colonized entire continents. A prime example is the North American continent, which is now the United States and Canada. There is also South America and the Latin countries. Australia, South Africa, and New Zealand were also settled at this time. The non-Jewish world proved to be excellent colonizers. The greatest achievements were in America, where a wild continent evolved within a few hundred years into the most technologically advanced country in the world.

It is amazing that while many nations tried to colonize and develop the Land of Israel, none succeeded. During the time of the Crusades it became a Christian goal to revive the Holy Land. There were so many Crusades and so many attempts. They all failed. Then the Moslems tried, and they also failed. At the start of this century the Germans also attempted and did not succeed.

It is noteworthy that the Land of Israel remained primitive in its development. Even in Egypt a more sophisticated civilization evolved. Syria and Iraq were also more developed than the Land of Israel. The Arabs who inhabited the Land of Israel were the most primitive and the least cultured of all their brethren. I remember the Land of Israel from my visit in 1935. Even then it was mainly desert, stones, sand, and water. This was after fifty years of Jewish colonization!

Yet as the Jews returned to the Land it slowly began to open up to them. Only now is the country beginning to bloom and prosper. If the Land had been developed by other nations, the Jewish people would not have had the opportunity to resettle in their ancestral home. The Land of Israel possesses a special holiness which makes it remain loyal to the Jewish people.

This loyalty of the Land resembles the concept of agunah, which literally means a woman who remains tied to her husband even though it is unknown whether he is still alive.[1] Although the years go by and old age gradually overtakes her, she still remains loyal to her absent husband. Such a situation with a woman is a grave tragedy, and we must do everything we can to help her. Yet in addition to the tragic aspect there is also a profound moral message. It is the loyalty of the woman to her marital state despite the adverse circumstances that is so inspirational. This is the ethical norm that is concealed in the concept of agunah. In this sense the Land of Israel has been an agunah as she has waited for her children to return.

Such being the case, there is an even greater question. Allowing that the Land will retain its loyalty to the Jewish people, will the people remain loyal to the Land? It is easier for stones and inanimate land to remain loyal than for humans, who can constantly express their freedom of choice. In halakhah we have the concept of agunah, but we do not utilize the word *agun* for a man. He has the freedom of choice and can always solve his inability to remarry by utilizing the heter me'ah rabanim [permission from a hundred rabbis]. This law was enacted by Rabbenu Gershom ben Yehudah [ca. 960–1028]; a man is prohibited from marrying an additional wife unless specifically permitted to do so on special grounds by at least one hundred rabbis from three different "countries."[2] I personally have never signed such a heter of one hundred rabbis, since I feel that the man's position should be symmetrical to the woman's in this situation. If the woman must wait, then the man must also wait.[3] I feel that the enactment of Rabbenu Gershom against having more than one wife must be parallel. One must be stringent not only as far as the woman is concerned but also regarding the man's marital status. I have therefore never signed a heter me'ah rabanim. Just as the man must also remain loyal to his wife, the people of Israel must also remain loyal to the Land. This was likewise a unique attribute which the Jewish people developed in their ongoing relationship with the Land of Israel.

1. On the halakhic status of the agunah, see Yitzchak Zev Kahane, *Sefer ha-Agunot* (Jerusalem: Mossad Harav Kook, 1954).

2. On the heter me'ah rabanim, see the *Talmudic Encyclopedia*, vol. 17, pp. 447–452.

3. Cf. Walter Wurzburger, "Rav Joseph B. Soloveitchik as Posek of Post-Modern Orthodoxy," *Tradition*, vol. 29, no. 1 (Fall 1994), p. 17.

16.02 American Jews and Israel

Related by the Rav in his address at the convention to mark the merger of the Mizrachi and the Ha-Poel ha-Mizrachi movements in the United States in 1957. Published in Ohr ha-Mizrach *[2], pp. 28–29. (Hebrew).*

The relationship of the Jew to the Land of Israel is much stonger than the feelings of other ethnic groups of immigrants in the United States toward their former homelands. Which Jews truly experience this deep attachment to the Land of Israel? It is only the first and second generations of American Jews who feel this devotion. The first generation of immigrants generally does not achieve material wealth. They help Israel with their deep sighs as they observe the struggles of the Jews in the Holy Land. Their sighs are piercing and heartfelt. As a result of these sighs, the second generation, which is generally wealthier than the first, contributes generously to Israeli causes.

The second generation of American Jews has inherited some of the vital Jewish spirit of the first generation. These feelings are expressed by their monetary contributions to the State of Israel. The second generation lags behind the first in many aspects of Jewish observance. However, the second generation gives expression to its Judaism by magnanimous donations to Israeli causes. I would say that the second generation compensates for its loss of considerable Jewish commitment by its generosity toward Israel. The second generation is sufficiently motivated to make these monetary contributions. However, its attachment to Israel is not strong enough to motivate them to physically contribute by becoming halutzim, pioneers in the Land of Israel.

"When you beget children and grandchildren and have been long in the Land" [Deuteronomy 4:25]—the second generation is truly rooted in the land. They are Americans, and their Jewish sparks are proportionately diminished.

The third generation is all the more embedded in American soil. They had little Jewish education and have no concept of Judaism. Who knows whether this nebulous commitment will be sufficient to maintain their continued connection with the Jewish people? This relationship is extremely weak, and I am not certain that it will not snap and be torn asunder because of the exigencies of the times.

This is the great challenge which faces us today. How can we influence the third generation and inspire commitment to the Land of Israel? I was recently told a story about two Jewish students on a college campus. They were reacting to the Sinai Campaign [the short war between Israel and Egypt; October 29–November 5, 1956]. One student declared regarding the Israeli victory: "Isn't it terrific!" The second responded: "Isn't it terrible!" The first was a second-generation American, while the second was a third-generation American. This is the great challenge that confronts us: How do we inspire the third generation toward Torah and Zion?

This commitment cannot be engendered by simple-minded gestures, such as reading modern Israeli literature or playing games like those played in *I Like Mike* [an Israeli play dealing with an Anglo-Saxon theme]. This will not influence the American youngster who lives in the midst of the highly developed and sophisticated Anglo-Saxon culture. Israelis do not comprehend how refined this culture is. Do Israelis really believe that they can rival the unprecedented technological developments in the United States?

East European Jews were transfixed by the mere reference to the State of Israel. These Jews had always been stateless. They never really felt an inner commitment to the lands in which they resided. They were constantly subjected to persecution and hardship in these countries. Therefore they were enchanted by the very mention of a Jewish state. However, the Jew born in the United States is totally at home in his country. He is an integral part of America and benefits from completely equal rights and unlimited opportunities. The American Jew is not captivated by the mere concept of a Jewish state.

In all of Jewish history there has never been a Jewish presence outside the Land of Israel that can compare with that of American Jewry. They are the most powerful and wealthy Jewish community in our history. There is no logical reason why they should willingly abandon this society for little Israel.

The only motivating factor which can inspire the American Jew toward Israel is the religious bond. The Jew's eternal faith and covenant with his true homeland cannot be weakened either by persecution or by American material success. The Torah has engendered an everlasting bond between the Jew and the Land of Israel. The stress in Torah and tradition on the primacy of the Land of Israel must be the basis of Zionist education in the United States. Only this approach will enable the third generation to inherit the traditions of their forebears. The State of Israel will then become a focal point in their spiritual perspective.

16.03 Contemporary Jewish Revival

Related by the Rav in his lecture on Hanukah, Boston, Mass., December 18, 1971.

In the prayer for Hanukah we recite: "When a wicked Hellenic government rose up against *amkha-Yisrael*" ["Thy people Israel"; *Daily Prayer Book*, trans. Philip Birnbaum, p. 92]. What does the expression amkha-yisrael mean? It could have been said that the Hellenic government rose up against "Israel" or against "Thy people." Why does the prayer stress "Thy people Israel"? What does this specific term express? Amkha means we belong to Thee. Amkha is a possessive noun. We belong to Thee even while we go astray and deviate from the righteous path. We are still committed to Thee even when we are guilty of certain offenses and certain sins. What comes to expression in Amkha is the old idea that "even though the people have sinned they are still called Israel" [Sanhedrin 44a]. A Jew, even when he sins, remains a Jew. What does this mean? What did our sages wish to express in this statement?

It means that there is an eternal commitment in the Jew to the Almighty. Sometimes it is a conscious commitment. Sometimes it is an unconscious commitment. However, there is a commitment which can never be annulled or severed. That commitment is like a heavy load pressing on the frail shoulders of every Jew. He may fight this commitment. He may hate it. But there is this commitment on the part of every Jew. The Jew basically cannot cast off this feeling. Habad call this *ha-ahavah ha-tiv'it*,[1] the natural love of God that every Jew possesses. Whether he has been trained or not, there is a natural instinctual drive and urge in the Jew to find God. Many Jews walk straight to that ultimate goal and move in the right direction. Some Jews are searching for God, but in their search move in the opposite direction. Of course, they are lost sheep. This is man's natural spontaneous urge and drive for God, but it comes to expression with more vigor in the Jew. That is the meaning of amkha. We belong to Thee, and there is no way we can free ourselves from Thee. That is the meaning of "rose up against Thy people Israel"—amkha-yisrael.

As a matter of fact, I will tell you frankly that some people think this is a beautiful idea but not valid in practical terms. Many a time I thought so myself. I began to doubt this philosophy that willy-nilly the Jew belongs to God. When I came to America, there was a tremendous assimilationist movement. It was assimilation in its most ugly and vulgar form. The first immigrants who came to America gave up everything. Then it seemed that Russian Jewry was completely lost. There was no general commitment on the part of the Jew. The observant Jew was a small and limited minority. There was no institution of Torah education in the United States. There were a couple of day schools, and even these were conducted in a desultory fashion. You could not be too optimistic about the philosophy of amkha-Yisrael.

Now, two things have happened which corroborate this philosophy. One thing is the awakening among the Jews of Russia. I really do not know if this is true. I am still skeptical. People who come from Russia tell me that it is true. I am still doubtful. Do you know why? It borders on the miraculous, because the revolution in Russia took place in 1917. That means that two generations have been raised in Russian schools that were atheistic from A to Z. Materialistic in outlook on the world and man, their teachings were particularly resentful of Judaism. I do not know why. Perhaps it is because Communism is a philosophy of atheism. Atheism is not something marginal and incidental. It is basic to the outlook of Communism. The Jew gave the world the concept of monotheism. A community founded upon atheism must hate a community which has brought the world the gospel of faith in God. Whatever it is, these Jews were raised as members of the Communist Russian society. If an awakening is taking place in Russia, the philosophy of amkha-Yisrael is correct one hundred percent. Again, I emphasize that I have doubts whether it is true. Perhaps it is limited to a small segment of Russian Jewry. However, if it is a movement, it validates the concept of amkha-Yisrael. After so many years of Russian education and training, young men are ready to cast off and shed the whole philosophy of Communism. They identify as Jews and are ready to go to Eretz Yisrael. Apparently, there is something to the Jew which is indicative of amkha-Yisrael. We belong to God, and no one can take us away from Him. This is very strange. Acknowledgment of being a Jew, be it secular or religious, is ipso facto an acknowledgment of belonging to God.

The second development that fortifies my faith in the philosophy of amkha-Yisrael is the remarkable commitment on the part of the American Jew to the State of Israel. It is also a miracle to me. I have told you many times that this phenomenon is not so simple. It is not simply a question of sympathy. It involves disagreeing with the government of the United States. We demand that the government of the United States adopt a policy which is friendly toward Israel. The American Jew of the 1930s was not ready for such an approach. He would have never taken the risk. It is something new to the American Jew. It is a new sense of pride, courage, and particularly a new awareness of his own identity. When you have this awareness, you know something else. No matter how unique each Jewish community is, and no matter now many languages we speak, there is a common destiny among all Jews across the globe. The American Jew did not have this feeling years ago. Even in the 1940s, during the Hitler Holocaust, the American Jew did not possess this awareness. Had he had the same awareness that he has now, millions of Jews could have been saved. He would have stormed the White House. [President Franklin D.] Roosevelt refused to receive a delegation of rabbis in 1943, when the extermination of the Jews had reached its height. If the Jews of 1943 had acted the way Jewish youth acts now in regard to Russia, they would have forced Roosevelt to act. Had he acted, a million Jews would have been saved. At that time in the 1940s, I thought that the American Jew had forgotten the concept of amkha-Yisrael. Now I am encouraged, and I am beginning to believe that a metamorphosis has taken place in the American Jewish community. There is pride and courage today. Particularly, there is the clear awareness that we belong to a great and eternal people, and that our destiny and commitment are one. This is amkha-Yisrael.

Of course, if we act like amkha, then the word Yisrael fits beautifully. Then we are truly amkha-Yisrael. What does Yisrael mean? What are the semantics of this word? "He said: No longer will it be said that your name is Jacob, but Israel [Yisrael], for you have striven with the Divine and with man, and have overcome" [Genesis 32:29]. What does it mean that you have contended, struggled, and wrestled with a powerful enemy, almost an omnipotent enemy? You have struggled with powerful and influential people, yet you have overcome them. In spite of all the pessimistic predictions, you emerged victorious. Why? Because of your commitment to amkha, to God and your people. No power in the world can break this commitment. When you have it, you are very powerful. You now have earned the name of Yisrael.

What was the secret of the victory of the Hasmoneans? Of course, they were helped by the Almighty. In addition, they possessed the secret of amkha. The Hasmoneans knew that they could never sever their affiliation with the Almighty. Even if this affiliation is a source of pain, suffering, and despair, it cannot be severed. It is certainly not a source of comfort and convenience. Still, we belong to Him. This absolute commitment gives power to a person. It is the strongest weapon that an individual or a community can wield. Because we are amkha, we are Yisrael. We contend with many and we prevail.

The concept of wrestling with a powerful enemy is central to Judaism. "Jacob was left alone and a man wrestled with him until the break of dawn" [Genesis 32:25]. What is the quintessence of Jewish history, not only in the last nineteen hundred years, but since the establishment of the Second Commonwealth? It is a story of twenty-three or twenty-four hundred years. If you wish to characterize this period, what is the motto of Jewish history? What is common to all ages and all eras? The verse that "a man wrestled with him until the break of dawn" is the answer. There is always somebody or something in opposition to the Jew. There were a number of issues. During the Second Commonwealth, the concept of the Sabbath was disliked by the Greeks and the Romans. There was also a story circulated in the Near East that in the Holy of Holies in the Bet ha-Mikdash [the Holy Temple in Jerusalem] the Jews had the head of a donkey. It was this donkey that was worshiped when the high priest entered this area on Yom Kippur. Josephus Flavius [ca. 38 C.E.–after 100] wrote his *Against Apion* [*Contra Apionem*] to refute this charge and other calumnies which were directed against the Jewish people. Apion was a famous anti-Semite in Alexandria.

Later, in the Middle Ages, there came the problem of the Talmud. The Talmud became the symbol of Jewish uniqueness which the Christian Church hated. How many times they burned the Talmud! Not only the Talmud, but they also burned those who studied the Talmud. There is a kinah [elegy] authored by Rabbi Meir of Rothenberg [ca. 1215–1293] describing such an event. We recite it on Tisha be-Av. "O Law that has been consumed by fire, seek the welfare of those who mourn for you" [*Authorised Kinot for the Ninth of Av*, trans. Abraham Rosenfeld, p. 161].

Then you have the blood libels regarding the baking of the matzah. You have no idea how much Jewish blood was spilled because of this recurring libel. Later the Jew became the symbol of capitalism. He was the moneylender, the Shylock. The great [William] Shakespeare [1564–1616] wrote *The Merchant of Venice*. This play had a tremendous impact upon gentiles. Do not fool yourself and think that Shylock was only an expression of art. Because it is art, it is more dangerous. The Jew was constantly called Shylock. I do not know if in America the Jew is called Shylock, but I remember that as a young boy, shekatzim [hoodlums] would run after me and call me Shylock. They did not know who Shylock was, but they knew that it was a bad word. Then the Jew became the representative of capitalism. [Karl] Marx [1818–1883], who was a Jew himself, said that the dollar was the Jew's god. Now, the object of hatred is the State of Israel. This tension is constantly present! "A man wrestled with him until the break of dawn"! I do not know when daybreak will finally come. We have lost many. On the whole, we still retain our identity and emerge victorious. We are still committed to the same goals that motivated our ancestors throughout the millennia. We still assemble from time to time to study the Torah. We are committed to the concept of amkha-Yisrael. We will never sever our relationship with the Almighty. When a wicked Hellenic government rises up against us, we will emerge victorious. The foolish Hellenic government thought, as [Leonid] Brezhnev [1906–1982, General Secretary of the Soviet Communist Party] thinks now, that it is possible to erase this identity. It was a mistake then, and it is a mistake now. We remain amkha-Yisrael!

1. The concept of *ha-ahavah ha-tiv'it* was expounded by the founder of Habad hasidism, R. Shneur Zalman of Lyady (1745–1813). See his *Likkutei Torah to Devorim*, Derushim le-Shemini Azeret, p. 83a, col. 2:2, and *Likutei Amarim: Tanya*, chaps. 18–19.

16.04 Attachment to Eretz Yisrael

Related by the Rav in his lecture on Parshat Shelah Lekha (Numbers 13:1–15:41) at the RCA Annual Convention, June 4, 1975.

Wherever the segulah [unique relationship] element is present, one cannot rationalize events. An example of this is the situation in Eretz Yisrael now. Basically our attachment to Eretz Yisrael and our faithfulness to the land is simply incomprehensible in logical terms; we must try to interpret it in metalogical terms. But I will tell you frankly, we know very little about metalogical categories. In logical categories, this closeness of people to land [the Jews to the Land of Israel] after nineteen hundred years of exile is maddening. It is simply mad. Do not forget that American Jews are today doing things out of a sense of devotion [to Israel] which may endanger their own security in America. The American Jew is usually very rational, a practical Jew, very utilitarian minded and pragmatically oriented. Now when I look at these same Jews, I see their excitement about Eretz Yisrael, and their readiness to attack anybody, even the President of the United States, for something that is not in the spirit of Zionism. I begin to think, Where is their logic? Where is their reason? Where is their practicality?

One is a manufacturer; another is a banker. After all, some are in businesses in which the turnover reaches tens of millions of dollars. In these endeavors they have clear minds. Many of them I know personally, and they have clear minds. Why do their minds become beclouded when Eretz Yisrael is placed on the agenda? Why do they want the gentiles to see Eretz Yisrael with the eyes of a Jew? The reason is because our relationship to Eretz Yisrael is that of segulah. Whenever segulah comes to the forefront, to the foreground, ratiocination resigns. You cannot rationalize events which revolve around segulah. There is an element of diminuendos, of the frighteningly strange, and of the hidden ineffable in the segulah's charisma.

16.05 John Foster Dulles

Related by the Rav in his lecture to a public assembly on Yom ha-Azma'ut at Yeshiva University, April 15, 1956. Published by the Rav as an essay entitled "Kol Dodi Dofek: It Is the Voice of My Beloved That Knocketh" [3], p. 22, and translated into English by Lawrence Kaplan [41], pp. 70–71.

We ought to take note of the "learned" explanation of our Secretary of State, Mr. [John Foster] Dulles [1888–1959], who also serves as an elder in the Episcopal Church, at a session of a Senate committee, that the Arabs hate the Jews because the Jews killed the founder of their religion. This "explanation" possesses profound, hidden symbolic significance. I am not a psychologist and certainly not a psychoanalyst; however, I do have some acquaintance with the Talmud. I remember well what our sages said about Balaam: "From his blessing you may learn what was in his heart" [Sanhedrin 105b; cf. Rashi on Numbers 24:6]. When a person speaks at length, the truth may at times slip out. When one of the senators asked the Secretary of State: "Why do the Arabs hate the Jews?" he really wanted to reply: "I myself, as a Christian, do not bear any great love for them. They killed our Messiah, and as a result lost their share in the inheritance of Abraham." However, an angel intervened or a bit was placed in the Secretary's mouth [as happened to Balaam, according to the sages' interpretation of the verse "and He put a word into his mouth" (Numbers 23:16; cf. Rashi ad loc. and Sanhedrin 105b)]. Instead of uttering the words "our Messiah" and "I myself," alternative terms slipped out of his mouth, and he said "the Arabs" and "Mohammed." In his subconscious he is afraid of the "terrible" fact that the Jewish people rule over Zion and Jerusalem. I find special pleasure in reading articles about the State of Israel in Catholic and Protestant newspapers. Against their will they have to use the name "Israel" when they report the news about Zion and Jerusalem, which are now in our hands. I always derive a particular sense of satisfaction from reading in a newspaper that the response of the State of Israel is not as yet known, since today is the Sabbath and the offices of the ministries are closed. I enjoy reading a news release from the United Press on Passover eve that "the Jews will sit down tonight at the Seder table confident that the miracles of Egypt will recur today." It is the voice of my Beloved that knocketh!

16.06 Asia and Israel

Related by the Rav in his address at the convention to mark the merger of the Mizrachi and the Ha-Poel ha-Mizrachi movements in the United States in 1957. Published in Ohr ha-Mizrach *[2], pp. 29–30. (Hebrew).*

Moshe Sharett [1894–1965], the former Prime Minister of Israel [1954–1955], journeyed to Asia in an attempt to gain the political support of the Asian nations for the State of Israel.[1] Upon his return, Sharett related that the Asian nations do not comprehend us. They cannot understand our viewpoint because they are not conversant with the Bible. If our Bible is alien to them, then the Asian states cannot conceive of our biblical quest for the Holy Land. If so, Sharett declared, then in their eyes the Jews are strangers in "Palestine." Then we are the aggressors who have stolen Arab lands.

Sharett's insight is well advised. Our information centers and attempts at persuasion must be religiously oriented and not simply political in nature. I would suggest that the responsibility for this aspect of Israel's policies be taken out of the hands of the political establishment. It should be assigned to rabbis, religious communities, and the spiritual leaders of the Jewish people.

This is the approach that will be most successful, because the conflict surrounding Israel essentially is of a religious nature!

1. Moshe Sharett later published a volume about this extended journey. See his *Mishut be-Asia: Yoman Masa* (Tel Aviv: Dvar, 1957).

16.07 Russian Resentment of Israel

Related by the Rav in his lecture on Parshat Va-Yigash (Genesis 44:18–47:27], Yeshiva University, December 16, 1980.

At first the Book of Genesis deals with the relationship of the Jews to the other nations. This portion culminates with the sudden attack of an antagonist whose name we do not know. He wanted to destroy Jacob entirely on that mysterious night. "And Jacob was left alone, and there wrestled a man with him, until the breaking of the dawn" [Genesis 32:25].

He did not succeed, but we are not sure that he will not come back someday. That event reflects the most mysterious phase in Jewish history. People who never met us, hate us. This is so strange! In order to love or hate another person, contact is necessary. If I have had no contact with another person, I have not communicated with him. I do not know him at all. So how can I love or hate him? The one exception to this is the Jewish people or the Jewish race. We have been hated by people who never lived with us or had any contact with us. At least Esau had complaints. I can understand his attitude, because he felt cheated by Jacob. However, who was this man about whom we read: "there wrestled a man with him until the breaking of the dawn"? Who was this man?

It was someone who had never seen Jacob before and did not know who he was. Yet this man had endurance and tenacity and continued his combat through the dark and lonely night. What motivated him? It is like asking what motivates the Chinese to be against the State of Israel. The answer is unknown. It does not make sense.

I understand very well what motivates the Arabs. I can even understand why Soviet Russia is opposed to the State of Israel. In certain respects, the State of Israel is in Russia's way toward achieving universal socialism. I hope that the State of Israel will not become a Communist or a socialist state. It will be a State based upon foundations of charity and justice. Such a state is resented by Russia.

There is something else which Russia resents. People had the strange illusion in the thirties, and even in the forties, that it was possible to change Hitler. Even many prominent Jews held this view. They were certain that Hitler could not be changed into a friend of the Jews, but they felt that he could become neutral instead of an enemy. At that time I told many people that they were making a mistake. Anti-Semitism was not just a minor plank in the program of the Nazis. It was the very heart of Nazism. Without anti-Semitism there would have been no Nazism. It was the very heart of Nazism. Anti-Semitism was the source of the energy the Nazis possessed. At that time they possessed a lot of vital energy. This enabled them to be so successful in their initial moves.

The same is true with Russia. Atheism, agnosticism, the denial of a metaphysical reality, and the negation of a morality given to us from a transcendental world are basic to Communism. The human being is nothing more than another animal—a civilized animal, but still an animal. There is no spirituality to the human being. It is not just a coincidence that Communism believes in all this. It is basic to the Marxist philosophy and its world picture. If a man has certain spiritual foundations, then the approach of the Communist party is wrong. If there is a metaphysical world, then Communism cannot succeed as a political theory.

In my opinion, the hatred that Russia has for Israel is a result of these factors. Eventually, one must admit that Israel is the representative of this metaphysical moral order. The Jews introduced to humanity the idea that our world is not just a mechanical system, but also a spiritual system. The revival of Israel as a state means the revival of the reign of principles of faith that the Communists cannot accept.

Some people still live with illusions. I recently received a letter advocating a change in our policies toward Russia. Instead of demanding that Russia let the Jews go, as Moses demanded of Pharaoh, we should stop requesting this. The Russians resent such demands. Why should the Jew wish to leave the Garden of Eden the Communists believe they have created in Soviet Russia? Instead we should persuade the Russians to grant religious autonomy to the Jews in Moscow. It is advisable that they should start to build yeshivas in Moscow, and each yeshiva should also have a mikveh. This will be financed and subsidized by the Russian government. You are laughing at me. That is exactly the content of the letter I received. It simply shows how stupid one can be. As a matter of fact, I was invited to be on the committee of this project. [Laughter.] Don't worry, I will not serve on the committee. Such proposals simply do not recognize the basic attitude and resentment of Communism toward Judaism.

While we may comprehend this type of enmity toward the Jews, the basic hatred cannot be explained in logical terms. "There wrestled a man with him," a man who never met Jacob before.

16.08 A Good Frenchman

Related by the Rav in a lecture on Parshat Vayechi (Genesis 47:28–50:26), Yeshiva University, December 23, 1980. Summarized and published in Divrei Hashkafah *[20:4], pp. 43–44.*

Alain de Rothschild of Paris told me the following story. There is really nothing new in it, but it sheds wonderful light on the story of Jacob and his insistence upon being buried in the Land of Israel.

[Baron] Edmond de Rothschild [1845–1934] was instrumental in developing the wine industry in Eretz Yisrael. He was responsible for the expansion of the settlements of Rishon le-Ziyon and Zikhron Ya'akov and was a focal figure in the developing Yishuv. He died in Paris, a year before his wife. Years later, it was decided to reinter his remains and those of his wife in Eretz Yisrael.

When the War of Independence [in Israel] was over [in 1949], they began to consider means to remove the bodies from Paris to Israel. Alain de Rothschild related to me that Charles DeGaulle [1890–1970; President of France, 1959–69] called in his cousin, James de Rothschild [the son of Baron Edmond], and excitedly told him: "I will tell you frankly. I do not understand you Jews. I always thought that the Rothschild family was devoted and loyal to France, that they were real Frenchman and only differed as to their religious commitment. But I would like to ask you to give me the real definition of who is a good Frenchman?"

DeGaulle himself answered his own question and said: "A good Frenchman is one who was brought up in French schools. A good Frenchman is one who fights for France in times of emergency. A good Frenchman is one who contributes to France and to its culture. And listen to what I am going to say now. A good Frenchman is one who dies and is buried in French soil. I cannot imagine a good Frenchman whose body is transferred somewhere else. I do not understand such an act. I knew the baron well and had unlimited trust in him. I always defended him against those who accused him of hypocrisy in his loyalty to France. But now I see that these accusations were correct. How can it be that you do not want him to remain buried in France? It is not only a reflection on him but on you and on the rest of the family as well. Actually I could forbid the reburial. All I have to do is call the magistrate in Paris and tell him not to grant permission. But I do not wish to start a fight with the Jews of France."[1]

This is exactly what Pharaoh said to Joseph. "And Pharaoh told Joseph: Go up and bury your father as he adjured you" [Genesis 50:6]. In other words, "Of course, I am disappointed that he will not be interred in Egypt. But what can I do, you took an oath to your father."

1. In 1954 the remains of Baron Edmond de Rothschild and his wife were reinterred in Ramat ha-Nadiv, near Zichron Ya'akov.

Zionism and Redemption

17.01 Opposition to Zionism

Related by the Rav when Rabbi Michel Shurkin was his student. Rabbi Shurkin was interviewed on March 27, 1993.

When Reb Chaim Soloveitchik was one of the roshei yeshiva in the Volozhin Yeshiva, he heard that there was a clandestine group of students who supported the ideology of the nascent religious Zionist movement. This was later to crystallize into the Mizrachi organization. Reb Chaim wanted to know who they were. He asked Reb Menachem Krakowsky[1] who the students were. The latter replied that he had taken a Torah oath not to reveal their names. Reb Chaim replied that such an oath was not binding, because it was "an oath to annul a precept" [Shevuot 3:8]. So intense was Reb Chaim's opposition to the notion of religious Zionism.

1. Rabbi Menachem Krakowsky was a leading student at Volozhin. He married Badana, the daughter of Rabbi Elijah Feinstein of Pruzhana. Her sister, Pesia, married Reb Moshe Soloveichik, the son of Reb Chaim. Rabbi Krakowsky later authored *Avodat ha-Melekh* on portions of Maimonides' *Mishneh Torah*. Following his death in 1929, his unpublished manuscripts remained with his widow. They were later destroyed in the Holocaust, during which his wife perished.

17.02 Reb Chaim's Love of Zion

Related by the Rav in an address to the annual convention of the American Mizrachi Organization. Published in Hamesh Drashot *[7:1], pp. 24–25, and* The Rav Speaks *[35:1], pp. 34–36.*

I had many doubts about the validity of the Mizrachi approach. After all, my roots are very deeply intertwined with the Oral Tradition and rabbinic scholarship. My entire world outlook was crystalized in the spirit of the Rambam and the Rabad and their conceptualization of talmudic topics.

Nevertheless, the Land of Israel occupied a major role in my house. My grandfather, Reb Chaim, was the first to halakhically analyze, define, and conceptualize on an extraordinary intellectual level the topics pertaining to the Land of Israel. These included such topics as the sanctity of the Land, the sanctity of partitions, temporary sanctification and eternal sanctification of the Land of Israel, the Entry of all the Jews into the Land, all its inhabitants, non-Jewish acquisitory rights in the Land, and so forth.

These terms represented not only concepts, abstract thoughts, and formal insights, but they also reflected deep-rooted emotions of love, yearnings and vision for the Land of Israel. Discussions of the sanctity of the Land of Israel, the holiness of walled cities, the sanctity of Jerusalem, were my lullabies, my bedtime stories. Reb Chaim was perhaps the greatest lover of Zion in his generation. He constantly delighted in the thought that after he married off all his children, he would transfer his rabbinate to one of his sons and then settle in the Land of Israel. There he would purchase an orchard and fulfill the agricultural laws which pertain to the Land of Israel.

Nevertheless, the love of Reb Chaim of Brisk for Zion and Jerusalem has no relationship to the Zionism of Chaim Weizmann [1874–1952, the first President of Israel] as it is expressed in his autobiography, *Trial and Error* [1949]. Just the opposite, they are in direct contradiction. If you think it is easy for me to get used to the partly heretical, partly "enlightened," and partly Russian-revolutionary testament of Chaim Weizmann, you are wrong. Particularly disturbing to me is the last chapter, where he develops his ideas about the spiritual content of the nascent State of Israel (so that, God forbid, it should not develop into a theocracy). An endless distance separates the outlook of Chaim Weizmann and the other secular leaders from my vision. I cannot understand their viewpoint. How can one dream about the rebuilding of the Land of Israel without the God of Israel?

17.03 My Uncle's Love of Zion

Related by the Rav in his eulogy for his uncle Rabbi Yitzhak Zev Soloveichik. Originally published in Ha-Doar, *Tishrei 9, 5724 (1963), p. 758, it was republished in* Be-Sod ha-Yahid vha-Yahad *[9:2], pp. 241–246, and* Divrei Hagut ve-Ha'aracha *[12:2], pp. 89–92. (Hebrew).*

My uncle [R. Yitzhak Zev Soloveichik, 1886–1960] was estranged from the secular overtones of the State of Israel. Nevertheless, this separation paradoxically was interconnected with his deep love for the Land of Israel, which was suffused with his experiencing its holiness. . . . My uncle may have disassociated himself from the state, but he still continued to pray for its well-being and was apprehensive for the welfare of its inhabitants.

When my uncle's love for the Land of Israel is comprehended, then the debate over his attitude toward the state becomes irrelevant. Let us ask whether there is a story about my uncle which illustrates his love for Zion. Is there something similar to the tale related by R. Yose b. Kisma [Avot 6:9]?[1] A person who does not know any better might ask: Was Reb Yitzhak Zev a Lover of Zion? Although many stories have been told about him, the answer to this question depends on how "Love of Zion" is defined. If Love of Zion is expressed by dialogues between American Jewish writers and their Israeli counterparts in luxurious hotels, then my uncle was not a Lover of Zion. These American Jewish writers excel in their absolute ignorance of anything Jewish and holy, while their

Israeli counterparts, on occasion, heap abuse and contempt on Judaism.

However if Love of Zion is expressed by living in the Holy Land, striking roots there, loving its soil and desiring its stones, sharing in the burdens of the community under siege, and being totally committed to the destiny of the Holy City of Jerusalem, then my uncle was a true Lover of Zion. He refused to leave the Holy City even when the enemy besieged its gates. He totally rejected all proposals to emigrate to safe cities outside the Land of Israel. This true love of Zion found its total fulfillment and realization in a "Man of Halakhah" who was in theological opposition to the State of Israel and separated himself from its ideology. He was the true lover of Zion, and not the Jew who lives comfortably in New York or Los Angeles and regularly flies back and forth between the United States and Israel.

Now let me tell you a story which is parallel to that of R. Yose b. Kisma. My uncle's eldest daughter and his son-in-law [Rabbi Yehiel Michal Feinstein] came to the United States and resided here in comfort and dignity. My uncle demanded that they return to Israel. When they tarried, he became angry and ceased corresponding with them. He only reconciled himself with them when they returned to the Holy Land.

I recall that when I was still a young child, carried on my father's shoulders, I would overhear my father and uncle discussing halakhic topics pertaining to the holiness of the Land of Israel. These topics included such themes as the sanctification of the land by Joshua and Ezra, the temporary and permanent sanctifications, and the sanctity engendered by the partitions in the Temple Court and Jerusalem. While formulating halakhic thoughts they were inspired by the prophetic visions of the Holy Land. Every word was filled with endless longing for the Land which is saturated by divine light and radiant energy. Yes, my uncle possessed deep love for the Land, although he opposed the State of Israel. Many American Zionists are committed to the State of Israel, but they are totally unwilling to dwell there. The mere thought of aliyah engenders within them a sense of dread and distress. Who is more preferable—my uncle or these American Zionists?

1. R. Yose b. Kisma related the following story: "I was once traveling on the road when a man met me and greeted me, and I returned his greeting. He said to me: 'Rabbi, from what place are you?' I said to him: 'I come from a city of sages and scholars.' He said to me: 'Rabbi, are you willing to live with us in our place? I will give you a million golden dinars, and precious stones and pearls.' I told him: 'Were you to give me all the silver and gold and precious stones and pearls in the world, I would not live anywhere except in a place of Torah'" (trans. of Avot 6:9 by Philip Birnbaum in his *Ha-Siddur ha-Shalem*, p. 532).

17.04 The Eretz Yisrael Jew

Related by the Rav in a lecture on "The Sanctity of the Land" in honor of Israel Independence Day, Boston, Mass., May 4, 1968.

It is quite interesting. Maimonides ruled that the sanctity engendered by the return [to the Land of Israel] at the time of Ezra was everlasting [Hilkhot Terumot 1:5]. This is not only in halakhah, but it is also an historical reality. The Jew has never severed himself from Eretz Yisrael throughout the generations. The Jews' attachment to Eretz Yisrael is actually amazing. At times, returning to Eretz Yisrael was as impossible as a flight to another galaxy. Throughout the Middle Ages, and even in modern times, such a return was impossible. Believe me, as a child in heder, I did not know the geography of Eretz Yisrael. I had no idea. Nevertheless, to me, my friends, and my generation, Eretz Yisrael was the most beautiful and richest land that existed. It was a land of endless light and sunshine. This is reflected in "El ha-Zippor," the first published poem of Hayyim Nahman Bialik [1873–1934]. The poem is addressed to a bird. They are inquiring of a bird that has returned in the spring, supposedly from Eretz Yisrael. You understand very well how much Bialik knew about the flight of birds and about geography. You see from the way he addresses himself to the bird and his inquiries about Eretz Yisrael that Bialik had no idea how the land looked. He knew nothing about the topography, flora, or fauna of Eretz Yisrael. He had no idea what it was all about. Bialik speaks about flowers. You only see flowers in the spring in Eretz Yisrael. Then they are smothered unless you cultivate and water the flowers twice a day. The climate there is very hot. He had no idea of the reality. Still, our attachment to Eretz Yisrael was simply incomprehensible in psychological terms.

I still remember as a child, when I was in heder and my rebbe was a Lubavitcher hasid. Somehow, suddenly the door opened, and a Jew came in with a red kerchief in his back pocket. He wore a long kapote down to his ankles, and the red kerchief was really a handkerchief. It was like a kerchief in that you could wrap something in it. This Jew was from Eretz Yisrael. Of course, all the teaching came to a stop. The rebbe immediately began to inquire about Eretz Yisrael. You know the stories which Jews from Eretz Yisrael used to tell years ago. They were fantastic! So much so that in Yiddish there is a colloquial expression that it is an "Eretz Yisroeldicker ma'aseh." It means that it is an exaggeration. So he told stories. However, my melamed was a clever Jew. Nevertheless, he was very impressed by the fact that he had the privilege to talk to a Jew from Eretz Yisrael. He sent us out of the heder and remained with the guest alone. Of course, we tried to eavesdrop. We heard our melamed ask the visitor: "Tell me the truth. Are you really from Eretz Yisrael?"

The guest answered: "What do you mean? I am certainly from Eretz Yisrael!"

My melamed then asked him: "Have your hands actually touched the stones of the Western Wall?" "Yes," was the quick response. My melamed, Reb Baruch Yaakov, grabbed his hands and kissed them.

This is what I remember. It is not just a story, but an episode that I witnessed as a young child in heder. Such stories have happened throughout the generations. When Ezra consecrated the Jewish land, he also consecrated the Jewish heart and the Jewish attachment and eternal commitment to Eretz Yisrael. The consecration was converted into an eternal attachment between the Jew and Eretz Yisrael. It was an even greater miracle than the actual consecration of the land itself.

17.05 Rebuilding Eretz Yisrael

Related by the Rav in his eulogy for Rabbi Zev Gold [4], p. 38.
(Hebrew).

I will never forget the evening in 5695 [1935] when I visited Rabbi
[Zev] Gold in Ramat Gan in Eretz Yisrael. He took me out to the
orange groves near his house. It was a beautiful night, the sky was
a perfect blue and there were endless stars. The bright moon of
Eretz Yisrael shone all over with an enchanted beauty. From afar
we could see the lights of the new all-Jewish city of Tel Aviv glistening in the dark. The lights were telling us the thrilling and intoxi-
cating news of the rebuilding of the Holy Land. Overwhelmed
with emotion, Rabbi Gold gazed toward the horizon and then
turned to me and said: "Whoever does not feel the presence of
God in Eretz Yisrael on this beautiful night while looking at this
magnificent moon and at these beckoning stars, breathing the
clear and pure air filled with the fragrance of blossoming growth,
and above all when looking at all the glistening lights of the city
that was built entirely by Jews, is simply blind."

Rabbi Gold continued: "Rav Yehudah Halevi [1075–1141]
was right when he said that prophecy flows unhindered in Eretz
Yisrael and we need only a proper vessel to receive its message"
[*Kuzari* 2:8–11].

As we stood there, Rabbi Gold picked up a small pebble and
kissed it, to fulfill Rav Abba's dictum in the Talmud that he would
kiss the rocks of Akko [Ketuvot 112a]. That night, I thought to
myself how insignificant I was compared to this special Jew who
was able to experience the glory of God through the grandeur of
the landscape of the land of Israel.

17.06 Mizrachi Leaders

Related by the Rav at a convocation honoring Mr. Moshe Krone, head of the Department for Torah Education and Culture of the World Zionist Organization, Yeshiva University, May 2, 1979.

I extend a welcome to Reb Moshe Krone, first of all, as the representative of a great movement, the Mizrachi movement. The Mizrachi saved religious Jewry from being forgotten in history as far as the restoration and the reconstruction of Eretz Yisrael is concerned. If not for the Mizrachi, this participation in the rebuilding of Israel would not have been accomplished. I am not out on a campaign to recruit members for the Mizrachi, but whatever is true should not be denied. I may at times be critical of certain methods employed by the Mizrachi leadership in Eretz Yisrael, now called the Mafdal, but on this issue the credit is all theirs.

As I see my life in retrospect and reminisce about events and experiences, I recollect certain incidents. I realize how basic the Mizrachi philosophy was and that the hashgachah [Divine Providence] has confirmed the truth of the Mizrachi outlook on the world.[1]

Rabbi [Norman] Lamm [president of Yeshiva University] spoke about mehalkhim [those who enter the outside world] and yoshvim [those who withdraw from the outside world]. The Mizrachi movement belongs to the mehalkhim. If not for the Mizrachi, we would have no share in the binyon haaretz [the rebuilding of Israel]. We would have been condemned by history to absolute anonymity. However, the Mizrachi wrote a glorious chapter in binyan haaretz.

In the mood of nostalgia, as I try to romanticize my memories, I see generations of Mizrachi leaders in Poland and Lithuania. I see Yehoshua Heschel Farbstein [1870–1948 of Warsaw and Jerusalem], Levi ha-Levi Levin Epstein [1865–1938 of Warsaw and Jerusalem], and Rabbi Isaac Judah Trunk [1880–1939]. The latter was the rabbi of Kutna and the son-in-law of Rabbi Shmuel Bornstein [1856–1926], the author of the *Shem mi-Shmuel*. Rabbi

Shmuel Bornstein was the son of Rabbi Avraham Bornstein
[1839–1910], the founder of the Sochaczew hasidic dynasty, and
the author of the *Avnei Nezer*. Rabbi Trunk was given an ultima-
tum: "Either you belong to me or you belong to the Mizrachi." He
left his father-in-law and the family of the great author of the *Avnei
Nezer*, and became very active in the leadership of the Mizrachi. I
recall the birth of the Hapoel Hamizrachi under the leadership of
Shmuel Hayyim Landau [1892–1928]. He was a strange person,
an enigmatic person, but a great person as well.

This was a group which dedicated itself to binyan haaretz.
They paid a high price for their idealism. Many of them were
thrown out of the shtiblach. Others were excommunicated. Many
Mizrachi leaders in small towns and villages were condemned to
loneliness. People would not extend greetings to them; they would
not talk to them. And still they carried on with their Mizrachi
activities.[2]

Nowadays, we have a state and there are questions of politics.
It is impossible to have a state and not engage in politics. Perhaps
the idealism of the Mizrachi as a movement is undermined
because of the politics. Whenever you have politics, the idealism of
the politicians is inferior to the idealism of the dreamers. Nevertheless, it was and is a great movement, and Reb Moshe Krone
represents, as far I am concerned, the basic ideals of the Mizrachi.

1. Cf. Rabbi Joseph Dov ha-Levi Soloveitchik, *Hamesh Derashot*, trans. David Telsner
(Jerusalem: Tal Orot Institute, 1974), pp. 19–24.
2. Cf. Ibid., pp. 19–20.

17.07 Israeli Youth in Boston

*Related by the Rav in his lecture on "Covenants in the Book of
Genesis" delivered to the Yeshiva University Rabbinic Alumni, Yeshiva
University, ca. 1955. (Yiddish).*

It is easy to be a loyal citizen of the country in which one resides.
The challenge to the Jewish people was for them to retain their loyalty to the Land of Israel during their long exile.

Let me be honest with you. I have noticed something that is a revelation to me. I observe the Israeli youth who come to Boston after receiving a secular Israeli education. When they first arrive in Boston they are extreme Israeli patriots. They cannot understand how Jews can live outside of Israel. In a year or two, however, many of them do not want to return to Israel. They seek every possible opportunity to delay their return. They rapidly lose their attachment to the Land of Israel, in contrast to the devotion of the Jews throughout the centuries. It is even unlike the feelings of many of the American religious youth who are desirous of going on aliyah.

Why is this so? It is a result of the secular Zionist stress on viewing the State of Israel from the perspective of loyalty to one's country. If so, the individual may also become a faithful American citizen. Germans in the United States retain very weak ties to Germany. This is also true of Americans of Czech or Polish origin, and other nationalities as well.

It is not so when a commitment to the Land of Israel results from an emphasis on the unique relationship between the Jewish people and the Holy Land. When one is taught to appreciate the singularity of the kinship of the Jewish people to its land, then this bond will survive even when the Jews are exiled for hundreds of years.

17.08 Halakhic Difficulties

Related by the Rav in his lecture on "Rashi on Aseret Hadibrot" at the RCA Annual Convention, June 30, 1970.[1]

Accepting the yoke of mitzvot is integral to our concept of conversion. The topic of gerut, or conversion, is very popular now. In Eretz Yisrael, they show miracles in that it is possible to convert without acceptance of the heavenly yoke but simply by relying on what will happen in the future. I do not like to talk about it, as I do not wish to discuss politics. However, this is more important than politics. I am very dissatisfied with the solution they have found. It has not enhanced our prestige. There was no sanctification of God's Name. The issue should have been fought out, and the Law [of Return] should have been amended to read that conversion is only in accordance with the Torah [giyur ke-din Torah]. Now it is suspended in midair. All right, you've solved this problem. Tomorrow you'll have another problem. There are another five challenges lined up. You can rely on *Ha-Aretz* [Israeli newspaper] and the League [Against Religious Coercion]. They are a group of sinners and infidels. I will tell you frankly, lately I have read editorials in *Ha-Aretz* that would have won prizes in Nazi Germany. These editorials are not criticisms of Orthodoxy, nor are they expressions of agnosticism. They are simply plain, mean hatred of Judaism.

This does not mean, however, that Orthodoxy has performed well. The prestige of Orthodoxy would have been enhanced if Mizrachi had quit the government. I am sorry to say so. I wrote so to [Hayyim Moshe] Shapira [1902–1970; Mizrachi leader and Israel's Minister of the Interior]. I did not want to publish my statement. I am not one of those about whom the sages say: "They live in Nisibis [in Mesopotamia], yet their net is spread in Jerusalem" [Pesahim 3b]. I do not like to give orders or instructions to those in Jerusalem. All I can say is that these are my thoughts. You may accept them if you wish. You also have a right to reject them. In my opinion, if the rabbis wish to improve things in Eretz Yisrael, redeem it, and make it more pious, we should go there. We should settle in Eretz Yisrael and then tell the Israelis what to do. I do not believe that in the diaspora we have the right to tell the residents of Israel what to do. However, as an observer and onlooker, I feel that we have emerged from the battle without dignity and glory. It is a temporary solution, but the problem will come again. We have lost a great deal. How can a conversion be valid when one lives in Nahal Oz, a kibbutz of Ha-Shomer ha-Za'ir [a socialist Zionist movement], where the kitchen is traif [unkosher], the Sabbath is not observed, and she herself [the convert] is married to a kohen [in violation of Jewish law]. How can she accept mitzvot? I cannot grasp it. You need the mind of one of the great sages of Israel to understand this. I am too stupid for this. [Laughter.]

I wish to emphasize something else. In an interview given by a certain rabbi to the Israeli press, he was asked how he could convert her if she was going to return to her husband, who is a kohen and therefore forbidden to her. He said that there are posekim who permit a convert to a kohen. Frankly, I am not a great scholar, but I am also not a great ignoramus. I challenge the rabbi to tell me who these posekim are. This is certainly a prohibition whose roots are in Torah law. How can posekim come and say that a convert is permitted to a kohen? Such a viewpoint is beyond and above me. I will be frank with you, there is freedom of interpretation in Torah study. However, such an approach is a fraudulent interpretation. I am sorry I have to say this. No one has ever said that a convert is permitted to a kohen. It is impossible!

I also wish to say something else. People know my attitude toward Eretz Yisrael. I consider the emergence of the State of Israel a miracle. It is the dam that slows the tide of assimilation. I know many Jews who were oblivious of their Jewishness. They woke up because Eretz Yisrael challenged them. Somehow they felt that they were summoned by Eretz Yisrael. God forbid, if anything should happen to Israel, a tide of shmad [apostasy] and assimilation will sweep through the world and overtake our people. I know all this. However, we are not ready to change the identity of our people. If it is a problem of whether the state should prevail or whether the identity of our people should remain, we will choose the latter. This is important for the Israeli leaders, and particularly the Minister of Justice, to know. After all, the Western immigration to Israel is recruited mainly among Orthodox young people. A very small number of immigrants to Eretz Yisrael come from Reform and Conservative circles. In order to please a small group of Jew-haters, it does not pay to lose the sympathy and the love of Orthodox Jewry.

All right, I do not know how I got onto this topic. I have enough problems as is. Nevertheless, I have to say this publicly. I do not like it when people try to cover up. Again, I am not telling the Israeli rabbis what to do. I am just expressing my own opinion—the opinion of a private person. Nevertheless, all my days I have grown up among the sages, and I know what conversion is. To make a mockery out of conversion is beyond me!

1. The Rav was alluding to two halakhic issues that had become causes célèbres on the Israeli scene. The first concerned the registration of Jewish nationality on the identity cards that are issued to residents of the State of Israel. Only a child born to a Jewish mother or a proper convert is a Jew according to the halakhah. In 1968, an officer in the Israel Defense Forces requested that his two children born of a non-Jewish mother be registered on their identity cards as Jews. When the Ministry of the Interior refused to accede to this request, they petitioned the Supreme Court to force the ministry to register the children as Jews. The court decided on January 23, 1970, by a majority of five to four, that the children should be so registered. Some of the judges stated that the concept of nationality on the identity card was a secular one and therefore the children could be considered Jewish from a secular viewpoint.

This decision aroused a strong protest in Orthodox circles. The law was subsequently amended by the Knesset to accept as Jews only those born of Jewish mothers or converted. However, it did not specify that the conversions had to be done in conformity with the halakhah. Thus non-Orthodox conversions performed outside the State of Israel would be sufficient for registration as a Jew on the identity card.

Another case concerned the permissibility of a female proselyte marrying a kohen. Such a union is explicitly forbidden by the *Shulhan Arukh* (Even ha-Ezer 6:8). To compound the situation, the couple resided in a totally nonreligious kibbutz. Thus, in addition to violating the prohibition of a kohen marrying a proselyte, the couple would also not be observing the other tenets of Judaism. In such circumstances, a conversion would be invalid because it would not allow for the observance of the precepts of Judaism on the part of the proselyte. Such observance is essential if a conversion is to be valid. In this particular case, the woman had already been converted by a Reform rabbi in Israel. She had petitioned the Israeli Supreme Court to compel the Interior Ministry to recognize the conversion. Rabbi Shlomo Goren, at that time the elected Ashkenazic chief rabbi of Tel Aviv–Jaffa, reconverted the woman in accordance with the Orthodox ritual. He permitted the conversion and union as a last resort because of pressure on the rabbinate by secular Israeli politicians. Rabbi Goren based his decision upon a responsum penned by Rabbi David Zevi Hoffmann [1843–1921], the rector of the Orthodox Rabbinical Seminary in Berlin. See the latter's *Melamed Leho'il*, vol. 3, responsum 8.

Following Rabbi Goren's conversion, the woman canceled her petition to the Supreme Court.

In a responsum on a similar question Rabbi Moshe Feinstein [1895–1986], the leading American posek, took the same position as the Rav. He also took issue with the ruling of the *Melamed Leho'il*. See Rabbi Feinstein's *Igrot Moshe*, vol. 4, Even ha-Ezer, responsum 4, pp. 313–314.

For the details of this case, see the *Jerusalem Post*, June 17, 1970. Jose Rosenfeld of the *Jerusalem Post* staff was most helpful in locating this source.

17.09 Death Is Absurd

Related by the Rav in his lecture on Parshat Hukat (Numbers 19:1–22:1), at the RCA Annual Convention, June 27, 1974.

Let us not forget something else. In the animal world the death of an individual is not tragic, because the existence of the genus is not menaced by the death of an individual. Basically, individuals do not exist in the animal world. There is no individualistic existence among the brutes and the beasts. The individual exists as a representative of the class. Hence the death of an individual is not considered a tragedy, because the class will continue to exist.

Among humans the situation is completely different. The individual does not lead a representative but an autonomous existence. The individual animal leads a representative existence. He exists for the sake of something else. What is this something else? The species, the genus, the class. He per se does not exist. These ideas were beautifully developed by Maimonides, even though they can also be traced back to Aristotle and Plato [*Moreh Nevukhim* 3:17 (Kapach edition, pp. 312–314)].

However, a human individual has his own right to existence. He exists not only as a representative, a messenger, an attorney, or a spokesman for someone. He exists on his own behalf. He has an independent existence. Among human beings the situation is completely different than in the animal world. The individual does not lead a representative but an individualistic autonomous existence. Each individual is a world unto himself. Each individual is a personality, a microcosm. The existential legitimacy is not the class or the species or the genus. It is to be found in the individual himself.

That is why the death of an individual is absurd and existentially abominable. I heard this story from somebody. It is a true story. It reflects our approach to death and confirms what I am saying.

The person who told me this story heard it from a certain European ruler behind the Iron Curtain. I must say the name of this ruler. It was [Nicolae] Ceausescu [1918–1989; President of Rumania, 1967–1989]. He visited [Anwar el-] Sadat [1918–1981; President of Egypt, 1970–1981] a few weeks before the tragic Yom Kippur [of 1973]. They discussed the matter of the next war. Everybody knew about it except Israel. So he warned Sadat not to start the war, because the Jewish army was superior. Sadat admitted that militarily it was a lost cause. But there was another reason for starting the war. Sadat pulled some newspaper clippings out of a drawer and gave them to Ceausescu.

Ceausescu took the clippings and saw that the script was unknown to him. It was not a Latin script. "What kind of paper is this," he asked Sadat.

"It's a Hebrew paper," Sadat answered.

"What's the name of the paper?"

"The big red letters say it's the daily paper called *Maariv.*"

"So what do you see here?" asked Ceausescu.

"Take a look," answered Sadat.

Ceausescu said to Sadat: "I can't read it. I don't know this language. It's like Chinese to me."

"Take a look at this picture," Sadat replied.

So he took a look and saw a picture of a young boy in uniform. So Ceausescu asked, "What are you showing me?"

"Do you know who this young boy was?" asked Sadat. "He is dead now. He was a soldier who was killed on the front, on the Suez Canal. The Jewish people mourn for him, and his picture is on the front page of the newspaper. Such a people cannot last long in a war of attrition. If every individual is dear to them, and they grieve and mourn for every individual, they will have to lose the war. No matter how wonderful their weapons are, they will ultimately lose the war."

That is exactly what I have been telling you. It is true. With all gratitude to [Richard M.] Nixon [President of the United States, 1969–1974] and [Henry] Kissinger [U.S. Secretary of State] for the separation treaties [with Egypt], nevertheless, these treaties are due to one factor. Even though they do not give too much protection to Israel, I am pretty sure that if there were a plebiscite in Israel now on the separation treaties, ninety-nine percent of the population would vote in favor. This would be the result even though ninty-nine percent of the population know that the treaties are not worth the paper they are written on. But the fear that young men might die is the main factor in this approach. The eagerness to save a life and to protect a young boy overrides every other logical consideration.

This is exactly what I have been saying. In Judaism, when someone dies, a whole world dies. A whole world collapses.

17.10 Wars Fought by Israel

Related by the Rav in his lecture on "The Duties of the King," at the RCA Midwinter Conference, January 18, 1971.

The Midrash says several times that the defeat of the Jewish people is as if the Ribono-shel-Olam [God: Master of the World] has been defeated. A victory on the part of the Jewish people is also a triumph for the Ribono-shel-Olam.[1]

I will give you an example. I do not know whether you have any idea of what went on during the Second World War on American college campuses and even in many public places. Missionaries suddenly emerged from all corners of the earth and converged on American Jewish young boys and girls. They told these youngsters that the Jews have made a fatal mistake by not accepting Christianity. You see how Jews are being punished now, and they will be completely exterminated.

It was a difficult task to explain to young people that the missionaries were wrong! The Jewish people were going through a long dark night of loneliness, destruction, and extermination. There was a possibility, heaven forbid, that Hitler would succeed in exterminating the Jewish people.

Then what did the gentiles say? They claimed that the covenant between Abraham and the Almighty had been, heaven forbid, abrogated. The covenant no longer belonged to the Jewish people. It had been given to another group, to another religion, to another faith, to another successor. The wandering Jew had finally reached an impasse.

You have no idea how the Name of the Almighty was glorified and extolled, and His Kingdom reestablished, by the establishment of the State of Israel.

I will tell you frankly, I have a lot of criticism as far as the State of Israel is concerned. I do not believe that we should subcribe to every policy of the government of the State of Israel. We should not deprive ourselves of independent judgment, understanding, and discrimination. However, the State of Israel has accomplished miracles not only for the prestige of the Jews in the world but also for the prestige of Judaism in the world. Now Christian theologians argue: Is the State of Israel the fulfillment of the prophetic pledge, or is it just an incident? Perhaps this new Jewish sovereignty is only a political event and has no prophetic significance. The mere fact that theologians, who until now never mentioned the word "Jew," are ready to argue over the State of Israel is in itself a great achievement. These are the very theologians who once actually denied that the Jew has any relationship to the Bible and to the Tanakh. They claimed that the Bible is for Christianity. "Who is Israel? Christians! What is Zion? The Catholic Church!" And so forth and so on. Now, willy-nilly, they cannot help themselves, and they must acknowledge the Jewish people and the Jewish state. All these events "come and flutter before the faces of the gentiles" and force them to rethink their positions [cf. Avodah Zarah 4b].

Whoever knows the recent theological literature sees how hard it is for them to understand this new reality. They do not wish to admit it. The State of Israel is truly a victory for the Ribonoshel-Olam. It is a Kiddush Hashem, a sanctification of the

Almighty's Name! "And I will be sanctified in you in the sight of the nations" [Ezekiel 20:41].

A political defeat of the Jewish people actually impairs, so to speak, the Kingdom of the Almighty. People then say of our Bible, prophets, and patriarchs that they are a hoax. They claim that all of Jewish history is nothing but a hoax. The Jews have fought for centuries, have shed their blood for centuries, and defended spiritual values for centuries. Nevertheless, the Jew has lived in a world of illusion, or perhaps delusion. That is what the gentile world thought during the Holocaust. Now the non-Jewish world does not say it anymore. Today they feel that perhaps there is sense to Jewish history. Perhaps this wandering Jew did have clairvoyance. Perhaps the promises of the prophets are coming true. Perhaps the Jewish Messiah is in the process of coming. Who knows! This is what goes through the gentile mind today. I am not talking about the people out on the streets, but the better and more intelligent minds.

When the Jew fights a war, it is not only for himself but for the Name of the Almighty. There are wars that do not contribute anything to the enhancement of the name of the Jewish people and the Almighty. These are selfish and destructive wars. They are not wars fought for the Almighty. However, a war which opens up before the world new horizons of Jewish thinking, hope, prophecy, and clairvoyance is a war fought for the Almighty. Not every war is to be glorified. Certain wars are unavoidable and inevitable, however, because they are wars fought for the Almighty.

As a matter of fact, I can tell you—and it is very hard to say—but in my opinion two wars that Israel fought enhanced the Name of the Almighty [the 1948 War of Independence and the 1967 Six-Day War]. I have doubts whether the 1956 war [the Sinai Campaign] was such a war. Why am I in doubt? Because we did not utilize or exploit the opportunity. We just lost so many people and withdrew to the old borders. I do not believe that Jewish prestige was enhanced by the Suez War in 1956. It was just simply a war, Ben-Gurion's war! Perhaps we were cheated by France and

England. It is possible. Perhaps America, led by [President Dwight] Eisenhower and [Secretary of State John Foster] Dulles, also cheated Israel. All right, this is a good excuse, and it creates extenuating and mitigating circumstances. That's all. It does not make the war of 1956 a war fought for the Almighty. However, I have no doubt that the War of Independence and the Six-Day War were wars fought for the Almighty. These wars changed the climate and enhanced the prestige of the Jew. In Judaism, the prestige of the Jew is identical with the majesty of God.

That is exactly what Maimonides meant when he said that the king "must fight the wars of the Almighty" [*Mishneh Torah*, Hilkhot Melakhim 4:10]. The king must understand and decide what kind of war he is going to fight. Is it just a war for expansion, or is it a war by which we will win a spiritual victory in addition to a political and military success? Is it a war that will defeat those who have denied our right to live and exist? Will we now be considered the heirs and successors of our forefathers, Abraham, Isaac, and Jacob? When the answer is positive, it is a war fought for the Almighty.

This is an important attitude. It is not only important for a king, but for any government. In my opinion, the 1956 war was a mistake. It did not achieve a spiritual victory for the Jewish people.

1. E.g., Isaiah 63:9, Ta'anit 16a, and Mekhilta to Be-shalah, Amalek, chap. 2 (15).

17.11 Pogroms and the Messiah

Related by the Rav in an interview with Levi Yitzhak ha-Yerushalmi. Published in Maariv *(Israeli daily newspaper), Erev Rosh Hashanah, Ellul 29, 5735 (September 5, 1975). (Hebrew).*

Let me tell you a story that I heard from my late father, my teacher, who heard it from his father, Reb Chaim of Brisk.

At the end of World War I, when Reb Chaim was in Minsk, the gentiles staged a pogrom against the Jews. One day, Reb Chaim was sitting with a group of Jews who were bemoaning the killings, the plundering, and the destruction of entire Jewish communities.

In the midst of their discussion, one of the Jews exclaimed: "If only we could be certain that these were the pangs of redemption that precede the coming of the Messiah." Before he was able to complete the sentence, Reb Chaim interrupted him and exclaimed: "I do not agree with you!"

Taken aback, the Jew responded to Reb Chaim: "What did I say, Rebbe, that you did not agree with. I barely said anything."

Reb Chaim replied: "You said too much! You implied that all the sufferings and sacrifices would be worth it if only we could be certain that these were the pangs of redemption. I do not agree with this approach because it is totally against the halakhah. The law is that saving lives [pikuach nefesh] cancels the entire Torah. Accordingly, it also cancels the coming of the Messiah. Who says that the Messiah will come only through the murder of innocent Jews? God has many ways to bring the Messiah, and certainly He does not have to bring him through the shedding of innocent Jewish blood."

This is the tradition I received from Reb Chaim of Brisk.

17.12 Jewish Sovereignity

Related by the Rav in his Yarhei Kallah lecture on the topic of "Rosh Hodesh," Boston, Mass., August 28, 1974.

Kiddush ha-Levanah [the Sanctification of the New Moon; *Daily Prayer Book*, trans. Philip Birnbaum, pp. 561–566] is symbolic of the historical destiny of the Jews. Despite the fact that we have been absent from the historical arena for a long time, we will return. Actually, we have not taken part in historical events, in historical development, for the last nineteen hundred years. We have not reappeared as yet. If you think the State of Israel means the reappearance of the Jew in the historical arena, then you are mistaken. If a [Henry] Kissinger [b. 1923, U.S. Secretary of State] can give an order to the Foreign Minister or the Prime Minister of

Eretz Yisrael to come [to Washington; capital of the United States] in September instead of November, then there is no real Jewish sovereignty. That was an order; it was not an invitation. Kissinger announced it [the visit] before the so-called invitation was even accepted.

Under such circumstances, there is no real independence, no real sovereignty. With the arrival of Moshiach [the Messiah], the Jewish people will reappear. We always say that Hazal [the sages] saw a symbol of Jewish history in a simple cosmic event like the steady disappearance of the moon and its sudden reemergence. To our naked eye, there is the moon's sudden reemergence and expansion until it reaches its full form. Hazal saw this as a symbol of Jewish history. We have disappeared, not just for a short while but for a very long time. Suddenly, when no one expects us to do so, we will reappear in full glory, in full glamour, in full splendor, the way the new moon reappears. As we recite in the blessing for the New Moon: "He ordered the moon to renew itself as a glorious crown over those He sustained from birth, who likewise will be regenerated in the future, and will worship their Creator for His glorious majesty."

17.13 Jewish and Universal Redemption

Related by the Rav in his Yarhei Kallah lectures on the topic of "Rosh Hodesh," Boston, Mass., August 28, 1974.

On one level the future redemption must be viewed as the realization of an historical destiny from solely a Jewish vantage point. On this level, never mind mankind. First of all, we are busy with ourselves. There is no doubt in our minds that the Jewish people need redemption very badly at this moment. I do not believe that the Jewish people have ever been in such great need of redemption as today. The need was never such an emergency or so urgent as it is now.

On one hand, there is an Amalek [cf. Exodus 17:8–16, Deuteronomy 25:17–19] in the persons of the Arab leaders who want to physically destroy Israel the way Hitler did. Do not believe all the stories about [Henry] Kissinger [b. 1923, U.S. Secretary of State]. Do not take them seriously. Forget about them. The Arab leaders want to destroy Israel. All right, they are ready to delay it for a couple of years, perhaps ten years, fifteen years. Still, they want to destroy Israel. Destroying Israel is not just the destruction of a political entity. It is the destruction of the people—men, women, and children. It is destruction the way Hitler did it. Do not forget, they had a good teacher. Hitler—may his name be blotted out—was an excellent teacher. He taught the world how to dispose of Jews. Until Hitler, no one knew how to dispose of Jews. Haman knew how, but he was a failure. So the world forgot about it. During the Middle Ages, no one knew how to dispose of the Jews. They put them in a ghetto. Now they know; you do not need a ghetto. You simply take the Jews and pack them into cattle cars, bring them to crematoria, and put them in the ovens. It is very simple and ingenious!

On the other hand, the threat of assimilation over here [in the United States] is frightening. Not only here, but in the whole Disapora and even in Eretz Yisrael we have this threat. When I say assimilation, I mean also in Eretz Yisrael. It is assimilation when a Hebrew daily newspaper can print an article by Shulamit Aloni [b. 1928, leftist Israeli politician] which is blasphemous. While the judges do not require all the witnesses to repeat the blasphemy [Sanhedrin 7:5], still I must share with you the gist of her article. She refers to the wicked matriarch Sarah who drove out Hagar when she was pregnant [Genesis 16:6]. Aloni bemoans the fact that the matriarch Sarah is a positive symbol for religious Jewry. This is blasphemy! This is not just heresy or Epicureanism. This is outright blasphemy! I have not heard any non-Jew or secularist speak like this. All right, they attack Orthodox Jews. We are vulnerable to attacks. However, such writings are simply Jewish self-hatred.

We therefore desperately need redemption for the Jewish people. We need redemption soon or, God forbid, our people will be lost. We will lose our spiritual identity, and our physical lives are also in danger. Had [Anwar el-] Sadat [President of Egypt] been victorious last Yom Kippur [1973, when he attacked Israel], he would have exterminated the entire Yishuv. It is not just a question of taking away political independence or destroying Israel as a political entity. It means that the very physical existence of the people is in doubt.

The Jewish people therefore need redemption now. Only afterwards can we discuss the universal aspects of redemption.

17.14 How Messiah Will Come

Related by the Rav in his Teshuvah Drashah, October 7, 1970. Published in Al ha-Teshuvah *[8:6], pp. 236–238, and* Soloveitchik on Repentance *[37:4], pp. 168–169.*

I heard from my father that Reb Chaim of Volozhin was once asked: "How will the Messiah come?"

He responded: "Let me tell you the following parable, and you will understand how the Messiah will come. On an ordinary weekday, I came home from the yeshiva after the morning prayers. My wife asked me: 'Chaim, are you ready to eat your breakfast?' I answered her: 'Relka, I have not finished preparing my lecture for today, and I cannot eat until I review the texts that I have to teach in the yeshiva.'

"'All right, Chaim,' she says, 'let it be. While you are preparing your lecture, I will go the market to buy a few things. In the meantime I will leave the soup cooking on the stove. Please be careful, Chaim, that it should not burn. Please be careful, I know you, and I am aware that you forget everything once you get involved in your learning.'

"My wife left for the market, and I opened my volume and started to study the appropriate texts. Suddenly, I look out the window and I see that the sun is shining with much greater brightness than ever before. What intensity! Then I hear the birds in the garden chirping a new tune, a stirring enchanted melody. I hear a commotion on the street. I look out my window and see Eli, the shoemaker, running and dancing. I call out: 'What is happening, Eli, why is the sun so bright? What are these enchanting songs of the birds? What has happened to the trees that are suddenly blooming with new leaves? What is happening?'

"Eli looks up at me and says: 'Rebbe, don't you know, the Messiah is here!' Immediately, I run to my closet to get my Sabbath clothes to wear to greet the King Messiah, and I take out my suit, and to my chagrin the jacket is missing a button! Last Saturday night it fell off, and when I told my wife to mend it she said to me: 'Why the rush? You will not need it until the next Sabbath.'

"Now I have to go forth to greet the Messiah with my jacket missing a button. While I am debating with myself whether to wear this defective jacket or whether I can go to greet the Messiah with my weekday jacket, my wife comes running home. She breathlessly cries out: 'Gevalt, Chaim, where are you! The soup has burned! You forgot to turn it off!' At that moment, I say to her: 'You foolish woman, we are going to greet the Messiah and you are worried about the soup?! Go and dress in your finest Sabbath clothes and come with me to greet the King Messiah.'"

This story, which I heard from my father, summarizes the whole saga of the redemption of the Jewish people. A Jew waits endlessly for the redemption, and then it comes unexpectedly. At that moment he discovers that a button is missing from the suit he has to wear to greet the Messiah.

COLLEAGUES AND
DISCIPLES

Speaking at the Sheva Berakhot *of Rabbi Nathan Kamenetsky and Shulamith Lifschitz at the home of the bride's parents, Rabbi and Mrs. David Lifschitz, June 20, 1954. (right to left) Rabbis Michael Bernstein, Joseph Soloveitchik, Nathan Kamenetsky, Mrs. Shulamth Kamenetsky, Rabbi David Lifschitz. Leaning forward is Rabbi Mordechai Elefant.*

Rabbi Michael Bernstein reciting one of the Sheva Berakhot *(l. to r.) Rabbi Nathan Kamenetsky, Dr. Samuel Soloveichik, Rabbis Joseph Soloveitchik and Michael Bernstein.*

The Rav with Rabbi Norman Lamm, ca. mid 1950s. Photo: Irwin A. Albert.

The Rav with Rabbi Norman Lamm, ca. mid 1950s. Photo: Irwin A. Albert.

First Chinuch Atzmai *Dinner, January 1956. (l. to r.) Rabbis Joseph Soloveitchik, Aaron Kotler, Mr. Irving Bunim. Photo: Chinuch Atzmai.*

Rabbis Solomon Sharfman and Joseph Soloveitchik, ca. late 1950s. Photo: Irwin A. Albert.

Streit's Matzoh Bakery, ca. 1960. (l. to r.) Rabbis Aaron Shurin, Joseph Singer, Chaim Bialik, Isaac Stollman, Aaron Soloveichik, Joseph Soloveitchik, Ben-Zion Notelevitz, Moses Poleyeff, and Aaron Zlotowitz.

Rabbinical Council of America's luncheon celebrating Rabbi Eliezer Silver's eightieth birthday (1961). Front row, (l. to r.) Rabbis Abraham AvRutick, Theodore Adams, Joseph Soloveitchik, Eliezer Silver, Pesach Levovitz. Back row (l. to r.) Rabbis Sidney Applbaum, Yehuda Gershuni, David Silver, Emanuel Rackman, Charles Weinberg, Louis Bernstein.

(l. to r.) Rabbis Moshe Dovber Rivkin, Joseph Soloveitchik and his nephew Yosef Soloveichik, at the latter's Bar Mitzvah, 1965.

Rabbis Joseph Soloveitchik and Joseph Burg (Israeli government representative of the National Religious Party), ca. 1974. Photo: Irwin A. Albert.

(l. to r.) Rabbis Ovadiah Yosef (Sephardi Chief Rabbi of Israel), Herbert
Dobrinsky (Yeshiva University administration), and Joseph
Soloveitchik, April 25, 1974. Courtesy of "Me-Brisk le-Yerushalayim,"
Rabbi Yosef Soloveichik, Arutzei Kodesh, Israeli Radio.

Rabbis Joseph Soloveitchik, and Shlomo Goren (Ashkenazi
Chief Rabbi of Israel), June 1976. Photo: Irwin A. Albert.

(l. to r.) Rabbis Shneur Kotler, Joseph Soloveitchik and Moshe Feinstein. In the background is Rabbi Pesach Levovitz. Courtesy of Jewish Action.

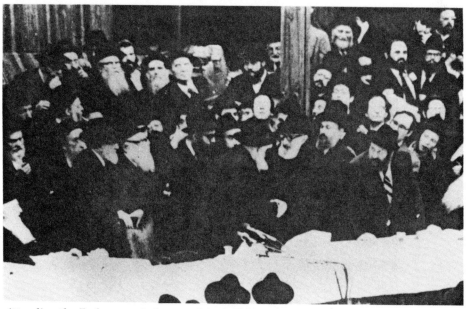

Attending the Farbrengen in honor of the Lubavitcher Rebbe's thirtieth anniversary as the head of Habad, *January 1980.*

Attending the Farbrengen in honor of the Lubavitcher Rebbe's thirtieth anniversary as the head of Habad, *January 1980. Courtesy of Jacques Gorlin.*

The Holocaust

18.01 Jewish Destiny

Related by the Rav in his lecture at Yeshiva University's Institute of Mental Health Project (undertaken jointly with Harvard and Loyola Universities to study religious attitudes to psychological problems), February 12, 1959.

The modern Jew does not try to forge his Jewish destiny but accepts it. Perhaps he does not really accept it, but sees it as foisted upon him. He has been thrown and tossed by the winds of circumstance into his Judaism. Bold, cruel, capricious fate has made him a Jew. The modern Jew tries to hide from his Judaism. I always recall the story of the prophet Jonah. When Jonah was fleeing God, he found it difficult to escape from the God of his loneliness as a Jew. He catches up with you. "But Jonah had gone down below the deck and was lying fast asleep" [Jonah 1:5]. He wanted to forget that he was traveling on a ship and the people were somehow trying to examine his background. "So the shipmates came to him, and said to him: 'Why are you sleeping? Get up and call upon your God! Perhaps God will think of us, so that we will not perish'" [Jonah 1:6]. Then you take verse 8: "Then they said to him: 'Tell us now, you who are the cause of our present distress, what is your occupation? Where do you come from? What is your country? To what people do you belong?'"

Sometimes we are pressed by the shipmaster, whoever he is, to acknowledge something about ourselves. It is a very embarrassing question. I lived in Germany many years. I knew assimilated Jews in Germany very well. These questions used to come up time and again. "What is your occupation? Where do you come from? What is your country?" Why should they ask a Jew these questions. Many Jews had lived in Germany even longer than the Germans themselves. Perhaps as early as the tenth century there was a Jewish community in Germany. Even Charlemagne [742–814] had dealt with Jewish communities.

Still, these questions came up. When these questions are asked, there is only one answer to be given. This answer can be given only by the person being asked. He must declare that he accepts Judaism not as a fate but as a destiny. This answer was given by Jonah the prophet. He understood that is was impossible to escape from God. Jonah told them: "I am a Hebrew; I revere the Lord, God of Heaven, who made the sea and the dry land" [Jonah 1:9]. The moment he gave this answer there was a complete change in his philosophy. Jonah now accepted his Jewishness as part of an intelligent destiny, and not simply as his fate.

18.02 Jewish Solidarity

Related by the Rav in his lecture at Yeshiva University's Institute of Mental Health Project (undertaken jointly with the Harvard and Loyola Universities to study religious attitudes to psychological problems), February 26, 1959.

Differences in the color of the skin, cultural diversity, economic discrepancies, language, dress, mores, and differences in the general social milieu must not dispel the feeling of solidarity which binds all Jews together. Whether they live in culturally advanced Western societies or in the Far East, Israel, or North Africa, the Jews must be united. Whether they live on Park Avenue or in the mellah in Algeria, they are all exposed to the same vicissitudes of history. I want you to know, this is not a prophecy of doom. No, it

is an approach based upon the idea that there is no aristocracy in
Judaism. I do not mean aristocracy in the sense of blue blood. I
mean aristocracy in the sense that no Jew can say that what happened to X cannot happen to me. I therefore resent it very much
when Zionist leaders like David Ben-Gurion [1886–1974; first
Prime Minister of Israel] begin to tell us how unreliable the
Diaspora is. I do not say that the Diaspora is very reliable. I say
something else: that the Diaspora is not reliable and the State of
Israel, too, is not reliable. If, God forbid, the day should come
when the American government and the American people become
anti-Semitic and start to pass anti-Jewish legislation, then we shall
have no shelter here. However, we will have no shelter in Israel,
either. This statement on the part of Ben-Gurion is ridiculous. I
have told Zionist leaders many times not to utter such thoughts
because they make no sense. The security and safety of Israel
depend upon Western society.

This is not a prophecy of doom. There is no security for a
people, just as there is no security for a human being. The American ideal that a man can find security is false. A man has no security as an individual, as I have explained many times. If a man has
a big bank account, does this make him secure? He is not secure,
because the vicissitudes of life are not only in the economic area.
Today I can move my fingers. The next day I cannot. Is this security? Who can secure me against illness? It is ridiculous when people speak about security. There is no absolute security. For the Jew
to claim security is equally incorrect.

I say this for many reasons. First of all, this is the prevailing
mood in Judaism. It is not pessimism. The Jew is never secure as a
person, and, on the other hand, the Jew is an optimist. It is a combination. The Jew thinks in dialectical terms. The thesis is right,
but the antithesis is also right. The thesis is right in that no one is
secure. The antithesis is also right in that man should feel secure as
far as possible. If you operate with a thesis and an antithesis, which
is dialectical thinking, then you do not operate with ultimates. You

do not have to say either this or that. You can develop a new approach.

My interpretation of Judaism is not objective. No person who interprets Judaism can be objective. Judaism is an experience. Experiences vary just as personalities vary. Therefore, my interpretation of Judaism is an outgrowth of my own personality and my own experiences. I lived for many years in Germany. The good years, the "seven good years" as we say in the biblical language [Genesis 41:26].[1] Germany in the twenties was ruled by social democracy. During this period, there were anti-Semitic outbreaks and violence from time to time in Poland and Lithuania. So German Jews who were assimilated Jews used to tell me: "What is happening in Poland cannot happen here. It is impossible." All German Jews were assimilated, whether they were pious or not. German Jewish society was integrated into German society far more than the American Jewish society is integrated into American society. Integration is a problem of years. It is not a result that can simply be brought about by changing one's language. It is a question of mores and a way of thinking. Do not forget that German Jewish society was almost as old as German civilized society itself. Of course, Hitler was on the scene a little bit at that time. But he was more of a comic figure in 1926 and 1927. No one paid serious attention to him. He was a crackpot from Vienna who did not speak a decent German. He spoke a grammatically wrong, faulty German. This is a fact. He never learned how to speak German properly, even when he was the leader, the Fuehrer of the German people. The Jews believed that the anti-Semitic outbreaks of Eastern Europe could not happen in Germany. At that time, I always felt a certain sense of complacency and security among German Jews.

Yet it happened in Germany. To say that Germany is different from all other nations is ridiculous. I knew many Germans, good Germans and bad Germans. They were a very cultured people. As far as culture was concerned, they were second to none. Who wrote beautiful books about ethics if not the Germans? They wrote about the categorical imperative and that man should sacrifice himself for the categorical imperative. Even a "necessary lie" should not be uttered, even to save one's life. It was [Johann Gottlieb] Fichte [1762–1814], the famous German philosopher, who insisted on this. Still, it did happen in Germany.

Why is it so? Because human beings can be either devils or angels. We are all human beings. I am not sure that even in Israel a Hitler is impossible. Even in Israel it is possible. We too are human beings. With all our charismatic endowment, we are still human beings. A human being is not reliable. That's all! You know what David said: "All men are liars" [Psalms 116:11]. He was right. It does not mean that you should not trust man, but that you also should remember this sentence. You know the rabbinic expression: "Honor him, but suspect him" [based upon Kallah Rabbati, chap. 9]. Pay him respect, but watch out! It does not mean so much to watch out for pickpockets, but rather for the vicissitudes of life. There are biological vicissitudes and also historical vicissitudes. At certain times a nation may go crazy, may run amok. This may happen not only with individuals, but also with an entire nation. We saw it with Germany.

Therefore, Jewish history calls out for the solidarity effect. Yes, disaster for one community must alarm all other Jewish communities and summon them to defensive action. Even if the community struck by disaster is distant from and strange to the other Jewish communities, all must react. If one community finds itself in trouble, it is one world for all the Jews. They all have a common destiny. One Jewish community must help another, not out of sympathy and pity, but because of the Jew's distinct feeling of involvement with the fate of other Jews. This is so regardless of the endless geographical, cultural, and political distance between these communities. If a Jew tries to desert his people and flee the common destiny, he is dragged back by a cruel and cynical fate. I feel impelled to refer you again to the story of Jonah, which is impregnated with symbolism. He is dragged back to God whom he tried to flee and desert.

1. Rabbi Soloveitchik lived in Germany from 1926 to 1932.

18.03 Man-Satan

Related by the Rav in the Tonya Soloveitchik Memorial Lecture on "Purim Ideas," Yeshiva University, March 4, 1974.

Who is Amalek [Exodus 17:8–16]? A man who personifies total evil. It is a man to whom immorality becomes the norm. Who is Amalek? Of course, it most probably was a wandering Bedouin tribe. However, the biblical verse is quite serious when it says that "God has declared an eternal war against Amalek, throughout the generations" [Exodus 17:16]. I would say it was beneath the dignity of God to declare an eternal war against a Bedouin tribe. Amalek will only be defeated at the commencement of the messianic era. No one will be able to defeat Amalek. The final defeat of Amalek will take place when the King Messiah arrives.

So who is Amalek? It is not just a Bedouin tribe. It is not a race, a specific group, or a nationality. It is man who went berserk. Man who incarnates total evil. It is Man-Satan. Man can be created in the image of God or in the image of Satan. It is Man-Demon.

I once heard from my father, in the name of my grandfather, that Amalek is any people or group who are committed to one purpose: the destruction of the Jewish people.[1] Such a group is to be classified as Amalek. If one writes on its banner, "Let us cut them off from being a nation; that the name of Israel may be no more in remembrance" [Psalm 83:5], he aquires the status of Amalek. The commandment of "surely erasing the memory of Amalek" [Exodus 17:14] is applicable to him or to them.

Quite often Amalek, or Man-Satan, succeeds in his attempt to gain power and to cause untold suffering to millions or hundreds of millions of people. I believe that our generation has encountered a few of them. Most of you are young, but I am speaking of people as old as I am. There is no doubt about it that Hitler was Amalek. I am speaking in halakhic terms. Hitler and his entourage were Amalek. There is no doubt that Stalin had the status of Amalek.

He too was the incarnation of total evil. I have doubts about the "generous" Mr. Leonid Brezhnev [1906–1982; general secretary of the Soviet Communist Party, 1964–82] and about Mao Tsetung [1893–1976; chairman of the Chinese Communist Party, 1943–76]. I do not know. I have serious doubts about them. Intuitively, I feel that they are also the incarnation of evil and Satan.

1. For a detailed analysis of this view, see the Rav's "Kol Dodi Dofek," tranlated by Lawrence Kaplan, in *Theological and Halakhic Reflections on the Holocaust*, edited by Bernhard H. Rosenberg and Fred Heuman (Hoboken, N.J.: KTAV, 1992), pp. 98, 116–117, fn. 25.

18.04 Determined Anti-Semites

Related by the Rav in his lecture on Hanukah, Boston, Mass., December 18, 1971.

In the prayer for Hanukah we state: "When a wicked Hellenic government rose up against Thy people Israel" [*Daily Prayer Book*, trans. Philip Birnbaum, p. 92]. What does *ke-she-amedah* mean? The literal translation means "rose up." What does it mean to rise? Why did they have to rise? What does this verb convey? There are many terms that could have been used. However, *ke-she-amedah* means determination. It is not just a decision. When you make a decision, you may either carry it out or renege on it. You may change your mind. If there is a feeling of determination, however, then it must be done. If this is your major objective, then you say *ke-she-amedah*.

For instance, I want you to understand, for Hitler anti-Semitism was not a secondary policy or a peripheral approach. It was the major objective in the wicked philosophy of Nazism. The destruction of the Jews was a major objective. The same is true with atheism in Marxism. We do not understand why it is necessary for Marxism and socialism to adopt an atheist philosophy. I do not know. That is a different problem. However, atheism is not just an incidental or peripheral doctrine in Marxism and Communism. It is the very foundation of Marxism and Communism. Why this is so, I have never been able to understand. You know that in

Germany there were religious socialists. Yet they never succeeded in attracting the masses. The Communist socialist society is usually an atheistic society. To them atheism is actually a religion unto itself. It is a kind of idol.

Ke-she-amedah means that to the wicked Hellenic government the destruction of Judaism was not just incidental. It was a major objective. I want you to know that anti-Semitism is never marginal for an anti-Semitic movement. It is central. We do not know why. For instance, there was the German National People's Party.[1] They were conservative, and represented the German capitalists and industrialists. There was no need for this party to be anti-Semitic. Yet they were, and it was the central idea in their political world philosophy.

That is exactly the concept here in *ke-she-amedah*. The wicked Hellenic government may have had many problems. However, a central problem for it was the subjugation of the spirit of the proud Judeans who did not want to surrender to the Greek culture. There was determination on the part of the Hellenic government, and this goal was central to its outlook. They were relentless in pursuing this goal. That is *ke-she-amedah*.

There was no need for Hitler to have been an anti-Semite. He could have gotten everything without his anti-Semitism. It is quite possible that he might have won the war had it not been for his anti-Semitism. Driving the Jewish scientists out of Germany denied him the chance to develop the atomic bomb before America. It is quite possible that anti-Semitism was actually responsible for Hitler's downfall. Of course, he fell before the atomic bomb was produced. He could have gotten it first, however. It was quite possible. Yet his anti-Semitism undid him.

1. For more information about the German National People's Party, see William L. Shirer, *The Rise and Fall of the Third Reich* (New York: Simon & Schuster, 1960), index.

18.05 Forced to Dance

Related by the Rav in his lecture on Parshat Sh'mot (Exodus 1:1–6:1), Yeshiva University, December 30, 1980.

The method employed by the sonei yisrael ["haters of Israel"] throughout the generations has not only been to oppress the Jew but also to discredit him in the eyes of the world. They want to prove to the world that the Jew is a subhuman, an immoral being, and therefore does not deserve the sympathy of other people.

As a matter of fact, that is what happened during the Holocaust years in Poland and Lithuania. I believe that several people have told me this story, and I have also read it. The Nazis would suddenly grab some Jews off the street and order them to dress up nicely in their festive clothes. They would then assemble them in a hall, usually in one of the finest hotels in Warsaw. The tables in the hall were set with delicious foods. It was actually impossible to obtain such precious items at such times. There was an orchestra and the Jews were forced to dance. During the feast, the Nazi photographer kept on taking pictures. Afterwards, the Nazis would take the Jews from the hotel to Treblinka to be destroyed in the ovens of the crematorium.

What was the idea behind these actions? We found out after the war why they did such things. I do not remember whether the information was in the documents of [Hans] Frank [1900–1946, Nazi governor of Poland] or [Joseph] Goebbels [1897–1945, Nazi Minister of Propaganda]. They wanted to show that the Jews were subhuman, that the Jews themselves did not care about Treblinka and Auschwitz. Had they cared, how could they have arranged banquets at a time when their brethren were suffering? They had no sympathy for fellow Jews who were suffering in the concentration camps at the very time they were feasting.

This was exactly the method employed by Pharaoh, the king of Egypt. He wanted to show that the Jews were not worthy of sympathy in that the Hebrew midwives themselves had no sympathy for the little ones. They were killing them at birth because they were afraid of what the king of Egypt would do to them if they refused to comply with his instructions. [Thus by implication, if the midwives showed no sympathy for their young ones, Pharaoh need not display sympathy for the Jewish children.]

18.06 Idolatrous Faith in Man

Related by the Rav in his lecture on "The Profundity of Jewish Folk Wisdom," at the RCA Annual Convention, June 20, 1977. This lecture was reconstructed in Reflections of the Rav *[33:6], pp. 59–70. This portion is summarized on pp. 68–69.*

We may have trust in man, confidence in him, but we may not have faith in him. Faith connotes absoluteness, and no man is worthy of absolute faith. The concept of faith is only applicable to God. . . .

I was young at the time, but I felt that we were wrong in our relationship to a certain person. Our relationship to President [Franklin Delano] Roosevelt bordered on idolatry. Had it not been an idolatrous relationship, we would have saved hundreds of thousands, perhaps millions, of Jews from the concentration camps and the crematoria. The fact is that we did not exert any pressure. The State Department would call in the American Jewish leaders and tell them not to circulate the stories about the extermination of the Jews in the crematoria. The State Department claimed that these stories would have hampered the war effort. I do not understand why this was so. Yet the Jewish leaders accepted it.

A layman once suggested to me that we should include another Al Het in our Yom Kippur confessional: "for the sins we have committed in being unresponsive to the cries of our brethren in Europe who were being brutally slaughtered." He was quite right! I am not blaming anybody. I am blaming myself. Why didn't I act like Mordecai when he heard the news about the evil decree issued by Haman and Ahasuerus? Why didn't I "go out into the center of the city and shout bitterly and loudly" [Esther 4:1]? Why didn't I shout, yell, and cry? Why didn't I tear my clothes like Mordecai? Why didn't I awaken the Jewish leaders? I am not blaming anybody. This was the punishment for our being idol worshipers. Our faith in Roosevelt bordered on idolatry.

And let me tell you, Roosevelt was a great President. If not for Roosevelt, it is quite possible that Hitler would have won the war. Roosevelt's open support of England before America entered the war greatly aided the powers then fighting the Germans. Roosevelt did a lot for the liberalization of America. If not for Roosevelt, labor would not have gained the positions it did gain later. Roosevelt did a lot for the world and for America, but he failed miserably as far as the Jews were concerned. Let me tell you, if Roosevelt had been President in 1948, the State of Israel would never have come into existence. [Harry S.] Truman was the messenger selected by Divine Providence to be the President at that time.

Why did Roosevelt disappoint us? Because we worshiped him! If we had been critical of him, we would have had the courage to tell him: "No, you are wrong." After all, there is no reason why saving Jews from the crematoria would have interfered with the war effort. If we had the courage, we would not have acted like cowards. We would have acted differently in regard to the problems of saving the Jews of Eastern Europe and the status of the Land of Israel at that time. However, we had faith in Roosevelt instead of only confidence. We worshiped him, and as a result Roosevelt disappointed us. That is the punishment for worshiping idols.

18.07 The 1943 March on Washington

Related by the Rav in his lecture on Parshat Sh'mot (Exodus 1:1–6:1), Yeshiva University, December 30, 1980. Summarized and published in Divrei Hashkafah *(20:5), p. 50.*

During the Holocaust years, American Jews were very, very indifferent. At least they acted as if they were indifferent. They were afraid of [Franklin Delano] Roosevelt and did not act properly. American Jews apparently did not identify with their brethren in

Auschwitz and Treblinka. Had they felt identity with these people, then they would have yelled, shouted, and complained. When the Agudat Harabanim [Union of Orthodox Rabbis of the United States and Canada] organized a march on Washington, Roosevelt refused to see them. It was the day before Erev Yom Kippur, and yet Roosevelt refused to see them. [The march took place on October 6, 1943.][1] Nothing helped! Roosevelt let Henry Wallace, who was then the Vice-President, receive the delegation of the Agudat Harabanim. The Jewish people just did not react to the event. As a matter of fact, many, particularly the Jewish press, enjoyed the spectacle. Five hundred rabanim went to Washington. These rabanim sent a delegation consisting of five rabbis to meet with the President, but he did not receive them!

I must say that the American Jew of today is different. There is boldness, and there is courage. They have simply changed their attitude. They are not as afraid of the non-Jewish community as the East European Jew was. There is also a stronger sense of Jewish identity in America today. This does not mean that we have won the battle; that is another separate story. But there is a stronger sense of identity today!

1. For a detailed account of the march, see Aaron Rakeffet-Rothkoff, *The Silver Era: Rabbi Eliezer Silver and His Generation* (Jerusalem: Feldheim, 1981), pp. 219–221. Cf. Raichel Horowitz, *The Bostoner Rebbetzin Remembers* (New York: Mesorah, 1996), p. 112.

18.08 Interned Yeshiva Students

Related by the Rav in his lecture on "Covenants in the Book of Genesis" delivered to the Yeshiva University Rabbinic Alumni, Yeshiva University, ca. 1955. (Yiddish).

Our covenant with God is not limited to its legal aspects; it also engenders a metaphysical reality in which the Jew constantly identifies with the past. The Jew is psychologically closer to the past than the non-Jew.

During World War II, I was sent an article that had appeared in an Anglo-Jewish newspaper. It described the visit of an Englishman to a facility in which aliens were interned. It seems that the quarters were inhabited by yeshiva students. The visitor reported that the students were learning about Rabban Yohanan ben Zakkai and his encounters with the emperor Vespasian in the first century [C.E.]. That was all the students were discussing even though [U.S. President] Franklin Delano Roosevelt was meeting with [British Prime Minister] Winston Churchill in Casablanca at that very time [January 1943]. The visitor was amazed that the yeshiva students were oblivious to major contemporary events. Their attitude seemed to confirm the argument of Professor Arnold Toynbee [1889–1975; in his *Study of History*, 10 vols., 1934–54], that the Jews were a fossil people.

An aquaintance of mine in England sent me this article. He wanted me to respond to its conclusion. I never answered the letter. However, the refutation is simple. It is a reality of Jewry's metaphysical existence that the Jew is closer to the past than to the present. We have all experienced this in our sermons. We think that our ideas and organization of concepts are clear, yet the audience does not respond. The minute we utilize biblical metaphors the audience warms up. The Jew experiences the episodes of Abraham, Moses, and King David better than he does current events. That is a result of our unique covenant with the Almighty!

18.09 The Cat on Yom Kippur

Related by the Rav on Tishah be-Av, Boston, Mass., August 9, 1981.

We read many memoirs today about the Holocaust. Six million Jews were destroyed. It is hard to enunciate such figures. And it was not only Jews that were exterminated, but Jewish homes. Each home was a bet ha-mikdash [Temple] in miniature. Each home in Lithuania, Poland, and White Russia had its own traditions. The private home of the Jew was like a bet ha-mikdash, and its sanctity had been responsible for the survival of the Jew since the destruction of the Jerusalem Temple close to two thousand years ago.

I begin to see images of some of the people whom I knew in my youth. One image I see is that of a carpenter. He was a short fellow and eked out a living from carpentry. In order to make ends meet, he also rented out a room in his house to my melamed. The carpenter was a simple Jew, not too much of a scholar. Yet as he worked at his carpentry, he would recite the Psalms. He had worked out a system so that whenever he completed some object, say a table, he would reach the final sentence of "Let every thing that hath breath praise the Lord" [Psalms 150:6]. He seemed like a plain Jew, yet my father, Reb Moshe, considered him one of the thirty-six saints who inhabit the world.

On Tishah be-Av we mourn not only the destruction of the bet ha-mikdash in Jerusalem, but also all these individual batei ha-Mikdash in miniature that were wiped off the map. The East European home was filled with tradition. The home was part of the Oral Tradition, Torah she-beal-peh. All of this has been destroyed.

I recently heard the account of a person who survived the Holocaust because he was deported to Soviet Russia. This saved him from being exterminated by the Nazis. His mother lived in Vilna, and she was a pious Jewish woman, as were all Jewish mothers before the war. Of course, she went to shul on Yom Kippur. By the time they reached the Maftir Yonah [the reading of the Book of Jonah] during the Minhah prayer, she was tired. She would leave the shul for about half an hour to go home and feed her cat. Every year this was the time she fed her cat on Yom Kippur.

After the liberation from the Nazis, her son returned to Vilna and spent Yom Kippur there. His mother and all her acquaintances had been killed by the Germans. The only one who met him was the cat. He felt that the cat was waiting for him to feed it the way his mother had every Yom Kippur before she perished.

People who survived have often told me that the sense of emptiness in their formerly vibrant home communities was unbearable. Anyone who knows what the Vilna shul was like on Yom Kippur before the war will appreciate how desolate it was when only a cat remained to greet you.

This was stark testimony to the destruction. The people, the homes, and the batei mikdash in miniature were all gone. Only the cat remained. For this too we mourn on Tishah be-Av.

18.10 The Church's Responsibility

Related by the Rav in his lecture on Hanukah, Boston, Mass., December 18, 1971.

Alexander of Macedon [356–323 B.C.E.] was actually the first missionary. He combined military tactics with Greek culture. He conquered a land not only to control it politically, but to implant Greek culture, ideas, and ethics. Of course, he failed. However, those who succeeded him retained the idea of spreading and disseminating Greek culture and philosophy. Of course, Judea refused. Judea resisted and did not succumb. As a result, religious persecution was initiated. Our refusal to comply with the missionary complex of the Hellenized Syrians was the reason for their beginning a religious persecution.

These people were really not Greeks. What, then, was responsible for their conduct? It was a product of the Greek mentality, culture, vanity, and pride. They believed that the whole world consisted of barbarians. Only the Hellenes were cultured.

In this connection, it is very important to understand what I told a member of the Catholic hierarchy from Rome. He claimed, not only that they [the Catholics] were not responsible for the Hitler Holocaust, but also that they had helped Jews during the Hitler period. In terms of statistics, it is very hard either to contradict him or to prove him right. Some did help, and some did not help. The priesthood in Poland cooperated with the Nazis and the Gestapo. There were only a few exceptions in Poland. As a matter of fact, I have read the memoirs of a Jew who was disguised as a Catholic during the Hitler occupation of Poland. He once went to confession, and confessed to the priest that he had saved a Jew. He said he did not know whether it was a good deed or a sin. He had saved this Jew from falling into the hands of the Gestapo. The priest declared that it was a venal sin, and that next time he should deliver such a Jew into the hands of the Gestapo.

There were a few priests in Poland who helped Jews. Not too many, but there were some. In Italy, the situation was much better. The Italian priests helped. Not all, but many. To say that the Catholic Church stood up and courageously protected the Jews would be a gross exaggeration.

However, I told him something else. I said that I could not argue with him about statistics or numbers. That I knew of certain incidents, both positive and negative. I also agreed with him that Hitler was not a Christian. He kept emphasizing this to me. Of course, Hitler was not a Christian. He was a pagan, even worse than a pagan. None of Hitler's friends were pious Christians. However, I said, if we think about the Holocaust engendered by Hitler, we must acknowledge that millions of Christians witnessed it. These people were decent, civilized, and cultured. They included people from Germany, Japan, Holland, and the Baltic countries. They witnessed the slaughter of six million Jews, among them little babies and infants! The Nazis used to swing them against brick walls and smash their skulls.

How was this possible? After all, many people cannot see a wounded dog without getting excited and trying to help the dog. Yet here they were able to observe the systematic murder and extermination of the old, the middle-aged, of children and infants! It was due to something else. It was due to the preaching of the Church throughout the centuries and the millennia. Over the past nineteen hundred years the Church has taught that the Jew was cursed by God because he had rejected the Messiah. That the Jew was a wandering Jew because he had no home. That the Jew was responsible for the fact that the Messiah has not yet returned a second time as he is supposed to. Finally, the idea that the Jew is subhuman is a Catholic idea. Of course, you may point out a few theologians in the Catholic Church who are more conscientious and careful. Usually, however, these are the ideas about the Jews that were supported, if not, cultivated by the Church. They were implanted in the Christians by the Church.

And so, I said to him, perhaps now you realize that it was a mistake, even a terrible error. Yes, Hitler was not a Catholic. If not for your doctrine of the eternal wandering Jew, however, Hitler could not have succeeded. If not for your constant and continued preaching that the Jew blocks the arrival of your Messiah, the Holocaust could not have taken place. Perhaps you are not directly responsible. But indirectly you are responsible. You are the culprit! If not for your teachings, such cruelty could not have taken place. Directly, perhaps you are right. I would not call Hitler a Christian. Indirectly it was your fault.

Similarly, it was not the Greeks who persecuted the Jews at the time of the Hasmoneans. Yet we recite in the prayer: "When a wicked Hellenic government rose up against Thy people Israel to make them forget Thy Torah and transgress the laws of Thy will" [*Daily Prayer Book*, trans. Philip Birnbaum, p. 92]. Greece was not directly responsible for the religious persecution of the Jews at that time. Indirectly, however, it was Alexander's mission, the pride of the Greeks, and their contempt for everybody else that brought about the evil conduct of the Hellenized Syrians. And that is why the prayer refers to them as the "wicked Hellenic government."

Religious Sensitivity

19.01 The Blessing of Thanksgiving

Related by the Rav to his Talmud Class at Yeshiva University, February 6, 1969.

The Mishnah states: "R. Judah says: If one sees the Great Sea, one should say, Blessed be He who made the Great Sea" [Berakhot 9:2]. While the Great Sea can perhaps be either the Atlantic Ocean or the Mediterranean, it is probably the latter. I was born in the continental part of Europe and had never seen the sea. I had no idea what it looked like. I remember that I was grown up when I went to Danzig [Gdansk, Poland]. I saw the [Baltic] sea for the first time, and it made a tremendous impression upon me. From afar, it looked like a blue forest. I was used to forests from Russia. When I drew closer and saw that it was the sea, I was overwhelmed. I made the benediction of "Blessed be He who wrought creation," which is recited when "one sees mountains, hills, seas, rivers, and deserts" [Berakhot 9:2]. This blessing came from the depths of my heart. It was one of the greatest religious experiences I have ever had. It was my first encounter with the sea. It was a summer day, and the water was perfectly blue. It looked just like a Russian forest.

I feel that these blessings should only be recited when the individual truly feels the need to do so. . . . Similarly, regarding illness, the blessing of thanksgiving for one who has recovered from an illness should only be recited if the person was in danger [Berakhot 54b]. It depends upon what kind of sickness. If you take infectious diseases, which are today controlled by antibiotics, then there generally is no danger. Years ago it was different. I remember that I was sick with a middle-ear infection. It was very dangerous, because it was the pre-antibiotic era. I was confined to bed for six weeks. This was before sulfa and any other such drugs. All they gave me was aspirin. Of course, I made the blessing when I recovered. Nowadays, however, such illnesses are minor.

Certainly, when there is a possibility of complications one must recite the blessing. Nine years ago, when I was operated on, of course, I recited the blessing when I recovered.

19.02 The Baltic Sea

Related by the Rav in his eulogy for Rabbi Moshe Dovber Rivkin[1] at Congregation Moriya, New York, N.Y., December 14, 1976. (Yiddish).

I remember how enthused I was the first time I saw the Baltic Sea. I was born in Russia and never saw a major body of water in my youth. It was a beautiful sunny day in the month of Iyar [April–May], after Pesach, when I went with a cousin to the Baltic Sea in Danzig [Gdansk, Poland].

I remember that the water was blue, deeply blue. From afar it looked like a blue forest. It resembled the aboriginal forests near Pruzhana, where I was born. When I came close and realized it was the Baltic Sea, I was overwhelmed by its beauty. Spontaneously, I began to recite the Psalm [104] of "Bless the Lord, O my soul." I did not plan to do this. Yet the words flowed from my lips. "O Lord, my God, Thou art very great; Thou art clothed with glory and majesty" [Psalm 104:1]. "There is the sea, vast and wide" [Psalm 104:25]. It was a religious reaction to viewing the majesty of God's creation. When I recited the blessing upon seeing the sea, I did so with emotion and deep feeling. I deeply experienced the words of the benediction: "Blessed be He who wrought creation" [Berakhot 9:1]. Not all the blessings that I recite are said with such concentration. It was more than simply a blessing, it was an encounter with the Creator. I felt that the Shekhinah [Divine Presence] was hidden in the darkness and vastness of the sea. The experience was unique and unforgettable; the blessing welled out of me.

Since then I have seen the ocean many times. I still recite the benediction if thirty days have elapsed since I last saw it. Nevertheless, since that first time it has become a routine blessing; a cold blessing [mitnagdisher brachah] like those recited by the mitnagdim who were opposed to the hasidic movement.

1. Rabbi Rivkin, a leading disciple of Lubavitch, was rosh yeshiva in Brooklyn's Mesivta Torah Vodaath for close to fifty years.

19.03 Religious Experience

Related by the Rav in his lecture to the Yeshiva University Rabbinic Alumni on Parshat Bereshit (Genesis 1:1–6:8), October 20, 1971.

Who taught me religious sensitivity? I will tell you frankly, they speak about Brisk. People describe Brisk as consisting of brains only, no heart. They claim that Reb Chaim had a brain like anyone else, and also a brain in place of his heart. This is wrong, completely wrong. Reb Chaim was a very sensitive person when it came to religious sensitivity. There are sensitivities in other realms, but I am speaking about religious sensitivity. Reb Chaim's religious experiences were powerful and dynamic. He never spelled it out because he could never externalize his experiences. I cannot externalize my religious experiences either. He never told people and never confided in people about his emotional life. Yet his personal experiences were overwhelming.

Actually I received this tradition from my father and grandfather. I saw enough of their religious experiences that I can easily remind myself of how Reb Chaim used to say the Avodah on Yom Kippur. How he chanted the description of "the kohanim and the people, who were standing in the Temple court" [*High Holiday*

Prayer Book, trans. Philip Birnbaum, p. 816]. Reb Chaim was not visible at that time. He used to be somewhere in Jerusalem. He moved back in time, perhaps nineteen hundred years backward. He found himself for a short while in the Temple court with the kohanim and the people. If only you could have observed the change in his facial expression and in the melody as he began to say: "All this took place when the Sanctuary was firmly established" [ibid., p. 828]. This was beautiful, but now it is just a vision and not a reality. "All this took place when the Sanctuary was firmly established. The high priest ministered, his generation watched and rejoiced. Happy the eye that saw all this!" [ibid.]. However, "the iniquities of our fathers destroyed our sacred home" [ibid., p. 830]. Now the reality is just the reverse. How Reb Chaim would change from enthusiasm to sadness and grief, to nostalgia. As a matter of fact, if you take the tune for "the kohanim and the people," it is a tune full of nostalgia. That is why in America, where this religious sensitivity is lacking, they do not care whether they sing the refrain of "the kohanim and the people" to the traditional tune or to the tune of Eichah [Lamentations]. It does not matter much to them.

19.04 Private Emotions

Related by the Rav in his lecture on the "The Abridged Havinenu Prayer," at the RCA Midwinter Conference, February 7, 1968.

Jews do confess, but confession is a private matter between the individual and the Almighty. In my opinion, this is because of the Jew's typical modesty and shyness. The noblest and most exalted feelings that the Jew experiences must remain like the Ark of the Covenant, concealed behind the curtain. "And the curtain shall separate for you between the Holy and the Holy of Holies" [Exodus 26:33]. The sanctuary of the human person is his emotional life, not his logical life. The Ark is with us in each person's emotional life, concealed behind the curtain. This aspect of the human being is protected from the eye of the cynic, the glance of the skeptic, the ridicule of the so-called practical and realistic man.

The Jew, as a father, never spoke of his love for his children. Never! I want to tell you something. My relationship with my father was very close. He was my rebbe. I had no other rebbe. Whatever I am intellectually is due to him. He was very close to me, and I was very close to him. There was an existential unity between us. Nevertheless, he never told me that he liked me. He never kissed me, and I never kissed him. I remember that on one occasion I was departing, and it was doubtful whether I would ever see him again. We just shook hands and he said: "Go in peace, and let God be with you." As a matter of fact, someone watching this cold, chilly scene of father and son parting said: "That's the Brisker lomdus!" [Laughter.] The truth is that we did not spell out our love for our children in objective terms. Neither did Jews as husband or as wife spell out their love for each other. No matter how much devotion, dedication, mutual trust, and love bound them to each other, they could not speak about it. This love was nurtured in privacy. "It is there that I will set My meetings with you and I shall speak with you atop the cover, from between the two cherubim that are on the Ark of the Testimonial-Tablets" [Exodus 25:22]. [Only in the privacy of the Holy of Holies is such a rendezvous possible.]

Apparently, the same method was applied in our relationship with the Almighty. We never told anybody and never wrote about our love and dedication for the Almighty. We have not told anybody about our great romance with the Almighty and His with us. There is no literature about this. The only book we have on this topic is Shir ha-Shirim [Song of Songs], and it is couched in symbols. Only through such symbolism could our romance with the Almighty be presented.

However, I do not believe that we can afford to be as reluctant, modest, and shy today as we were in the past about describing our relationship with the Almighty. Why? The reason is simple. In the past, this great experience of the tradition was not handed down from generation to generation through the medium of words. It was absorbed through osmosis; somehow, through silence. We used to observe. I observed my father praying on Rosh Hashanah. That is an experience I will never forget. If on Yom Kippur I feel deficient in my own dedication, piety, and enthusiasm, no philosophical ideas can help me at such a time. If I want to inspire myself, I must visualize my grandfather Reb Chaim reciting his prayers on these Holy Days. I still recall that as a young child on Yom Kippur I observed his recitation of the refrain: "When the priests and the people, who were standing in the Temple court, heard God's glorious and revered Name clearly expressed by the high priest with holiness and purity" [Musaf service for Yom Kippur, trans. Philip Birnbaum, p. 816]. He was then a man completely consumed by nostalgia and yearning. This emotion was passed on from generation to generation simply through observance and viewing. Today in America, however, and in the Western world, this is completely lost. The father cannot pass it on to his son. The father does not possess these emotions, because he never observed and experienced them. He cannot expect his son to receive something he himself does not possess.

Therefore it is up to the Yeshiva and the teacher to open up the emotional world of Judaism to the students. I do not know how one can do so. Believe me, I have told you many times that before Rosh Hashanah and Yom Kippur I can teach my students the laws and the philosophy of these Holy Days. I am not a bad teacher. However, I cannot transmit my recollections to them. If I want to transmit my experiences, I have to transmit myself, my own heart. How can I merge my soul and personality with my students? It is very difficult. Yet it is exactly what is lacking on the American scene.[1] That is why American Jews do not pray as they should— and I am speaking of those who pray three times a day. There is no true avodah she-be-lev, worship of the heart, when it is only a mechanical recitation. The American Jew does not experience Rosh Hashanah and Yom Kippur as the Jew of old did. He observes these days, but he does not truly experience their sanctity, and particularly the nearness to God.[2]

This is exactly our greatest need in the United States—to feel and experience God's presence. It is not enough to eat matzah; we must feel the experience of the mitzvah. One should not only study Torah, but should actually experience it as a great drama and redeeming act which purges the personality. That is exactly what is lacking in the United States.

1. Cf. Shalom Carmy, "On Eagle's Flight and Snail's Pace," *Tradition*, vol. 29, no. 1 (Fall 1994), p. 31, fn. 22: "The Rav once remarked in my hearing that old-time Gedolim refrained from talking about themselves, but that the disconnection of modern man from living examplars of religious existence has made self-revelation an educational necessity."
2. Cf. Haym Soloveitchik, "Rupture and Reconstruction: The Transformation of Contemporary Orthodoxy," *Tradition*, vol. 28, no. 4(Summer 1994), p. 129, fn. 98.

19.05 Experiencing the High Holidays

Related by the Rav in an article published in Ha-Doar, *1 Sivan 5720 (1960), p. 520. Republished in* Be-Sod ha-Yahid veha-Yahad *(9:6), pp. 415–416; and* Divrei Hashkafah *(20:20), pp. 248–249. (Hebrew).[1]*

There is much that I have studied and taught about the Days of Judgment and Mercy, Rosh Hashanah and Yom Kippur. I have discussed the concepts of these days with my late father, who was my teacher. I have often lectured on the halakhic, aggadic, and philosophical nature of these special days to my congregants, students, and colleagues. I also possess many manuscripts which I have written on these themes. Nevertheless, my true understanding of these days is shaped by my childhood experiences, which I must constantly recall from the distant past. My joyful spirit is revived when these memories once again become tangible. Only then can I supplicate the Almighty and pour out my uneasy soul to Him. At that moment, I feel that the presence of God hovers over me in the image of the pleasurable smile of a beloved mother.

When I once again visualize my late father sitting and studying on Yom Kippur night, then I feel the true meaning of this sacred day. My father studied, in his intimate and modest fashion, the laws pertaining to the sacrificial service of Yom Kippur. He chanted the text to a tune that was both melancholy and joyful. When these sounds pierce my consciousness from the distant past, I am overcome with intense yearnings for that faraway world of my innocent childhood, which is so different from my present tainted one. My love is awakened and my spirit is sparked. Only then am I inspired to recite from the depths of my being the blessing of the sanctity of the day: "Our God and God of our fathers, pardon our iniquities on this Day of Atonement" [*High Holyday Prayer Book*, trans. Philip Birnbaum, p. 610].

When my eyes focus on my forebears as they stooped in total submissiveness when they confessed their sins before the Almighty, then my absurd pride is shattered. I sense a hidden hand throwing cold water on me which purifies and purges my enfeebled soul. In a moment I return to the dawn of my existence and find myself standing next to my father in the midst of a congregation of Habad hasidim engrossed in their prayers on the first night of Rosh Hashanah. I can feel the unique atmosphere which enveloped these hasidim as they recited the prayers by which they proclaimed Him their King. The older hasidim termed this night the "Coronation Night" as they crowned Him as their King. These poor and downtrodden Jews, who suffered so much during their daily existence, were able to experience the enthroning of the Almighty and the true meaning of the Malkhuyot [Kingship] prayers of the Rosh Hashanah liturgy. True, the knowledge of Judaism that I have subsequently acquired has deepened and broadened these experiences. It has placed them in a more profound and meaningful framework. Nevertheless, the emotions and the comprehension of an innocent youngster are still concealed in the depths of my soul.

1. Regarding the importance of this brief essay, see Aharon Lichtenstein, "The Rav at Jubilee: An Appreciation," *Tradition*, vol. 30, no. 4 (Summer 1996), p. 55. Rabbi Lichtenstein considers this essay "the single best introduction to the Rav's thought."

19.06 Two Unique Nights

Related by the Rav in a Memorial Lecture for Rabbanit Tonya Soloveitchik entitled "The Story of the Exodus," Boston, Mass., March 30, 1974.

In my experience—that is, in my experiential, not intellectual, memory—two nights stand out as endowed with unique qualities, exalted in holiness and shining with singular beauty. These nights are the night of the Seder and the night of Kol Nidrei. As a child I was fascinated by these two nights because they conjured a feeling of majesty. As a child I used to feel stimulated, aroused, and deeply inspired. I used to experience a strange peaceful stillness. As a child I used to surrender, using the language of the mystics, to a stream of inflowing joy and ecstasy. In a word, as a young child I felt the presence of kedushah [holiness] on these nights.

Of course, it is hard for me now, when I am old, to describe the state of mind of a sensitive young child. I cannot describe these feelings in general childish categories. I can only proclaim the experiences of my childhood days in retrospect by using the categories of an adult mind.

Paradoxically, I must say that these emotions and experiences, however naive and childish, have always been the fountainhead of my religious life. My religious life has always been a colorful life. This achievement I derived from my childhood experiences and not from my intellectual accomplishments.

I can still hear the sound of the melody of Yaknahaz [the order of reciting Kiddush and Havdalah when a festival falls on Saturday night], which I heard most probably at the age of four (1907) when my grandfather recited Kiddush on the Seder night which happened to coincide with Motzoay Shabbat [Saturday night]. I can still hear his deep voice, the rolling *resh*, and his chanting the words: "As thou hast made a distinction between Sabbath sanctity and festival sanctity, and hast hallowed the seventh day above the six days of work, so hast Thou set apart and sanctified Thy people Israel through Thy holiness." Finally, he concluded the blessing with the words: "Who makes a distinction between the degrees of holiness." These words gradually faded away, or shall I say gradually transposed themselves into another melody—a melody of silence. The hasidim say that the most beautiful melody is the silent melody.

As a child I used to muse for hours over the meaning of "Who makes a distinction between the sacred and the secular." I was fascinated by that phrase. I loved the sanctity of the sacred days of the Sabbath and the festivals. I cherished every spark of holiness of the festivals. I hated the everydayness and the gray routine of the weekdays. I can understand the hasidim who are not anxious to recite the Vehu Rahum Yehaper Avon prayer ["And He, being merciful, forgiveth iniquity"] on Mondays and Thursdays. Whenever they can, hasidim delete this prayer. This prayer represents the heart of weekdayness, devoid of any trace of festivity. Hasidim long for redemption, for a world that is entirely good and suffused with sanctity. The long Tahnun [Supplication for Pardon] prayer intrudes upon these emotions!

Likewise the night of Yom Kippur had a very strange impact on me. This feeling still inspires me today, and it will remain with me forever. On the night of Yom Kippur I felt that I was confronted with something beautiful and exalted. I felt that I was in the presence of what mystics call a redeeming reality. I was ready to wash myself and cleanse myself so that I could be embraced by this reality. The whole nature of Yom Kippur night seemed to me to be exalted and beautiful. Out of everything I saw that night, I could perceive the mystery of the Almighty. I was too young to understand ideas and the need for atonement. However, even as a child, I felt spiritually clean. I still remember the stirrings in my childish heart in response to the recitation of the She-hehi-yanu ["Who has given us life and sustenance"] blessing following the Kol Nidrei prayer.

I understand that you are probably wondering why I am telling you all this. The reason is obvious. All these memories lie at the root of my religious Weltanschauung and experience. Without them, I would have missed the ecstasy accompanying religious observance and the depth of religious meditation and thinking.

19.07 Fusing Emotion and Intellect

Related by the Rav in his lecture on "The Role of the Rabbi" to the Yeshiva University Rabbinic Alumni, May 18, 1955. (Yiddish).

Between Pesach and Shavuot we mainly read the weekly Torah portion from the Book of Leviticus [Vayikra]. This book was often misunderstood, and some Jews thought that they could live a corrupt life. All they had to do was to bring sacrifices to expiate and cleanse their sins. The truth is that the individual must be pure before he brings the sacrifice.

This cathartic purity can only be achieved if the emotion goes hand in hand with the halakhah. This makes our task much more difficult. It is impossible to study the Torah while standing on one foot. We have no instant ceremonies. Every religious experience must be based on halakhah. The religious emotion must originate from the fusion of the intellect and the halakhah.

When I taught my class in the Yeshiva the laws of preparing food for the Sabbath, we illustrated how a housewife should act in this matter. By discussing a temporal matter of this kind, we uncovered half of the Sabbath laws that are detailed in the *Shulhan Arukh*, Orah Hayyim. We must comprehend what Jewish law demands of us so that our religious life will have depth.

Even on the night of the Pesach Seder, when we have so many ceremonies, we must understand the components of the Seder on both the intellectual and the halakhic level. Which ceremonies are delineated by Torah law, and which are ordained by rabbinic law? Why is the Hallel divided so that we say the first part before the repast and the remainder after the meal? What is the difference between the daily charge to recall the going out from Egypt and the unique commandment on the Seder night to retell this story? What are the details of the requirement to drink four cups of wine?

There is so much that we must study to truly appreciate and properly discharge the demands of the Seder night.

In relation to Rosh Hashanah, we must comprehend the various sounds of the shofar. What is the difference between those that are blown before the Musaf prayers and those that are sounded after Musaf? What is the nature of the sanctity of the two days of Rosh Hashanah?

By understanding the halakhah, we can augment our philosophical approach to Judaism. To speak about Jewish philosophy without knowing the halakhah is like speaking about the philosophy of nature without knowing mathematics.

19.08 High Holiday Emotion

Related by the Rav in his Teshuvah Drashah, October 7, 1970. Published in Al ha-Teshuvah *(8:6), p. 200, and* Soloveitchik on Repentance *(37:4), pp. 133–134.*

Here I am, sitting in my classroom trying to explain the concepts of Yom ha-Kippur to my students. We learn about the mahzor [High Holiday prayerbook] with its liturgical poems and about the laws and customs pertaining to the Days of Awe. If there is a need, I also give them philosophical explanations. From an intellectual point of view, there is much that I can transmit to my students from what I received from my forefathers and mentors about the significance of the day and about the sanctity of the Days of Awe. What I cannot give them, however, are my personal emotional experiences that I have experienced on these days. I cannot lift them into the world of emotion that a Jew has to feel when he says the Zikhronot [Remembrance Prayers], when he declares the words "And the Lord God will sound the shofar and march amid the storms of the south" [Zechariah 9:14]. How can I transmit to them the feelings that I felt when I heard my grandfather, Reb Chaim, recite the prayer after the description of the Temple Service with so much emotion and fear: "All this took place when the sanctuary was firmly established. The high priest ministered, his generation watched and rejoiced" [*High Holiday Prayer Book*, trans. Philip Birnbaum, p. 828]. You could tangibly feel that at that moment Reb Chaim was in a totally different world, as if he had left Brisk and had been transported back to the Jerusalem of thousands of years ago. This experience of feeling the emotion of the sanctity of the day is lacking for American Jewry.

19.09 Fear and Joy

Related by the Rav in his Teshuvah Drashah, September 1975. Summarized and published in Yemei Zikaron *(17:12), p. 240 (Yiddish).*

Rosh Hashanah possesses aspects of both fear and joy. This duality was reflected in the behavior of our great rabbis. My great-grandfather Reb Yosef Baer would fast by day on Rosh Hashanah. Yet he would be in an ecstatic and joyful mood at the repast on Erev Yom Kippur. On the other hand, my grandfather Reb Chaim was cheerful on Rosh Hashanah and terror-stricken on Yom Kippur.

There were similar differences between the hasidic masters. Some of them celebrated Rosh Hashanah as a festival, with all the joy of Pesach, Shavuot, or Sukkot. Others observed it as the Day of Judgment, with the stress on awe and trepidation.

Similarly, on Yom Kippur there were two approaches to the sanctity of the day. I remember that when I first arrived in Germany, I was shocked by the joyful tunes that were sung as part of the liturgy [on Yom Kippur]. They were in stark contrast to the apprehensiveness and fear that permeated the synagogues in Eastern Europe on this day. Nevertheless, I realized that both approaches were correct. There is also great joy on the day that our sins are forgiven.

19.10 Fasting on Yom Kippur

Related by the Rav in his lecture entitled "Rashi on Aseret Hadibrot," at the RCA Annual Convention, June 30, 1970.

There are mitzvot which we observe because of an inner need, urge, yearning, and quest. One finds self-fulfillment and realization in their observance. In such instances, one does not act under pressure or divine decree.

Let me give an example from my own life. When I fast on Yom Kippur, I am completely unaware of the prohibition of "You shall afflict your souls" [Leviticus 23:27]. I do not fast because of any normative pressure. I simply find delight, joy, and happiness in fasting, praying, and cleansing myself. I would be the most unhappy person in the world if the great privilege of "You shall afflict your souls" were denied me. People have many phobias. One of my greatest fears as I get older is that I will be forced to break the fast because of health factors. Such a traumatic experience would be tragic or even fatal for me. I pray to God that it should never happen.

19.11 Communicating Judaism

Related by the Rav in his lecture on "The Future of Jewish Education in America," at the Lincoln Square Synagogue, New York, N.Y., May 28, 1975.

The av zaken teaches the yeled zekunim how to act and discipline his thoughts. We must devote a lot of time to teaching Gemara. We are not just teaching a text but how to think halakhically, how to conceptualize and to define. I want to tell you that as far as lomdut is concerned, American Jewish children are very bright and brilliant. Sometimes I do not believe my own eyes when I consider their fantastic accomplishments. I am speaking from experience, because I have been a melamed of Gemara my entire adult life.

However, besides teaching the yeled zekunim discipline, the av zaken teaches him something else—the romance of Yahadut.

He teaches the child how to experience and feel Yahadut. Yahadut is not only discipline. Yes, we start with that, to discipline the child on all levels, on the physical level, on the social level, on the emotional level, and on the intellectual level. Above all, he teaches the child how to experience Yahadut, how to feel Yahadut. That is what my melamed taught me.

A Jew is not only supposed to know what Yahadut stands for and to have knowledge of Yahadut; he is also called upon to experience Yahadut, to live it, and to somehow engage in a romance with the Almighty. Knowing about Yahadut is not enough; it is a norm to be implemented and experienced. It is to be lived and enjoyed. It is a great drama which the yeled zekunim must act out after observing the av zaken.

Studying the Torah she-ba'al peh, the Oral Tradition, and complying with its precepts are the greatest pleasures a person can have. It is an exciting and romantic adventure. It is the most cleansing and purging experience a human being can experience. The av zaken teaches the yeled zekunim how to live and to feel Yahadut.

Let me make an admission here; I will confide in you. This is the toughest of all jobs, the most difficult of all tasks. I know from my own experience how difficult it is. I am not modest; I am far from being modest. I know that I am a good teacher. I can teach halakhah. I can explain the most abstract concepts. I can popularize the most complex talmudic debate and break it down into its component parts. I can explain and elucidate abstract ideas.

For instance, before Rosh Hashanah and Yom Kippur I used to study with my students (your rabbi [Rabbi Stephen Riskin] can confirm this) the halakhot pertaining to the Yomim Noraim [Days of Awe]. From time to time I would reach out for the aggadah or for philosophical ideas with which to elucidate the philosophy of those solemn festivals. If necesssary I would also introduce a modern idiom in order to explain certain aspects of the sanctity of these holy days [Kedushat ha-Yom]. All these tricks I know.

But one trick I have not mastered. One thing I cannot do to perfection is to tell my students how I felt on Rosh Hashanah and Yom ha-Kippurim when I was their age. The emotions I experienced, and not what I knew about it. I knew a lot, and they know a lot. But what I felt on these days! How I lived it! I am unable to share with them what I experienced, for instance, when the shaliakh tzibbur [cantor] used to chant and sing: Veha-kohanim veha-am haomdim ba-azarah ["When the priests and the people who were standing in the Temple court"; from the Avodah, the procedure of the Temple service, which is recited as part of the Musaf of Yom Kippur; *High Holiday Prayer Book*, trans. Philip Birnbaum, p. 816]. If you know the melody, you will agree that there is so much nostalgia, so much longing and melancholy in this tune, in the melody of Veha-kohanim veha-am haomdim ba-azarah. I felt as if I had been transferred in time and space into a different world. I felt that I was in the Bet Hamikdash [Holy Temple]. How can I explain this to my students? I can tell them about it but I cannot pass on my experiences to them!

Or how can I pass on the emotion I felt on Kol Nidrei night when the congregation responded amen to the chanting of the Shehehiyanu blessing. It is difficult to transfer experiences and not just concepts; to give over themes and not just numbers. To pass on feelings, to tell the story of both inner restlessness and serenity, to relate the narrative of joy and awe, of trepidation and at the same time equanimity in one's heart, one must not use words. Words cannot explain it. Instead an unusual medium must be utilized: silence. That melamed of old in my heder knew how to pass on his emotional acquisitions, his ecstatic experiences, and his mystical outlook on life. He knew how to pass this on to his pupils without saying a single word.

Of course these experiences can only be passed on in the fashion that one passes on a contagious illness. How do you communicate a disease? Through contact! And contact is the secret of passing on the experiences of Yahadut. The skill of somehow communicating with the soul of the person is not through the spoken word but through the art of silence.

However, it is very difficult. I have not entirely succeeded in passing on this part of Yahadut. But your teachers in your high school will. They will be more successful. They will arrange the rendezvous between the av zaken and the yeled zekunim.

19.12 Teaching a Hasidic Text

Related by Rabbi Menachem Genack in an interview, January 25, 1993. The incident was originally related to the author by Yaakov Haber, who heard the story while a student of Rabbi Genack.

In the summer of 1969, a number of Rabbi Joseph B. Soloveitchik's students traveled to Boston to study with him. The Rav felt that his students were mastering the intellectual aspects of the rabbinic tradition, but did not truly comprehend its emotional nature. With the aim of intensifying the emotional experience, the Rav announced that he was interested in teaching the *Likkutei Torah*, authored by the founder of Habad hasidism, Rabbi Shneur Zalman of Lyady [1745–1813]. The Rav chose the section that began with a commentary on "I am my beloved's, and my beloved is mine" [Song of Songs 6:3; *Likkutei Torah* to Deuteronomy, Parshat Reah, 32a].[1] Soon afterwards, the Rav learned that one of his closest students, who was a confirmed mitnaged [opponent of hasidim], was not exactly pleased with the choice of this topic.

Upon hearing of the student's objections, the Rav recounted the following tale, which was based upon a short story [entitled "Zwishen Zwei Berg," i.e., "Between Two Mountains"] by Isaac Leib Peretz [1852–1915]. The Rav described his great-grandfather, Rabbi Joseph Dov ha-Levi Soloveitchik [1820–1892], the author of the *Bet ha-Levi*, who was a stalwart mitnaged. The *Bet ha-Levi* had a student who had become a devotee of the hasidic movement. This student became the Bialyer Rebbe and was anxious for Rabbi Soloveitchik to appreciate the hasidic movement. Time and again he invited the *Bet ha-Levi* to join him at a gathering of his hasidim.

After many refusals, Rabbi Soloveitchik finally consented to accompany his student. In the heart of the winter, the odd pair, one a mitnaged and the other a hasid, made their way through the heavy snow and blustering winds toward the *shtiebel* where the gathering was taking place. Upon arriving, the two entered a room filled with song and spiritual delight. As the tunes of the hasidim grew louder and more intense, the sun suddenly peeked out of the clouds and shined forth over the *shtiebel*. Then the Rebbe began to speak, and his followers huddled around him to digest every word. After the words of Torah, the hasidim once again broke out in tumultous song until the whole building shook. Suddenly, the snow melted, the grass sprouted forth, the barren trees bloomed again, and the birds joined the hasidim in praising the Almighty.

As the hour was late, the *Bet ha-Levi* glanced at his watch and suddenly told his student in a sharp tone: "Nu, nu, it is time for the Minhah [afternoon] prayers." The spiritual rapture of the gathering was broken, the weather outside once again turned bleak, the trees once again became bare, and the earth returned to a barren wilderness.

After finishing the story, the Rav turned to the student who was not happy about studying a classic hasidic text and exclaimed: "This story is about you!"

The same incident was thus related by Rabbi Menachem Genack in his article: "Walking with Ramban," Tradition, vol. 30, no. 4 (Summer 1996), pp. 186–187.

One summer, the Rav gave a few shiurim on *Likkutei Torah*, by Rav Shneur Zalman of Lyadi, the founder of Lubavitch hasidism. He said it was important to study *Likkutei Torah* in order to properly appreciate the grandeur of Rosh Hashanah. When he sensed that some of us were resistant to learning the hasidic work, the Rav related an apocryphal story, "Between Two Mountains," written by the classical Hebrew author, Y. L. Peretz.

The story describes the encounter of the Rav's great-grandfather, Rabbi Yosef Dov Soloveitchik (the author of the *Bet ha-Levi*, for whom the Rav was named), and the Bialyer Rebbe, a former talmid of his who had become a hasidic rebbe. The Bialyer Rebbe, filled with passion and religious fervor, had cajoled his master, the *Bet ha-Levi*, to come to visit a gathering of the Rebbe's followers. As Peretz tells the story, the song and warmth of the hasidim melted the outside snow and caused the trees to bloom and the birds to chirp. The cold Russian winter twilight was transformed by the ecstasy of the Hasidim into a bright spring day. As sunset approached, the *Bet ha-Levi*, who had a profound and analytical mind and was devoid of undisciplined emotion, looked at his watch and interrupted the song to remind the assembly that it was getting late and it was time to daven Minhah. Suddenly, the glorious spring faded and reverted to the cold winter. The Rav then looked at me and said, "That's you." To the Rav, it was important to communicate both the logic and the passion of the Torah.

1. These details were provided by Rabbi Aharon Lichtenstein during his eulogy for the Rav on April 22, 1993 in the Jeshurun Synagogue in Jerusalem. See the published version of the eulogy in *Mesorah*, no. 9 (February 1994), p. 32.

19.13 Two Traditions, Two Communities

Related by the Rav in his eulogy at the conclusion of the sheloshim (thirty-day mourning period) for the Talne Rebbetzin, Rebecca Twersky, the mother of his son-in-law, Rabbi Yitzhak Twersky. Published as "A Tribute to the Rebbetzin of Talne," Tradition (32:5), pp. 76–78.

People are mistaken in thinking that there is only one masorah, and only one masorah community, the community of the fathers. It is not true. We have two masorot, two traditions, two communities, two shalshalot ha-kabbalah [chains of tradition]—the masorah community of the fathers and that of the mothers. "Thus shalt thou say to the House of Jacob [= the women] and tell the children of Israel [= the men]" [Exodus 19:3], "Hear, my son, the instruction of thy father [musar avikha], and forsake not the teaching of thy mother [torat imekha]" [Proverbs 1:8], counseled the old king. What is the difference between these two masorot, these two traditions? What is the distinction between musar avikha and torat imekha? Let us explore what one learns from one's father and what one learns from one's mother.

From one's father one learns how to read a text—the Bible or the Talmud, how to comprehend, how to analyze, how to conceptualize, how to classify, how to infer, how to apply, etc. One also learns what to do and what not to do, what is morally right and what is morally wrong. Father teaches son the discipline of thought as well as the discipline of action. Father's tradition is an intellectual-moral one. That is why it is identified with musar, the biblical term for discipline.

What is torat imekha? What kind of a Torah does the mother pass on? I admit that I am not able to define precisely the masoretic role of a mother. Only by circumscription may I hope to explain it. Permit me to draw upon my own experiences. I used to have long conversations with my mother. In fact, they were monologues rather than a dialogue. She talked and I "happened" to overhear. What did she talk about? I must use a halakhic term in order to answer this question. She spoke of *inyana de-yoma* [the affairs of the day]. I used to watch her arranging the house in honor of a holiday. I used to see her recite prayers. I used to watch her recite the sidra [weekly Torah portion] every Friday night; I still remember the nostalgic tune. I learned much from her.

Most of all I learned that Judaism expresses itself not only in formal compliance with the law but also in a living experience. She taught me that there is flavor, a scent, and a warmth to mitzvot. I learned from her the most important thing in life—to feel the presence of the Almighty and the gentle pressure of His hand resting upon my frail shoulders. Without her teachings, which quite often were transmitted to me in silence, I would have grown up a soulless being, dry and insensitive.

The laws of Shabbat, for instance, were passed on to me by my father; they are part of musar avikha. The Shabbat as a living entity, as a queen, was revealed to me by my mother; it is a part of torat imekha. The fathers knew much about the Shabbat; the mothers lived the Shabbat, experienced her presence, and perceived her beauty and splendor.

The fathers taught generations how to observe the Shabbat; the mothers taught generations how to greet the Shabbat and how to enjoy her twenty-four-hour presence.

The [Talne] rebbitzen, as I mentioned before, was one of the few women to whom the maternal masorah, torat imekha, was entrusted. She represented the masorah community with great loyalty and dedication. She was devoted, a good keeper of the treasure that was put in escrow with her, and she knew how to guard it and to transmit it to another generation. She was an outstanding teacher, even though she was a woman of few words. She taught, like my mother, how to feel the presence of God. She taught how to appreciate mitzvot and spiritual values, to enjoy the warmth of a dedicated life. In a word, she taught everything that is included in the torat imekha.

Permit me to say a few words about her background. She was the daughter of a small-town rabbi in Bessarabia at the turn of the century. He was a saintly man; she was his beloved daughter. From my conversations with her, I inferred that her father somehow resembled my maternal grandfather, who was a rabbi in a small town in Lithuania. Their lives were dedicated unreservedly to two objectives: the study of the Torah and charity [helping people]. The sociological reality at that time was quite unique: the whole community was one family, and the teacher of the community was the patriarch of the family. She told me—something I also used to do—that she used to sit in her father's room for hours, listening to the humming of the traditional tune of Talmud study. Sometimes, when he was engrossed in the analysis of a difficult halakhic theme [sugya], he used to address himself to her, to Rivkaleh, trying to convince her that he, not his opponent, was right. She absorbed Torah by osmosis. She inhaled it together with the oxygen of the room. The very weave of the tender personality of that little girl became saturated with Torah.

Only such a woman is worthy to be admitted to the masorah community and to be trusted with the great treasure of torat imekha.

.

The Study of Torah

20.01 Generations Merge

Related by the Rav in a talk delivered at the Pidyon ha-Ben of Zev Karasick on March 20, 1974 at the Windermere Hotel, New York City. Zev was the son of Rabbi Mark Karasick, a student and personal assistant of the Rav during this period. The grandfather, Rabbi Joseph Karasick, started his studies with the Rav, as one of his earliest students at the Yeshiva, in 1942.[1]

This talk was later adapted for publication by Rabbi Abraham Besdin and was initially printed under the title: "The First Jewish Grandfather" [30]. It was later revised and published in Man of Faith in the Modern World: Reflections of the Rav *[39:1], pp. 21–23.*

"R. Akiva declared that the father transmits to the son comeliness, strength, wealth, wisdom, years, and the number of generations before him [*mispar ha-dorot*]" [Eduyyot 2:9]. In the mesorah community, in this fraternity of the committed, there need not be any generation gap, any splintering of ranks. There is, rather, a sharing of ideas and ideals which span and unite countless generations. This is the secret language of *mispar ha-dorot*, of uniting generations. Each newborn Jewish child enters an extended historical family where he will be reared by the wisdom and teachings of great Torah personalities.

Whatever I have said now is not just an abstract idea but an ongoing experience for me. Let me say that I constantly experience the secret of *mispar ha-dorot*, of combining, uniting, and merging many generations into one community. This idea becomes real every time I enter the classroom at the Yeshiva. In the Yeshiva years play no role, centuries have no significance, and different generations can successfully communicate with each other.

My classroom is crowded with boys who, as far as age is concerned, could be my grandchildren. I enter the classroom as an old man with a wrinkled face and eyes reflecting the fatigue and sadness of old age. You have to be old to experience this sadness. It is the melancholy that results from an awareness of people and things which have disappeared and linger only in memory. I sit down; opposite me are rows of young beaming faces with clear eyes radiating the joy of being young. When I enter the classroom I am filled with despair and pessimism. I always ask myself: Can there be a dialogue between an old teacher and young students, between a rebbe in his Indian summer and boys enjoying the spring of their lives? I start the shiur without knowing what the conclusion will be.

Whenever I start a shiur, the door opens and another old man walks in and sits down. My students call me the Rav. He is older than the Rav. He is the grandfather of the Rav. His name is Reb Chaim Brisker [1853–1918]. Without his method of study, no shiur could be delivered nowadays.

Then the door opens quietly again and another old man comes in. He is older than Reb Chaim because he lived in the seventeenth century. His name is Reb Shabbetai ha-Kohen [1622–1662], the famous Shakh [from the initials of his book, *Siftei Kohen*]. He must be present when civil law, or *dinei mamonot*, is discussed when we study Baba Kamma or Baba Mezia. Then more visitors show up, some from the eleventh, twelfth, or thirteenth centuries. Some even lived in antiquity. Among them are Rabbi Akiva [ca. 50-135], Rashi [1040–1105], Rabbenu Tam [ca. 1100–1171), the Rabad [ca. 1125–1198], and the Rashba [ca. 1235–ca. 1310]. More and more keep on coming in.

What do I do? I introduce them to my pupils, and the dialogue commences. The Rambam states a halakhah, and the Rabad disagrees sharply. At times the Rabad utilizes harsh language against the Rambam. A boy jumps up to defend the Rambam against the Rabad. In his defense the student expresses himself rashly, too outspoken in his critique of the Rabad. Young boys are wont to speak in such a fashion. So I correct him and suggest more restrained tones. Another boy jumps up with a new idea. The Rashba smiles gently. I try to analyze what the young boy meant. Another boy intervenes. Rabbenu Tam is called upon to express his opinion, and suddenly a symposium of generations comes into existence. Young students debate earlier generations with an air of daring familiarity, and a crescendo of discussion ensues.

We all speak one language—"The whole earth was of one language and of common purpose" [Genesis 11:1]. We enjoy each other's company, speak one language, and pursue one goal. All are committed to a common vision, and all operate with the same halakhic categories. A mesorah collegiality is achieved. It is a friendship, a comradeship of young and old, spanning antiquity, the Middle Ages, and modern times. The Mishnah [Eduyyot 2:9] concludes that "the number of generations before him" leads to "the appointed end"—*ve-hu ha-ketz*. This unity of generations, this march of centuries, this dialogue and conversation between antiquity and the present will finally bring about the redemption of the Jewish people. *Ve-hu ha-ketz!* The messianic realization will come about because of this great dialogue of the generations.

Let me tell you, at the conclusion of the shiur, which can sometimes last three or even four hours, I emerge young. Younger than my pupils. They are tired and exhausted. I feel happy. I have defeated age. I feel young and rejuvenated. In the mesorah experience, years play no role. Hands, however parchment-dry and wrinkled, embrace warm and supple hands in a commonalty, bridging the gap which separates the generations.

Thus, the old ones of the past continue their great dialogue and rendezvous of the generations. This forges an enduring commitment to the mesorah. *Ve-hu ha-ketz*—this is the secret that will lead to the messianic redemption.

1. This event was described by Rabbi Joseph Karasick in a letter to the author, dated May 13, 1996.

"My son Mark invited the Rav to the Pidyon ha-Ben, not knowing if the Rav could attend. If the Rav would attend, Mark thought that he would remain only a few minutes. Mark did not dream that the Rav would speak.

"When the Rav arrived, there were about two hundred guests present. The Rav not only stayed the entire evening, but also pulled out a manuscript from his pocket and indicated that he would speak. He spoke for about three-quarters of an hour. It was an electrifying speech in which he set forth the relationship between the generations both on a personal and an academic level. The talk absolutely mesmerized the audience. The talk was enhanced by being given in a closed, warm, and intimate environment. This was unlike the Rav's public derashot and shiurim, where there always was a huge audience present."

20.02 The Divine Presence

Related by the Rav in his Teshuvah Drashah, October 7, 1970. Published in Al ha-Teshuvah *[8:6], pp. 208–209, and* Soloveitchik on Repentance *[37:4], p. 142.*

There are times when I learn Torah very late at night. As is well known, the night is especially beneficial for the study of Torah [Avodah Zarah 3b]. The Torah we master at night is clearer and sharper in our minds. There are times at night when I feel as if someone [the Divine Presence] is standing behind me, bending himself to look over my shoulder to peer into the talmudic text at the topic I am studying at that moment. At times, he nods his head in agreement with the explanation I am attempting to develop. If I have been able to survive what has happened to me during the past three years since my wife died on the eleventh of Adar II, 5727, it is only because I relate to the principle of Torah from heaven not merely as an article of faith but also as a living and tangible reality.[1]

1. The date of death is erroneously stated as the thirteenth of Adar II in *Al ha-Teshuvah*, p. 209.

20.03 Learned Drashot and Simple Jews

Related by the Rav in his annual Yahrzeit Shiur in memory of his father, Rabbi Moshe Soloveichik, Yeshiva University, January 18, 1972. (Yiddish).

I remember as a child that my father would deliver two drashot a year, on Shabbat Teshuvah [before Yom Kippur], and Shabbat ha-Gadol [before Pesach]. It would be wonderful if this were also the norm for American rabbis. As a matter of fact, I will let you in on a secret. My grandfather did not even give these two drashot. When Reb Chaim first arrived in Brisk, he gave one drashah on Shabbat ha-Gadol and one drashah on Shabbat Teshuvah. Then he said that these drashot had exhausted him, and he ceased to engage in public preaching.

My father always gave these two drashot each year. What did the drashot consist of? My father dealt mainly with difficult texts in the Rambam [Maimonides]. He always analyzed complicated and complex rabbinic topics. Yet the shul in Khaslavichy was packed. It was a large, spacious Bet Medrash. It could accommodate over one thousand people, but it was always crowded beyond its capacity. Among the people there were some lomdim [rabbinical scholars] who could follow the intricacies of the drashah. Perhaps there were anywhere between a hundred and a hundred and fifty such scholars. Yet hundreds of non-learned Jews were also present. Many were poor Jews who barely knew how to pray. Peddlers, shoemakers, tailors, and porters were in the huge crowd. You should have seen how their eyes were totally fixed upon my father. You might imagine that my father was telling them a simple story instead of a profound drashah. They seemed to have endless joy from his presentation and the atmosphere in the shul during the drashah. Yet I can guarantee you that most of these Jews did not understand one word of my father's drashah.

Their participation was not a fulfillment of the command to study Torah. These simple Jews were not on the level of the hundred or hundred and fifty scholars who were also present. The latter fulfilled the precept of Torah study. They engaged in a give-and-take with my father. They questioned and answered and engaged in a dialogue with my father. These participants were true lomdim, and among them were hakhmei Yisrael, outstanding sages. However, while the other thousand listeners did not discharge the precept of Torah study, they certainly fulfilled the charge to be involved with Torah study. There is no greater achievement than to be involved with Torah study while standing for two hours and intently listening to a drashah which one does not comprehend. That is the meaning of the blessing "La'asok be-divrei Torah"—to be involved with Torah study.

The truth is that this concept is stated in an open gemara. I do not have to tell you stories: "R. Zera says: The merit of attending a lecture lies in the running. Abaye says: The merit of attending the kallah sessions [public assemblies at which the Oral Tradition was expounded] lies in the crush" [Berakhot 6b]. Rashi explains that "the majority of the participants did not comprehend the lectures or could not properly repeat them afterwards." Yet they were rewarded for enduring the rush and crush engendered by the massive crowds at these public assemblies. They were rewarded for the hard benches on which they had to sit during the lectures. They gained merit because of the crowdedness and uncomfortable conditions they had to endure. This was truly the fulfillment of the precept to be involved with the study of Torah.

20.04 A Disciplined Inner Life

Related by the Rav in his lecture on "The Future of Jewish Education in America" at the Lincoln Square Synagogue, New York, N.Y., May 28, 1975.

There is a third kind of discipline which the av zaken, the old father, teaches the young child, namely a disciplined inner life. The Torah is not interested only in human physical actions, whether on an individual physiological level, such as eating, or on the social level, such as manufacturing or selling goods. No, the

Torah is also interested in the inner activities of the Jew, in his emotional life. We think the Torah is only concerned with the Jew's hands, legs, mouth, and digestive organs. True the Torah is concerned with these physical aspects, but it is also concerned with the Jew's feelings, sentiments, and emotions. The Torah knew very well that some emotions that a person experiences, such as hate and envy, are disjunctive, and the Torah requires that we disown such emotions, reject them, and drive them out of our personality. If an emotion is destructive, then man is capable of rejecting it.

Let me give you a personal example. I am not bragging about myself, but I cannot draw on the experience of someone else. I have to draw on my own experience. I was very envious as a child, very envious. I was envious of my friends, because I was not a bright child. It is true. Some called me stupid. This impression was created because I was intellectually honest. I would declare that I did not understand a topic when I did not truly understand it. I was very envious of another child in the heder, who was reputed to know one hundred pages of the Talmud by heart. In truth he was a faker, "Izak the faker." I was terribly envious of him. I remember my father called me in once and told me that envy is a *middah megunah*, a deplorable trait, a bad habit. This emotional enemy is known as *lo tachmod*, "you shall not covet" [Exodus 20:14] and *lo titaveh*, "you shall not desire" [Deuteronomy 5:18]. These emotions have been forbidden by the Torah.

I began to train myself to overcome it, and I succeeded. Now there is no kinah, no envy, in my heart. I mean, I am bad enough, but there is no envy in my heart. On the contrary, I rejoice in the success of my fellow man. The Torah demands from man a disciplined inner life. On the contrary, we know of constructive cathartic emotions, such as sympathy, love, and gratitude, which should be integrated into one's personality. One has freedom not only to control his physical acts but also to control his emotional life.

This kind of discipline of the inner life is also taught by the av zaken, the old father, to the yeled zekunim, the intelligent, bright, talented Jewish child.

20.05 The Halakhic Methodology

Related by the Rav in his lecture on the "The Abridged Havinenu Prayer," at the RCA Midwinter Conference, February 7, 1968.

I always find it hard to explain to non-Jews exactly what rabbinic lomdut [learning] is. This is the hardest task I ever face. I must explain to the gentile that the halakhah is not law or ritual. It is also not only an ethical norm. These terms are familiar to the non-Jewish world. However, the halakhah is more than all these definitions. The halakhah is a method of thinking, a unique approach to the world, and a mode of understanding. There is a methodology, logic, and epistemology in the halakhah. When I speak about halakhic methodology, it is beyond their comprehension. Not only non-Jews but most Jews do not understand this concept. I am speaking about Orthodox Jews, members of the Orthodox Union [Union of Orthodox Jewish Congregations of America] and lay leaders in their synagogues. The situation has improved today thanks to the influence of the Yeshiva. Nevertheless, the average American Orthodox Jew does not understand that the halakhah is not just the *Shulhan Arukh*. It is not just a code of don'ts and dos, you shall not and you shall. Of course it comprises such elements, since it is a practical code. However, it extends into intellectual infinity. It embraces a world. It is very hard to explain. As long as we do not succeed in imparting these concepts to our laymen, the Orthodox rabbinate cannot claim any real success.

The concepts of halakhah and lomdut do not just separate Jews from non-Jews; they are also the distinction between Orthodox Jews and non-Orthodox Jews. If you only explore the halakhah historically, it is not halakhah anymore. What we must stress is the conceptual analysis of the halakhah which dates back to Reb Akiva Eiger [rabbi of Posen, Germany, 1761–1837], the Vilna Gaon [Reb Eliyahu of Vilna, 1720–1797], the *Netivot* [authored by Reb Yaakov Lorbeerbaum on *Shulhan Arukh*, Hoshen Mishpat; ca. 1760–1832], the *Kezot* [authored by Reb Aryeh Leib Heller on *Shulhan Arukh*, Hoshen Mishpat; ca. 1745–1813]; the *Shakh* [authored by Reb Shabbetai ha-Kohen on the *Shulhan Arukh*, 1621–1662]; the *Taz* [authored by Rabbi David ben Shmuel on the *Shulhan Arukh*, 1586–1667]; the Rabad [of Posquières, France, 1120–1198], the Ramban [Nahmanides, 1194–1270], and the Ba'alei Tosafot [the authors of the Tosafot commentary on the Talmud and Rashi, 12th–14th centuries].

It is not only the halakhah which dates back to antiquity, for the method dates back as well. It comprises its own system of understanding, mode of thinking, conceptual analysis, a method of discrimination, organizing, classifying, and comparing topics. This is exactly the heart of what we refer to as hokhmat ha-Torah, or Torah wisdom.

20.06 The Halakhic Thought System

Related by the Rav in his lecture on "The Future of Jewish Education in America," at the Lincoln Square Synagogue, New York, N.Y., May 28, 1975.

Halakhah is not just a book of rules. It is not just the *Kitzur Shulhan Arukh*. It is a system of thought, lomdut, a unique way of thinking and interpreting the world. What is colloquially known as lomdut is an intellectual frame of reference, a unique way of thinking. Halakhah is universal. It interprets every phenomenon, every event. We have categories; we have concepts; we have methods of our own.

Let me tell you something. I am fairly well conversant with philosophical analysis, the most modern philosophical analysis. I can tell you that our methods and the unique word structure in our system of lomdut do not lag behind any contemporary philosophical system. I am not speaking in an apologetic manner; I have never engaged in apologetics. I do not defend Yahadut. I think that Yahadut should be aggressive and not on the defensive. We have developed in the yeshivas a methodology in the areas of defining, abstracting, classifying, demonstrating, and postulating talmudic concepts. This methodology is not behind the most modern philosophical analysis. If anything, we are ahead of them. Our instruments of thought are far more precise and finer than the instruments of, for instance, John Dewey [1859–1952; U.S. philosopher, psychologist, and educator] or William James [1842–1910; U.S. psychologist and philosopher]. Again this is not an apology.

20.07 Nahmanides

Related by the Rav in his Yarhei Kallah lecture on the topic of "The Ramban's Critique on the Sefer ha-Mitzvot *of the Rambam," Boston, Mass., September 1, 1976.*

The Ramban [Moses ben Nahman, also known as Nahmanides; 1194–1270] had one of the most creative minds. I will tell you, many times when I see the [the text of the] Ramban, I have the impression that Reb Chaim [Soloveitchik] is saying it.[1] The Ramban was the pioneer in the analytical approach to halakhah which stressed conceptualization and analysis. The Ramban was the pioneer. Then there were those influenced by the Ramban: the Ran [Nissim ben Rueben Gerondi; ca. 1310–1375], the Rashba [Solomon b. Abraham Aderet; ca. 1235–1310], and the Ritba [Yom Tov b. Abraham Ishbili; ca. 1250–1330]. Then this method became an undercurrent. It was picked up again by Reb Akiva Eiger [1761–1837], the *Kezot* [authored by R. Aryeh Leib Heller, ca. 1745–1813], and the *Netivot* [authored by R. Jacob Lorbeerbaum, ca. 1760–1832]. The *Netivot* utilized this method even more than the *Kezot*. It was perfected by Reb Chaim. It is not that Reb Chaim came from nowhere. There was a tradition of this shitah of havanah, this approach of conceptual analysis.

However, the pioneer and originator of this approach was the Ramban. Then the Ramban applied it not only to halakhah but also to aggadah [nonhalakhic rabbinic teachings], drush [homiletics], and mahshavah [philosophical thought]. The Ramban was very daring in mahshavah, extremely daring. He had so much courage. There is always something new in his thinking, and he is rarely repetitious. The Ramban could spend so much time defending the Ba'al Halakhot Gedolot [a halakhic code dating from the geonic period], but at the end he says that the Rambam is right. Only the Ramban could do this. So if you spend time learning the Ramban, accept his system. There are certain differences between the systems of the Ramban and the Rambam, but they do not differ too much.

1. The Rav's grandson, Rabbi Mayer Twersky, wrote: "The Rav *zt"l* vividly described that when he would close his eyes and listen to a passage from the novellae of Ramban, he would, in his mind's eye, see Rav Chaim standing before him."

See "A Glimpse of the Rav," *Tradition*, vol. 30, no. 4 (Summer 1996), p. 84.

20.08 The Torah Highway

Related by the Rav to his Talmud Class at Yeshiva University, December 9, 1976.

I am proud when my own insights and interpretations are later discovered in the rishonim [early authorities] or the early aharonim [later authorities].

My great-grandfather, Reb Yosef Baer of Brisk [1820-1892], always said that when you travel on a main highway you meet other travelers. When you go on a side road you meet nobody. In other words, when your original ideas are correct, you will encounter others who think your way. However, if you do not uncover support for your thesis, it may very well be incorrect.

20.09 The Study of Nezikin

Related by the Rav in his lecture on Parshat Mishpatim (Exodus 21:1–24:18), Yeshiva University, February 3, 1981.

It is very strange. There are many concepts that are not written down but are very indicative of Jewish life in the last few hundred years in Eastern Europe. It was by sheer association that I reminded myself of this when I was listening to the Torah reading of Parshat Mishpatim [Exodus 21:1–24:18]. Throughout Eastern Europe, the Sabbath of Parshat Mishpatim was the Sabbath of the

Hevra Shas. After all, every shul in Eastern Europe had a Hevra
Shas in which the Talmud was studied. Groups of people would
come every night and study. The annual festival of the Hevra Shas
in every town was on Parshat Mishpatim. The town where I was
brought up as a young boy had twelve synagogues. On the Sabbath
of Parshat Mishpatim, they would come and take over the synagogues. The Hevra Shas represented the Torah she-be'al peh, or
the Oral Tradition. The Torah she-biktav, or the Written Torah,
would be read in the morning in the synagogues, and the Oral
Torah would be studied in the afternoon. The Sabbath drashah, or
sermon, focused on the Oral Torah and was traditionally delivered
in the afternoon before the Sabbath Minhah prayer. The morning
was set aside exclusively for the Written Torah. The afternoon was
devoted to the Oral Torah. For this reason there was an issur [pro-
hibition] against reciting Tehillim [Psalms] on Sabbath afternoon
during the time that the drashah was being delivered in the bet
medrash by the hakham [sage] of the city [Shabbat 16:1; 116b].
The Sabbath afternoon until after Minhah was devoted to the
study of the Oral Torah. After Minhah, they did not study until the
conclusion of the Sabbath because Moshe Rabbenu died on a late
Sabbath afternoon. Once a sage dies, his house of study is suspended [Moed Katan 22b]. When the rebbe dies, the drashah is
abrogated and there is no bet medrash.

Anyway, the Hevra Shas in Europe functioned mainly on Sabbath afternoons. This was the time for the drashah—the Oral
Torah. Nevertheless, when it came to choosing a special Sabbath,
the Hevrot Shas, throughout the large and small towns of Eastern
Europe, somehow felt that the Sabbath of Parshat Mishpatim was
their Sabbath. It is a very strange feeling. They could have chosen
any Sabbath, but no, they only chose the Sabbath of Parshat Mishpatim. There were no exceptions to this practice among the hevrot.
Apparently, Parshat Mishpatim is representative of the Torah she-
be'al peh, or Oral Tradition. Not Parshat Yitro [Exodus 18:1–
20:23] or Parshat Tezaveh [Exodus 27:20–30:10] or Parshat
Kedoshim [Leviticus 19:1–20:27], but only Mishpatim.

This was not just a minhag [custom], but it was integrated into our awareness of Torah she-be'al peh. As a matter of fact, the young boys who studied Talmud preferred the talmudic division of Nezikin ["Damages"], which covered the topics of Mishpatim, over other tractates, such as Zevahim and Hullin. In Lithuania we never studied Hullin. In Volhynia [a border area between Lithuania and Poland], they sometimes studied selected chapters of Hullin with little boys. In Lithuania proper these chapters of Hullin were never studied. I never studied Hullin with my father. I know Hullin because of osmosis. I swallowed Hullin as a little boy. [Laughter.] Are you laughing because I know Hullin or because I do not know it? [Laughter.] They did not even study the tractate of Shabbat. I have introduced the study of this tractate into the Yeshiva curriculum. I have insisted upon the study of the tractates of Shabbat, Niddah, and Mikvaot. The minhag was not like this. The minhag was and still is to place the emphasis on Nezikin. The last mishnah in Baba Bathra already states: "He who would be wise should engage in the study of the civil laws, for there is no branch of the Torah more comprehensive than they; for they are like a welling fountain" [Baba Bathra 10:8]. In the tractates of Nezikin one can sharpen one's mind and develop precision and depth in its comprehension.

As a young boy I began studying the Talmud by learning the chapter of Ailu Meziot [the second chapter] of Baba Metzia, and then I studied Shenaim Ohazim [the first chapter] of Baba Metzia and Merubah [the seventh chapter] of Baba Kamma. I still know these chapters of Nezikin. Apparently, Nezikin is permeated with a certain spirit and strength which inspires the student of Torah. It helps him develop not only his intuition but his intellect. There is a special capacity that the Almighty implanted in the laws and concepts of Nezikin. It is inspiring on all levels, both the emotional and the intellectual. From all viewpoints Nezikin is the most fundamental of the six divisions of the Mishnah and Talmud.

As a matter of fact, apparently Hakhmei Yisrael [the great rabbinical scholars] felt this and gave preference to learning Nezikin.

Actually, the best rabbinic volumes were composed on Nezikin. Reb Aryeh Leib Heller [1745?–1813] wrote his classic *Kezot ha-Hoshen* on Nezikin [*Shulhan Arukh*, Hoshen Mishpat]. Reb Jacob Lorbeerbaum [1760–1832] later devoted a major portion of his classic *Netivot ha-Mishpat* to a critique of the *Kezot ha-Hoshen*. Both of these great rabbis also wrote other volumes, but none achieved the fame of their works on Nezikin. The author of the *Kezot ha-Hoshen* authored a similar volume entitled *Avnei Milluim* on the *Shulhan Arukh,* Even ha-Ezer. But this volume was not as outstanding as his work on Nezikin. That is the truth. As a matter of fact, the accusation circulated that Reb Aryeh Leib Heller's son-in-law, Reb Solomon Judah Leib Rapoport [1790–1867], really wrote portions of the *Avnei Milluim.* He had become a pioneer of the Haskalah and Wissenschaft des Judentums in Eastern Europe. Similarly, the author of the *Netivot ha-Mishpat* also wrote *Havvat Da'at* on *Shulhan Arukh,* Yoreh Deah. However, the *Havvat Da'at* is not nearly as well known as his volume on Nezikin. The hashgahah [Divine Providence] willed that the best commentaries be written on Nezikin.

Reb Aryeh Leib Heller actually revolutionized advanced rabbinic learning in Lithuania with his *Kezot ha-Hoshen*. He himself was a melamed, a teacher of Talmud, in Lemberg [Lvov]. Some of the baalei batim [laymen] claimed that he was a bad melamed, so they fired him. During the winter he had no fuel in his home. So he would get into bed and cover up with his blanket and say a shiur. This is a true story. He had no money for heat. He and the author of the *Netivot* revolutionized the learning of Seder Nezikin. The latter was a wealthy man. Reb Jacob Lorbeerbaum married twice, each time to a wealthy woman. They supported him. He served as the rabbi of important Polish communities. Nevertheless, he had plenty of difficulty in his rabbinical positions. With it all, these two volumes changed the entire method of studying Nezikin.

The only one who wrote and did not give preference to Nezikin was Reb Akiva Eiger [1761–1837]. I may be mistaken, but you do not see in his selection of topics any preference for any division of the Talmud. My grandfather, Reb Chaim, who revolutionized talmudic study thought that his strength was concentrated in his novellas on the topics of writs or documents [shetarot], which again is in Nezikin. He also felt that his strength was in Tumat ha-Mes ["The Impurities of the Dead"] and Ohalot ["Tents"].

Anyway, there was a general preference for Nezikin, which was introduced by the Almighty in last week's parshah of Mishpatim.

20.10 The Study of Torah

Related by the Rav in his address on "Gerut (Conversion)" to the Yeshiva University Rabbinic Alumni, Yeshiva University, June 19, 1975.

My credo regarding the Torah and the way Torah should be taught is based upon the Torah itself. I have been a rosh yeshiva or a teacher of Talmud all my life, or at least the major part of my adult life. I have taught many, many people, and when I teach, time comes to a stop for me. I do not look at the timepiece, the clock, or at my wristwatch—I just teach. I do not know how to explain it, but teaching has a tremendous and a very strange impact upon me. When I teach Torah, I feel the breath of eternity on my face. Even now, in my old age, teaching Torah and giving shiurim relieves me of the fear of death and all the gloomy and depressing moments which elderly people go through. When I teach Torah, I feel rejuvenated and as if I were twenty-five or thirty years old. If not for the study and teaching of Torah, I would have lost my sanity in the year of my triple mourning in 1967 when I lost my mother, brother, and wife. I was on the verge of mental collapse and breakdown. I did not break down; I emerged victorious. That victory over despair was due to one thing only, I would say—my overwhelming dedication to Torah and teaching Torah. I am not trying to brag or to boast; I am telling the truth. I was sick that year and the following year. I felt somehow that because of teach-

ing Torah I was not alone and that I had somebody. That somebody was invisible, but I felt His presence, I could confide in Him.
There was somebody on whose shoulder I could cry, and there was
somebody from whom I could almost demand words of solace and
comfort.

People do not know—and again, please take it in the proper
spirit, I am not bragging—how busy I am and what my schedule is.
They know I teach shiurim here [in New York]. All right, fine, I say
shiurim three times a week in the Yeshiva. And you know that these
shiurim should be an hour and a half each. It never happens that I
get through with the shiur in an hour and half. So two hours,
sometimes three hours, and sometimes the shiur is even more than
three hours. It is very strange; the boys in my class are very young,
perhaps a quarter or a third of my age. Yet they come out
exhausted and I come out refreshed after the shiur. Then I return
to Boston. Every Friday morning, from half past eight for three
hours, until half past eleven, I study with my son-in-law [Rabbi
Isadore Twersky]. Saturday—believe me that I cannot afford to
take a nap on Saturday afternoon. I have not taken a nap on Saturday afternoon for the last, I would say, twenty years, because I
study with Moshe [Twersky, his grandson] three hours at least,
and I study with Mayer [Twersky, another grandson] two and a
half hours. The same with Sunday and the same with Monday; and
I simply have no time sometimes to sit down and relax.

The cathartic impact on me of studying Torah is rooted in the
wondrous experience I always have when I open up the gemora.
Somehow, when I open up the gemora, either alone or when I am
in company as when I teach others, I have the impression, do not
call it a hallucination, as if I hear, so to say, the soft footsteps of
somebody invisible. He comes in and sits down with me, sometimes looking over my shoulders. It is a simple idea, not mystical at
all. Our sages already stated that "the Presence of God dwells
among [those who occupy themselves with the Torah]. . . .
Whence can it be shown that it applies even to one? Because it is
said: 'Wherever I permit My Name to be mentioned, I shall come

to you and bless you' [Exodus 20:21]'" [Avot 3:7; Berakhot 6a]. We all believe that the One who gave us the Torah has never deserted the Torah. He simply walks and accompanies the Torah wherever the Torah has, let us say, a rendezvous, an appointment or date, with somebody. The Giver of the Torah is there!

Therefore, for me the study of the Torah has never been simply a formal religious duty that mandates an intellectual act or performance. The satisfaction I derive from it is much more than the fulfillment of a mitzvah alone. It is true regardless of how important a role the intellect plays in the study of Torah. You know very well that I place very much, a great deal, of emphasis upon the intellectual understanding and analysis of the halakhah. You know that this is actually what my grandfather Reb Chaim introduced. You know, and I can tell you and I have told it so many times, and I will tell it again. Our methodology, our analysis, our manner of conceptualizing, inferring, classifying, and defining concepts of halakhic matter do not lag behind the most modern philosophical analysis. I happen to know something about modern philosophical analysis. We are far ahead of it, because the tools we employ to analyze a talmudic discussion are the most modern. The logical tools and the systemological implements which we employ in order to analyze a sugya, or talmudic subject, for study, whether in Baba Kamma or any portion of Shas, are the most modern. They are very impressive. My grandfather had a great share in this achievement. Anyway, we avail ourselves of the most modern methods of understanding, abstracting, inferring, classifying, defining, and so forth and so on. So there is no doubt that the intellect plays a tremendous role in the study of Torah. However, this study is more than simply an intellectual performance. It is a total, all-encompassing, and all-embracing involvement of the mind and heart, will, and feeling—the very center of the human personality. The emotional side of man, his logical bent, the volunteristic impulses can all be usefully employed in plumbing the depths of Torah.

The study of Torah is basically, for me, an ecstatic experience in which one meets God. And again I want to say that what I have just told you is not just mysticism or due to my mystical inclinations. It is not so, but the Talmud expresses this very idea. Our sages equate the study of Torah with revelation, the great event and drama of God's revelation on Mount Sinai. This event is reenacted, restaged, and relived every time a Jew opens the Talmud. The rabbis declared that a ba'al keri [one who has experienced a seminal emission] may not study the Torah. The reason is, as they taught:

> "And make them known to your children and your children's children" [Deuteronomy 4:9], and it is written immediately afterwards, "The day that you stood before the Lord your God at Horeb" [Deuteronomy 4:10]. Just as there it was in dread and fear and trembling and quaking, so in this case too the study of Torah must be in dread and fear and trembling and quaking.
>
> Berakhot 22a

What must you make known unto your children and your children's children? You must tell them about what took place at Horeb. The Torah does not say that you should only make the halakhot known to them. More than that! The Torah requires you to tell them about your rendezvous with God. It means that they should experience exactly what you experienced when you stood before thy God in Horeb with fear, awe, and tremor in your hearts—trembling! So must every Jew, when he engages in Torah study, stand before God in fear, awe, and terror. That is why a ba'al keri may not study Torah; this is the reason! It is not that the tumah impurity impairs him, but that such a person is not in a mood to experience the presence of the Almighty—to experience revelation every time he engages in the study of Torah. So if a Jew cannot experience revelation when he is busy studying Torah, then this pursuit is forbidden to him. That is the reason for the prohibition that a ba'al keri may not study the Torah. In other words, the study of the Torah is an ecstatic, metaphysical performance and an act of surrender to the Almighty.

20.11 The Majority of One's Knowledge

Related by the Rav in his annual Yahrzeit Shiur in memory of his father, Rabbi Moshe Soloveichik, Yeshiva University, January 11, 1970. (Yiddish). Summarized and published in Sheurim Lezekher Abba Mari Zal *[16:1], vol. 2, p. 15.*

Now, we must analyze what is meant by the concept of "the majority of knowledge." For instance the Rambam states [Hilkhot Talmud Torah 5:9]:

> When his teacher dies, the student must rend his garments until his heart is laid bare. These tears can never be properly repaired. This concept applies when the deceased was his main teacher, from whom the student received the majority of his knowledge. However, if the student did not receive the majority of his knowledge from this teacher, then this law does not apply. Under such circumstances, the teacher is considered his colleague rather than his master.

At first glance, it would seem that the concept of the majority of knowledge should be reckoned simply on the basis of quantity. If I studied one hundred folios of the Talmud with one teacher and ninety-nine with another, then the former is my master and the latter my colleague. Somehow, I intuitively feel that this is not the proper explanation. My own experience suggests a different explanation. I had only one rebbe muvhak [master teacher]. I had a number of melamdim but only one rebbe—my father. I can testify about myself that the majority of my knowledge is from my father. That which I know, I know because of my father. When I think about my father, I enumerate in my mind the various talmudic tractates I studied with him. It was not the majority of them, although it was a substantial portion. If it is simply a question of quantity, then perhaps I have studied more folios of the Talmud on my own than with my father. It is already twenty-nine years since he died. During this period, it is true that I have studied a great deal on my own. It seems to me that quantitatively I have learned more on my own than with my father. I can even list exactly the tractates that I studied with him. We started with Baba Kama and Baba Mezia; Baba Bathra, Sanhedrin, Shevuot, and Makkot followed in the Nezikin division of the Shas. In the Nashim section we studied Gittin, Kidushin, Nedarim, Nazir, and Sotah. In Kodashim, it was Zevahim, Menahot, Me'ilah, Bekhorot and Temurah. In Tohorot we studied Kelim, Oholot, and Yadayim, while in Zera'im it was Berakhot, Peah, Terumot, Maaser Sheni, and Bikkurim. I am not certain whether it was more or less than the majority of the knowledge that I attained. It seems that quantitatively it was not a formal majority.

You know the conditions under which we studied together. It was truly a period which could be characterized by the ruling of Maimonides that "a person only masters the majority of his knowledge at night" [Hilkhot Talmud Torah 3:13]. It was the time of the ascendency of the Bolsheviks and the Russian Revolution. Food was not available and we suffered the pangs of hunger. The entire family lacked for food. There was also a shortage of sources of illumination. About all we could use in the house was some low-grade oil which gave off a terrible odor as it burned. You could not learn near such an odor.

It was impossible to study at home because it was too cold. At least in the bet medrash there was proper light and heat. After the evening prayers, we would go up to the bet medrash where we could study. During the winter months, Maariv would be as early as four in the afternoon or half past four. My father and I remained in the bet medrash until 1:00 or 2:00 a.m. You did not wish to return home because of the warmth and light in the bet medrash. My mother once said that after her death she should be eulogized in the same way that the Vilna Gaon lamented his wife. The Gaon declared at her death that she had suffered more than he because of their dedication to Torah study. She had suffered both from hunger and the cold. He had only endured hunger, however, since he had enjoyed the warmth of the bet medrash. That is how it was during this pericd of endless nights in Europe.

Nevertheless, during those difficult nights I mastered the majority of my Torah knowledge. This is not to be understood in solely quantitative terms. It means the attainment of the essence of my knowledge. To put it simply, during these difficult nights my father enabled me to stand on my own two feet in the discipline of talmudic study. My father gave me the key with which to open the world of lomdut; he taught me how to comprehend and analyze a rabbinic text. How to submerge oneself in the understanding of the commentary of a rishon [early authority, ca. 1000–1500]. How to extract, with the guidance of a rishon a gem of perception that was hidden in three words of Tosofot. How to exhaust oneself in the study of rabbinic literature. My father taught me the method by which "to understand and discern . . . all the teachings of Thy Torah" [Morning Prayer, blessing before the Shema]. Whether I studied five hundred or six hundred folios of Talmud with my father is not really relevant. What is crucial is that he gave me the key to understanding. Therefore, my father was my rebbe muvhak, and the majority of my knowledge is from him. This is what our sages refer to as the "handles of the Torah."[1]

Today I am studying Eruvin, which I did not learn with my father. Nevertheless, when "I clear the jungle of difficulty in this tractate and chart a path toward the inhabited areas," I feel my father's guiding hand. My ability to chart a course of understanding in Eruvin is due to him.

This is the concept of the majority of knowledge. It is difficult to articulate this idea. Perhaps a story will clarify it. When I was a youngster, I met Reb Yeruchem Levovitz [d. 1936; mashgiah (spiritual supervisor) of the Mir Yeshiva] in Vilna. One time I was sitting before him in the midst of a group of people. Reb Yeruchem was speaking about my grandfather Reb Chaim. This took place shortly after my grandfather's death [in 1918], and Reb Yeruchem was speaking about Reb Chaim's uniqueness. Reb Yeruchem expressed an idea which has remained with me until today. He declared that Reb Chaim was unequaled in his generation because he alone possessed "the soul of the Torah." Reb Chaim was able to dialogue with the soul of the Torah. He was always able to discern where the truth was. He possessed sensitivity and was attuned to the Torah. Reb Chaim could instantly place his hand on the pulse of the Torah. Possessing encyclopedic knowledge or being exceptionally skillful in dialectical thinking is not sufficient [Berakhot 64a]. It was Reb Chaim's being in total harmony with the heart of the Torah that made him unique in his time. It was like a doctor who can immediately place his hand on his patient's pulse. When taking the hand of the Torah, a rabbinical scholar must at once feel its pulse. This was Reb Chaim's genius, and this ability is the heart of the concept of the majority of knowledge. That is what I received from my father.

Reb Chaim's intuition and instant perception of the Torah made him unique. Of course, one must study a great deal to gain the wisdom of the Torah. However, this sensitivity and perception must come first if one is to truly achieve Torah knowledge. Reb Chaim would always compare his approach to analyzing a difficult [passage from the writings of] Rambam [Maimonides] to a traveler in the dark of night. He sees a light flashing on the horizon. The light goes on and off, and is too distant to be of any use to the traveler at this point of his journey. Nevertheless, at least he knows that he is traveling in the right direction. Reb Chaim declared that this was the way he felt whenever he began to analyze the Rambam. Intuitively, he knew he was moving in the right direction even when his thesis was not yet completely formulated. This perception is the basis of the majority of knowledge. Perhaps it can also be called the essence of knowledge. Who is a rebbe muvhak? The person who endows us with this perception and sensitivity. Once you possess this notion, you can develop your intellect and construct beautiful architectural structures of Torah thought and reasoning. First, however, you must experience the sight of the small candles or stars on the horizon. They flash on and off and attract you toward them. Once you reach them you have achieved the majority of your knowledge. On a popular level, we refer to this concept simply as lomdut. It is how we study and not so much what we study. It is the ability to see between the lines of rabbinic writings. You can push aside the potsherds and extract the pearls hidden within. This is the essence of the majority of knowledge.

1. Eruvin 21b and Shir ha-Shirim Rabbah 1:8. Cf. Maimonides, *Moreh Nevukhim* (Yosef Kapach ed.), pp. 9–10.

20.12 The Hundred and First Time

Related by the Rav in his annual Yahrzeit Shiur in memory of his father, Rabbi Moshe Soloveichik, Yeshiva University, January 11, 1970. (Yiddish).

Let us analyze the statement of the Talmud [Hagigah 9b] elaborating upon the verse: "Then you will return and see the difference between the righteous and the wicked, between one who serves God and one who does not serve Him" [Malachi 3:18]. The Talmud asks if "the righteous" is the same as "one who serves God" and "the wicked" the same as "one who does not serve Him"? The answer given is that "one who serves God" and "one who does not serve Him" both refer to those who are perfectly righteous. However, "one who repeats his chapter a hundred times is not to be compared with one who repeats it a hundred and one times."

The explanation of this talmudic passage is found in the *Likkutei Amarim* [*Tanya*] of Reb Shneur Zalman of Lyady [1745–1813]. Sometimes I must be a hasid and cite hasidic sources. The *Likkutei Amarim* [1:15] explains that the norm during the talmudic period was for the student to review the material being studied one hundred times. It was a time when the Oral Torah was not committed to writing and therefore had to be studied orally [Gittin 60b]. Our sages were pedantic about mastering the exact language of the oral traditions. Evidently, this could only be achieved by reviewing the material one hundred times. The students had to transmit the Oral Torah to the next generation. Therefore, under the supervision of their teachers, they would go over the lectures one hundred times. Once the students completed this task, they were dismissed and free to return home. The teachers were confident that the pupils now comprehended the material and would always be able to cite the texts correctly. The student who finished this process and knew the intricacies of the Oral Tradition certainly discharged his obligation of "learn them, and be careful to perform them" [Deuteronomy 5:1]. He also fulfilled the charge "to meditate therein day and night" [Joshua 1:8]. This student was finished and could now go home and devote his time to other matters.

However, there was another kind of student, the one who would not go home. He would review the material a hundred and one times. The rebbe did not require this additional study. The mashgiah [spiritual supervisor] did not demand this devotion. The student knew the material as well as the students who stopped after one hundred times. The truth is that there is a limit to how many times you can review the same material. One more time, at this point, will not enable you to gain additional knowledge. You can learn new material, but you cannot review the same text all the time. If the sages instituted the concept of one hundred times, they knew what they were doing. This is the maximum you should do. If so, why did the student remain to go over the material the hundred and first time? And if our sages spoke of a hundred and first time, it also means that the student would review it a hundred and second time and many more times as well. The night would go by, and the bet medrash would empty out as the students returned home. They had discharged their obligations and the next day would start their new studies refreshed and healthy. Only this individual remained in a corner of the bet medrash and continued his intensive study. It is the hundred and first time, the hundred and second time, the hundred and third time, and the hundred and fourth time. Why? What is accomplished by this?

I have never really understood the answer to this question. However, I have experienced scenes of action that have clarified the approach of our sages for me. Because of these experiences I am able to comprehend the quest of the student who went beyond the required one hundred times.

I recall how on Rosh Hashanah night after Kiddush and the holiday repast I saw my father, and even Reb Chaim, sitting over an open gemora of Rosh Hashanah. They both had the habit of placing their right hand on their left shirt sleeve as they leaned over the text. They would sing the words of the Mishnah and the Gemara as they read them from the text. I can recall my father on Kol Nidrei night doing the same with the Yoma talmudic text. They recited these words with so much enthusiasm and ecstasy that they could not stop. They both certainly knew these texts by heart. Yet they insisted on reciting every word from the printed text. They could not pull themselves away from the text. The Torah drew them closer. The Torah became like a magnet. Even if they knew the passages totally by heart, they still could not depart from the text. They could not leave the Gemara. It was as if they were tied to the Gemara.

This was exactly the same sensation that was experienced by the student who refused to depart even after he had repeated his chapter one hundred times. It was like Reb Chaim, who could not stop studying talmudic topics even though he knew them to the limit. They felt that studying the Torah was a rendezvous with the Shekhinah, the Divine Presence. Therefore, they constantly sought to prolong the experience. They just could not bring themselves to close the text.

In general, people have a mistaken impression of Reb Chaim and my entire family. There is a general feeling that they lacked emotion and only stressed the intellect. This is absolutely not so. I never met a greater oved hashem [servant of God] than my grandfather Reb Chaim. I remember as a child how overwhelmed I was when I observed Reb Chaim reciting the Avodah [the account of the Temple service in the Musaf additional prayer] on Yom Kippur. My young soul was struck with wonder when I heard Reb Chaim enthusiastically and ecstatically chant the words recited by the high priest: "O Lord, Thy people, the house of Israel, have transgressed and sinned against Thee" [*High Holiday Prayer Book*, trans. Philip Birnbaum, p. 822]. He would continue with "When the priests and the people, who were standing in the Temple court, heard God's glorious and revered name clearly expressed by the high priest with holiness and purity." Reb Chaim would chant these words to the widely used tune in his baritone voice. There was endless joy in his voice. You felt that Reb Chaim was actually standing within the precincts of the Temple and was actually looking at the kohen ha-gadol [high priest]. There was so much delight and enthusiasm in Reb Chaim's voice. You could see that he was totally reliving these happenings in the Temple. Modern philosophers speak about religious experiences. Yet they cannot truly comprehend this term, because they never observed Reb Chaim on Yom Kippur. To Reb Chaim these were not aspects of the Avodah that took place in the Temple some nineteen hundred years earlier. Reb Chaim was standing with the kohanim and the people, and he could hear the voice of the kohen ha-gadol. Reb Chaim would continue singing the Avodah with great joy. You could feel his happiness as he chanted the refrain describing the "smiling countenance of the high priest as he safely left the Holy of Holies!" [ibid., p. 828].

Suddenly, Reb Chaim's entire mood changed as the inspiring description of the kohen ha-gadol came to an end. You could feel the catastrophe of the destruction of the Temple in his voice. The Avodah continued: "All this took place when the sanctuary was firmly established. The high priest ministered, his generation watched and rejoiced. . . . However, the iniquities of our fathers destroyed our sacred home, and our own sins retarded its restoration" [ibid., pp. 828–830]. At that moment Reb Chaim's nostalgic emotions of ecstasy and joy abruptly ended. He was now overwhelmed by sorrow-clouded pangs of mourning for all that had been destroyed. "At this time, we have none to guide us as in the days of old; we have neither the high priest nor the altar for the offering of sacrifices" [ibid., p. 830].

Yes, Reb Chaim was the true oved hashem. You observed it while he prayed. Nevertheless, the most sublime moments in his service of God were during his study of Torah. Reb Chaim could not pull himself away from the rabbinic texts, and this was his ultimate fulfillment of "the righteous . . . that serve God." The student who can learn the same Gemara text even after one hundred times is the true servant of God. The Gemara is a magnet. It is like a conspicuous star which guides the wayfarer on his journey.

20.13 Relearning Is Harder

Related by the Rav in his Teshuvah Drashah, October 3, 1973. (Yiddish).

There is a rule in life which is true in many instances. Our sages tell us that "it is harder to relearn well something that we once knew and then forgot than to master a new topic" [Yoma 29a]. I have experienced this many times. As you know I am a rosh yeshiva. Most of the time I teach tractates which I really do not know very well. I prefer to teach my students material that will enable me to be a student as well. I work out topics that are new to me as a rosh yeshiva. When I work out a new topic, I generally succeed in mastering its intricacies. It takes effort, diligence, and logical thinking. I am now learning a new topic in the Yeshiva about "If a man engages artisans" [Baba Metzia 6:1]. I never studied this topic as a rosh yeshiva, but I learned it when I was an eight-year-old child in heder. My melamed was a Habadnik, a wonderful and dedicated Jew. Nevertheless, neither of us really understood the sixth chapter of Baba Metzia. He taught me hasidut in a proper fashion. I am thankful to him, because if not for his teachings I would not have an understanding of hasidut. I would be lacking a great treasure if not for this melamed. Many of my drashot and lectures are based upon hasidic philosophical thoughts that were implanted within me when I was a child of eight and nine. These seminal concepts still open new vistas of understanding for me. Nevertheless, when it came to the talmudic chapter of "If a man engages artisans" [entitled Ha-Sokher et ha-Umnim], I could have had better teachers than my Habad melamed.

Today I am working out this chapter. It is difficult because we lack some basic rishonim [early authorities] on this chapter. In general the yeshivas do not really study this chapter. The semester ends when they are still caught up in the study of the second chapter of Baba Metzia, Eilu Metziot [Baba Metzia 2:1]. They never reach the sixth chapter. Nevertheless, I achieve results in my efforts to master this somewhat new topic of "If a man engages artisans."

However, when I try to rework a topic which I once knew well and have allowed to slip away, it is always much more difficult. It takes me a lot longer to prepare a shiur which I must reconstruct from the past than to develop a new lecture. This is human nature. It is difficult to build a new house—"Who is the man who has built a new house" [Deuteronomy 20:5], but it is even more difficult to reconstruct an old one.

YESHIVA UNIVERSITY

RIETS Faculty, ca. 1944. Standing (l. to r.) R. Joseph Arnest, R. Ephraim Steinberg, Samuel Sar, R. Samuel Volk, R. Joseph Weiss, Norman Abrams.
Sitting (l. to r.) R. Judah Levine, R. Aaron Burack, R. Isacc Rubenstein, R. Abraham Selmanowitz, R. Joseph Soloveitchik, R. Moses Shatzkes, R. Samuel Belkin, R. Judah Weil, R. Samuel Gerstenfeld, R. Moses Poleyeff, R. Chaim Shunfenthal. Photo: Y.U.

RIETS Ordination Board - (l. to r.) Rabbis Samuel Belkin, Chaim Heller, Joseph Soloveitchik, Moses Shatzkes, ca. 1956. Photo: Irwin A. Albert.

Chag haSemikhah *(l. to r.) Rabbis Chaim Heller, Samuel Belkin, Moses Shatzkes, Joseph Soloveitchik, ca. 1958. Photo: Y.U.*

Yeshiva Faculty Members, (l. to r.) Rabbis Avigdor Cyperstein, Joseph Soloveitchik, Jacob Lessin, ca. late 1950s. Photo: Irwin A. Albert.

Reception in Honor of the Rav's return to the Yeshiva following his ill health, February 1960. (l. to r.) Rabbis Samuel Belkin, David Lifshitz, Dean Samuel Sar, Rabbi Joseph Soloveitchik, Dr. Tovah Lichenstein (obscured), Rabbi Aharon Lichtenstein. Photo: Y.U.

Speaking at the Reception, February 1960. (l. to r.) Rabbi Joseph Soloveitchik (speaking), Dr. Tovah Lichtenstein, Rabbi Aharon Lichtenstein, Jacob Dienstag (Y.U. Library), and Rabbi Henoch Fishman (RIETS faculty). Photo: Y.U.

Reception for David Ben Gurion at Yeshiva University, 1960. (l. to r.) Dr. Samuel Belkin, David Ben Gurion, Rabbi Joseph Soloveitchik. Photo: Y.U.

Reception for Rabbi Louis Rabinowitz of Johannesburg and Jerusalem at Yeshiva University (l. to r.) Rabbis Samuel Belkin, Joseph Soloveitchik, Louis Rabinowitz. ca. 1966. Photo: Y.U.

Reception for Dr. Samuel Belkin at Yeshiva University, December 14, 1966. (l. to r.) Rabbis Joseph Soloveitchik, Samuel Belkin, Mendel Zaks, Photo: Y.U.

Rabbis Joseph Soloveitchik, Samuel Belkin, ca. 1975. Photo: Irwin A. Albert.

Listening to Dr. Belkin, ca. 1975. Photo: Irwin A. Albert.

*Rabbis David Lifschitz and Joseph Soloveitchik,
1977. Photo: Mark Weiner.*

(l. to r.) Rabbis David Lifschitz, Zevulun Charlop (Director of RIETS), Joseph Soloveitchik, ca. 1977. Photo: Y.U.

Menahem Begin visits the Rav. (l. to r.) Menahem Begin, Rabbis Joseph Soloveitchik and Israel Miller, ca. 1977.

Dedication of the Beit Medrash of the Yeshiva in honor of Mr. Joseph Gruss, May 17, 1979. At the table (l. to r.) Rabbi Joseph Soloveitchik, Dr. Norman Lamm, (the third president of Yeshiva University), Mr. Joseph Gruss. Photo: Y.U.

Yeshiva University

21.01 Boston to New York

Related by the Rav in his address at the convention to mark the merger of the Mizrachi and Ha-Poel ha-Mizrachi movements in the United States in 1957. Published in Ohr ha-Mizrach *[2], p. 28. (Hebrew).*

I am only a guest in New York. I regularly fly back and forth from Boston to New York. While aboard the plane I am often overwhelmed by the achievements of modern technology. The speed and exactness of the flight of the aircraft exemplify these accomplishments.

At times, when observing these technological strides, I feel lost as I fly between the heavens and the earth. Man loses his independence, and I feel like a worthless object in the vastness of the universe. "When I behold Thy heavens, the work of Thy fingers . . . what is man, that Thou are mindful of him? And the son of man, that Thou thinkest of him?" [Psalms 8:4–5].

After the plane lands at LaGuardia Airport, I go directly to the Yeshiva. I immediately enter the world of Abaye and Raba. It is a different world with totally dissimilar surroundings. If you should ask how I feel with this sudden change in my environs when I enter the Yeshiva, I will respond that it is a superb transition. When I enter the world in which the same topics are discussed that were analyzed in the academies of Sura and

Pumpeditha [in ancient Babylonia], I know that I am on firm and stable ground. In such endeavors there is perpetual truth. In the Yeshiva I am at home because I am grounded in the world of eternity.

21.02 Yeshiva University I

Related by the Rav in his address to the Yeshiva University Rabbinic Alumni, Yeshiva University, March 1, 1956. (Yiddish).

In addition to teaching at the Yeshiva, I consider myself a real friend of the institution. This is not just because I am a rosh yeshiva at Yeshiva University. It is much more than a matter of employment; it is, rather, that the Yeshiva redeemed my soul! It's true! You all know how difficult the American rabbinate is. The rabbi can lose his mind. The older European rabbis lost their heads in the slaughterhouses and butcher shops. The younger American rabbis lose them in cemeteries and wedding halls. Since I am half and half I would have lost my head in both places. Since I am half modern and half old-fashioned, I would have lost my head both in the slaughterhouse and the cemetery. [Laughter.]

The Yeshiva redeemed me and spared me from such a destiny. These last fifteen years [1941–56] I have been privileged to avoid falling in the sense of the fall of "the Nephilim [giants] were on the earth in those days" [Genesis 6:4]. In my whole life I have not accomplished as much spiritually as I have in these past fifteen years! There are days and nights when I do not leave my desk. I struggle to understand a [passage from the] *Bet Shmuel* [commentary on the *Shulhan Arukh*, Even ha-Ezer], the Ramban [Nahmonides] on the Torah, the *Milhamot* [*ha-Shem*] of the Ramban on the Rif [Rabbi Yitzhak Alfasi], or a midrash. My wife will testify to this. For this ability to devote my time to the study of Torah I am thankful to the Yeshiva. However, my real gratitude to the Yeshiva is because of another reason.

I may have very few good traits, but one trait which I do possess is my inability to imitate anyone else. I always want to be

myself and to display my unique dignity of having been created in
the image of God. The glory of the individual is exemplified by the
singularity of every human being. This concept is the motto of my
life. I never wish to wear the mask of another person in order to
ingratiate myself with the masses. I know the statement of the
sages that "If I am not for myself, then who is for me?" [Avot
1:14]. What our sages mean is that if I am not myself, I will not
succeed in acting like someone else.

I came to the United States and was thrown into Boston as a
rabbi. It was difficult. Laymen like to advise their rabbis. This is
true about the laity in Boston and even about my congregants in
Congregation Moriya [on the Upper West Side of Manhattan].
They advised me to Americanize and to adjust myself to the new
American circumstances. They wanted me to fit in. I fought them
bitterly. I knew that I would lose my originality if I tried to be what
I was not. I would lose my uniqueness, and ultimately the Divine
Image within me. I do not like to do what others can do better or
just as well. I wish to do that which I am unique at! This is not an
expression of haughtiness; no, it is a fulfillment of my intrinsic
human dignity and individuality.

Even when it comes to talmudic study I follow the same principle. I had a great rebbe—my father. My father had an even
greater rebbe—Reb Chaim. I learned a great deal from my father.
I can declare, like R. Eliezer: "Much Torah have I learned, yet I
have but skimmed from the knowledge of my teachers much like a
dog lapping from the sea" [Sanhedrin 68a]. As much as I received
from my father, I still manage to pass it on to my students in my
own unique fashion. I utilize my own vocabulary. True, I must say
about my father and grandfather that "we drink their water" [i.e.
benefit from their learning; Baba Metzia 84b]. Yet I am writing my
own Sefer Torah [Torah scroll], and I have my own unique *ketav
yad* [handwriting].

I do not enjoy it when my students speak in cliches and simply
parrot the concepts of Brisk. The same with my homiletical lectures. I do not utilize the rabbinical sources and quotations that

others generally use in their sermons. I rejoice in being alone and individualistic. If I am found wanting, then my achievements may very well be inconsiderable. However, if I am a pygmy, at least I am a pygmy who possesses the Divine Image. I must chart my own course. Our sages refer to Abraham as the "only one" [Sanhedrin 93a] because he was unique and paved a new way for mankind. I am always attracted to those Gedolei Yisrael [rabbinical scholars and leaders] who charted new courses. The same is true in my relationship with institutions. I am impressed by institutions that are pacesetters and innovative. In the Rabbi Isaac Elchanan Theological Seminary of Yeshiva University, I have discovered such an institution. This school is unique, and it is imbued with the honor and dignity of man created in the Image of God. This is the secret of my love for and commitment to the Yeshiva.

In order to explain what characterizes the uniqueness of the Yeshiva, I must utilize an historical parallel. In the last century there was Rabbi Samson Raphael Hirsch [1808–1888] in Germany. He was unique in both his intellectual ability and his emotional sensibility. He had an aesthetic appreciation and understanding of life. He struggled with the same problem we have today in the United States: how to preserve Torah Judaism in a secular environment. Rabbi Hirsch accomplished great things in Germany. Our problems today are even more profound and complex than those that he faced. Rabbi Hirsch struggled in 1860; today it is 1956 and we have so many more technological advances. Yes, we are attempting to solve our problems. We have made a start. What is the difference between our approach and that of Rabbi Hirsch? He developed an aesthetic and tasteful synagogue service that would appeal to the German Jew. He strove to unite fear of God with universal concepts. Rabbi Hirsch set as his goal the training of German Jews who would be frum [pious] and have universal understanding. However, in addition to combining the fear of God with worldly culture, the Yeshiva wants above all to stress the importance of the study of Torah. Our goal is to educate a generation of Torah scholars with secular knowledge. Rabbi Hirsch was satisfied to attract the youth to the synagogue, in which he developed a beautiful and aesthetic Judaism. This is exactly what many Orthodox Jews wish to do in New York. They want Judaism to be built on ceremony and beautiful sentiments. For example, they stress the lighting of Sabbath candles, the white tablecloth for the Sabbath table, the decorating of the sukkah, and transporting the etrog in a silver case. They desire a decorous prayer service and insist that all the worshipers sing together when the Torah scroll is removed from the ark!

Rabbi Hirsch succeeded in these endeavors. He insisted that his followers not shave during the three weeks [of mourning for the destruction of the Temple] and during sefirah [the period of mourning between Passover and Shavuot]. Many German Jews observed the entire Torah as a result of Rabbi Hirsch's efforts. They were careful about both minor and major laws. I lived for many years in Germany, and I observed these Jews. I knew a Professor Eugen Mittwoch [1876–1942], who was a professor of Oriental languages at the University of Berlin.[1] I saw him come to the university on Tishah be-Av in slippers and with a three-week beard. You have no idea how deep his commitment to Judaism had to be to do this. To wear a yarmulka at the University of Berlin was not like wearing one at Columbia University today.

These were great accomplishments in Germany. This type of Judaism was truly blossoming in the twenties and the early thirties when I was there. Tragically, it was cut down right after the start of its bloom. Many cultured, observant Jews were developed by this approach. Nevertheless, German Jews lacked the knowledge of Torah. All-encompassing dedication to the study of Torah was not stressed. German rabbis were frum. There is much we can learn from their piety and observance. They were zealous in safeguarding the Orthodox character of their synagogues. However, these German rabbis only knew a small portion of the *Shulhan Arukh* and the Bible. They studied such popular halakhic volumes as the *Hayyei Adam* [by R. Abraham Danzig, 1810, based on *Shulhan Arukh*, Orah Hayyim] and the *Kitzur Shulhan Arukh* [by R.

Solomon Ganzfried, 1864, an abridged *Shulhan Arukh*]. They had some slight knowledge of how to decide questions of Jewish law and also knew a little Jewish philosophy. They excelled in their external deportment, and their synagogues were graced with an aura of dignity.

There are many Jews in the United States, and among them our own rabbinical graduates, who desire that the Yeshiva follow the same course. They feel that the Yeshiva should stress the externals and produce "professional rabbis." Such rabbis would resemble the incense altar in the Tabernacle. They would emit a pleasant fragrance. However, they would never enter the Holy of Holies and achieve the knowledge of Torah represented by the Tablets in the Ark of the Covenant [which stood in the Holy of Holies]. I am certain that the Yeshiva would have an easier time raising funds if it followed this path.

The Yeshiva has another goal, however, and this is its greatness. It seeks to achieve the contents of the Ark of the Covenant. The Yeshiva's ultimate goal is to produce true rabbinical scholars. I do not wish to exaggerate, but I feel that the Yeshiva has the finest talmudic faculty in the world. No Yeshiva, including those in the State of Israel, has such an outstanding faculty. The roshei yeshiva here deliver lectures that could have been presented to the students in the Volozhin Yeshiva. I know what I am talking about in this respect. The language of the Yeshiva is the same as that utilized in all the yeshivot in consonance with the traditional approach to the study of the Oral Torah. Rabbinic literature is studied in full depth, and our goal is to educate first-class rabbinical scholars. Simultaneously, we wish to give these Torah students secular academic ability.

I have heard criticisms against the Yeshiva that we have not yet achieved the proper synthesis between Torah study and secular endeavor; between fear of God and worldliness. We have not achieved what the German Orthodox Jews called "Torah with derekh eretz [worldly occupation"] [Avot 2:2]. I claim that the true greatness of the Yeshiva is that it does not have this synthesis.

The truth is that there is no real synthesis in the world. If there is a contradiction between Torah and secular endeavor, then synthesis is not possible. If there is a thesis and anti-thesis, then no synthesis is possible. In general, a synthesis is very superficial. It is apologetic, it imitates others and the individual loses his uniqueness. In synthesis no one succeeds. Even our great teacher Rabbi Moses ben Maimon [Maimonides] did not succeed in his attempts at synthesis. The greatness of the Yeshiva is that it is a real Yeshiva and on the second level a proper academic institution. Both divisions function without synthesis and compromise.

My students go from my shiur on the first floor of the Yeshiva building to their college classes on the third floor. In my class, they study in depth such talmudic topics as whether the signatures of the witnesses or the witnessing of the actual delivery make the get [divorce document] effective [Gittin 23a], or whether going over the writing on a get document can validate the get [Gittin 20a]. Then they go upstairs to their college classes, where they study theories in mathematics and physics. I am proud when my student is both a Torah scholar and a good college student. If there were a synthesis, both achievements would be weakened!

In this concept, our Yeshiva is unique. It is not like other yeshivot. It is not like Israeli institutions. Let us not allow the Israelis to rebuke us. They have much to learn from us. Their so-called modern institutions have not produced Torah scholars. I am not overwhelmed by wonder at the establishment of a religious university [Bar-Ilan University]. It can be named after the Vilna Gaon, not just after Rabbi Meir Bar-Ilan [1880–1949; leader of religious Zionism]. Such an institution does not produce Torah scholars. The Catholics also have religious universities. I do not like to imitate others! We have a Yeshiva, and because the times demand it, we also have a university. These two divisions will not be synthesized. They will remain two institutions. It may be like a man with two heads, but it is better to have two heads than not to have one. [Laughter.]

This uniqueness of the Yeshiva is another reason why I am loyal to this institution. It is a reflection of my own thinking and commitment.

1. On Professor Eugen Mittwoch, see Mordechai Eliav and Esriel Hildesheimer, *Bet ha-Medrash le-Rabanim be-Berlin, 1873–1938* (Jerusalem: Leo Baeck Institute 1996), p. 79.

21.03 Yeshiva University II

Related by the Rav in his address at the Hag ha-Semikhah (Rabbinical Graduation Convocation) on April 12, 1970. The address was described in the Commentator *(Yeshiva University's undergraduate newspaper) on April 15, 1970; and excerpted and published in the* Commentator, *March 22, 1994, pp. 8–9.*

Yeshiva is an institution which has been opposed and challenged for a long, long time. This opposition to the Yeshiva is a result of the uniqueness of its singular contribution to American Jewish life. You will ask me, In what does this uniqueness express itself? What is it? I will answer you that its uniqueness is an idea, or, if you wish, a faith. If you wish to say so, the uniqueness consists of an adventure. What is this idea, faith, or adventure? It is the concept that the Yeshiva has proclaimed in three words: "It is possible!" That is the motto of the Yeshiva. What is possible? If you ask this question, I will tell you. It is possible to be a Jew, a loyal committed Jew, living a Jewish life. It is possible to be a talmid hakham, a scholar, because intellectual achievements play a great role in Judaism. One can be a scholar, a Jew committed to Torah she-be'al peh [the Oral Tradition] and Torah she-bikhtav [the Written Tradition]. One can be a Jew committed to the past, present, and future of Jewish history. A Jew committed to the eschatological vision of Aharit ha-Yamim [the end of days], and, at the same time, a member of modern society. A useful member, trained in all the skills, and able to live in the midst of modern society and not to retreat. Such an individual takes pride in the fact that he is singular and unique as a Jew. This is the idea that the Yeshiva has proclaimed in three words: "It is possible!" It is to this motto that we especially cling now.

I will tell you. I have been a teacher at Yeshiva for twenty-nine years. Next May, I will complete my twenty-ninth year as a teacher here. The Yeshiva has accomplished something which has been unknown in Jewish annals since the Golden Age of Spain. This accomplishment is the combination of talmid hakham with academician, a person trained scientifically in all the technological skills. I lived many years in Germany, and you probably have heard about the revolution that Rabbi Samson Raphael Hirsch [1808–1888] precipitated there. He was followed by Rabbi Azriel Hildesheimer [1820–1899], and it was a very impressive accomplishment. However, the accomplishment consisted of combining academic training with piety. One of my professors at the University of Berlin was Eugen Mittwoch [1876–1942], who was truly an *ehrlicher Yid* [pious Jew]. On Tishah be-Av he used to come to the Seminary for Oriental Languages at the university in sneakers! Remember that Berlin was not New York. Yes, in Germany I witnessed the combination and merger of academic modern training with piety and loyal observance.

However, what the Yeshiva is doing is something else. The Yeshiva has been more ambitious and more bold. It has proclaimed a higher goal, the combination of academic modern training with lomdut, with rigorous rabbinic scholarship at the highest level. The alumnus of the Yeshiva, whether he is a rabbi or a merchant, a lawyer or a doctor, is also a talmid hakham. Some to a lesser degree, some to a higher degree, but many are talmedei hakhamim. I am very careful and very cautious when I utilize the term talmid hakham. I mean that they are talmidei hakhamim in the sense that they are interested in the *Kezot* [*ha-Hoshen*, commentary on *Shulhan Arukh*, Hoshen Mishpat, by R. Aryeh Leib Heller, 1745–1813], the Rambam [Maimonides], or the *Hiddushei Rabbenu Hayyim ha-Levi* [on the Rambam, the classic work by the Rav's grandfather Reb Chaim Brisker]. The alumnus of the Yeshiva possesses this curiosity. The sign of a scholar is not so much the amount of knowledge he has as his inquisitiveness, curiosity, quest, interest, and commitment. I have seen many scholars with almost unlimited erudition but have doubted their scholarship. They were similar to what the Ramban [Nahmanides] calls a *hamor nosei' sefarim*, "a donkey loaded with many books" [in the introduction to Ramban's critical glosses on the Rambam's *Sefer ha-Mitzvot*]. The criteria of a scholar are commitment, curiosity, inquisitiveness, restlessness, exploration, and steady questing. This is exactly what all musmahei ha-Yeshiva have. I can testify that the level of the shiurim delivered at the Yeshiva have reached great heights. No other yeshiva here in America or in Eretz Yisrael has attained this level. I say this despite what some of the Mizrachi people claim about their yeshivot in Eretz Yisrael. I am little impressed by their statements. No yeshiva exceeds or transcends our school.

There are boys in our institution who are committed to Torah, *bekol libam u-vekol nafsham* [with all their hearts and souls]; with a fire and a passion unmatched in the history of yeshivot. When I see them, I am sometimes reminded of Bialik's "Ha-Matmid" [Hayyim Nahman Bialik, 1873–1934, Hebrew poet; his "Ha-Matmid" is about the diligence of the students at the Volozhin Yeshiva]. They are bright and sharp, and their precision and skill in text interpretation are simply admirable. I can tell you that sometimes I sit up studying days and nights. Many a time my son comes into my room and finds me asleep over the gemora. It is late in the evening. Why? It is not so much my diligence, but I am afraid of my pupils. If I come into the class unprepared, they will tear me apart. This happens quite often. At the same time, as far as modern education is concerned, they are academically well trained, on a par with any boys from Harvard, Yale, or Columbia. In addition, to their scholarship and knowledge, they possess a sense of commitment to Klal Yisrael the likes of which is hard to find.

When I came to America almost forty years ago, I found in Boston six young men who were Sabbath observers. The rest did not observe the Sabbath. There were some who did observe, but they observed not only the Sabbath, but Sunday, Monday, and Tuesday as well. They were octogenarians! I must tell you that three of these young men are now my brothers-in-law. Boston, which was an *ir ha-nidahat* [wayward city; Deuteronomy 13:13–19] as far as Orthodoxy was concerned, is today a stronghold of Orthodox striving and questing. In my shul at Maimonides [School], the average age of the worshipers is twenty-one! I am the oldest, the oldest in years, and I also consider myself the teacher of those who attend services. Boston is not an exception to the rule. I mention Boston simply because I live there, but you will find the same is true in New York, which is a much larger city. The fact is that we today are enjoying a renaissance of Orthodoxy. The average age in the Orthodox shul is below that in the Conservative synagogue. It is certainly below that in the Reform synagogue. They have failed to raise a new generation. We have succeeded. The fact that thousands of young men and women not only live Jewish lives, but think in Torah categories and talk the language of the Torah, and are committed to our tradition, is due directly or indirectly to our Yeshiva. Could I have ever dreamed twenty-five years ago that a bunch of boys from our Yeshiva and other yeshivot would occupy the quarters of the Federation of Jewish Philanthropies in New York, the sanctum sanctorum of Reform Jewry and make demands boldly and proudly! [The demands were for financial support of Jewish education.] You will see the "priests" of the sanctum sanctorum giving in to these young boys—and the same thing is happening in Boston. All this is due, directly or indirectly, to our Yeshiva. It is responsible for the renaissance of Orthodoxy, and I am not exaggerating. For the Yeshiva is not just an institution or a school; it is a movement, an idea, a challenge, it is a faith and an assurance that Torah can blossom and flourish in the Western Hemisphere, close to the skyscrapers of New York. The Torah can be cultivated, taught, and propagated in all societies and eras, no matter how powerful the opposition, and no matter how unfriendly the circumstances.

21.04 Educating the Stomach

Related by the Rav in the Tonya Soloveitchik Memorial Lecture entitled "The Nine Aspects of the Haggadah," Yeshiva University, March 23, 1977.

The Greeks considered eating an animal function. A man, they felt, should not exhibit animality. Aristotle could not undertsand how you could serve God with your stomach. Aristotle held that you can serve God only with your mind.

Jacob Schiff [1847–1920],[1] an American Jewish philanthropist, once visited the Yeshivat Rabbi Isaac Elchanan. He walked into a room where Rabbi Binyamin Aronowitz[2] was saying a shiur on Yoreh Deah [the division of the *Shulhan Arukh* that includes the dietary laws]. Old-timers still remember Rabbi Aronowitz. The philanthropist asked his guide: "What is the old man saying? What is he teaching his students?" The guide answered that Rabbi Aronowitz was teaching about *melihah* [how to salt meat in the kashering process]. Jacob Schiff declared that he did not support religious institutions that were interested in the stomach.

Of course the first section of Yoreh Deah is concerned with the stomach. No question about it! That is the greatness of Judaism. To teach the stomach, indeed the human body, to behave in the presence of God is more difficult than to teach the mind to behave properly in the presence of God. If you start with the mind you will fail; if you start with the body you might succeed.

1. Jacob Schiff, financier and investment banker, was raised in the Frankfurt spiritual community of Rabbi Samson Raphael Hirsch. In the United States, Schiff joined the Reform movement and Temple Emanu-el. Nevertheless he retained many ritual observances and was later active in the development of the Jewish Theological Seminary. For a discussion of Schiff's spiritual motivations see Moshe Davis, *The Emergence of Conservative Judaism* (Philadelphia: Jewish Publication Society, 1965), pp. 448–450.

2. Rabbi Binyamin Aronowitz (1864–1945) was a focal member of the Yeshiva's faculty. See Gilbert Klaperman, *The Story of Yeshiva University: The First Jewish University in America* (Toronto: Macmillan, 1969), pp. 82–83, 141, 164, 174; Jeffrey S. Gurock, *The Men and Women of Yeshiva* (New York: Columbia University Press, 1988), pp. 48, 49, 134; and *Sepher Yevul Hayovloth* (New York: Rabbi Isaac Elchanan Theological Seminary, 1986), p. 208.

21.05 A Lack of Sensitivity

Related by Rabbi Hershel Schachter, "Me-Peninei Rabenu, Zal,"
in Bet Yitzhak, *ed. Zvi David Romm and Azriel Rosner (New York:*
Student Organization of Yeshiva, 1995), p. 16.

Once the Rav attended the funeral of an eminent rabbi. After the
eulogies and while walking behind the funeral cortege as the journey to the cemetery began, the Rav was approached by a student
from the Yeshiva. He asked the Rav whether he could discuss a certain Torah topic with him. The Rav, surprised at the student's lack
of sensitivity, asked if this was a proper time to indulge in the joy of
Torah discussion. The student responded that it was, since he
wished to discuss an aspect of the Laws of Mourning with the Rav.

That afternoon, the Rav told his class about this episode. He
said that it reminded him of a story he had heard from Reb Chaim
Ozer Grodzinski [1863–1940]. A fire once broke out in Reb
Chaim Ozer's house in Vilna. Reb Chaim Ozer hurriedly tried to
save his rabbinic library from the flames. In the midst of the commotion, a young scholar approached Reb Chaim Ozer and asked
to discuss a Torah topic with him. Reb Chaim Ozer, taken aback,
asked whether this was an appropriate time to discuss Torah
themes, since the flames were still raging and the books had to be
saved. The young scholar replied that the topic he wished to discuss was *Isho mishum hitsav*—"whether fire involves liability
because of the human agency that brings it about" [Baba Kamma
22a].

21.06 Moral Choices

Related by the Rav in a talk to the National Association of Tradi-
tional Communal Workers, Yeshiva University, May 6, 1975.

We have definite halakhot to guide us in the ritual area. We actually
have an all-inclusive code, and a rich halakhic literature that guides
us in times of doubt and perplexity. However, there is a dearth of
objective principles that could provide us with counsel and guid-

ance whenever ethical man seems to be lost. When you have questions about prayer, you open up the *Shulhan Arukh,* Orah Hayyim. A great scholar will find it quickly. Someone who is not advanced in learning will take a little longer. But you will find either the law which explicitly suits this particular occasion or a similar law. When you have moral problems, however, it is very hard to open up an appropriate text. Where do you find guidance?

Apparently, there is a subjective element in making moral decisions. If one is confused, he can ask for guidance and counsel. Many times, I have been presented with such moral questions. I never give a yes or no answer. The questions may determine the future of the particular individual. I will explain the options but tell him that the final choice is his. These are occasionally the most important of problems. Many times when my own students ask me such questions, I explain to them what is involved. They have to understand the alternatives.

As a matter of fact, somebody has told me that [Henry A.] Kissinger [b. 1923, U.S. Secretary of State] told him that his job is to break down problems into several alternatives. He offers various solutions and then presents his analysis to the President [Richard Nixon, President 1969–1974]. The decision belongs to the President. This is also true of my counseling my students. I receive many such questions. I would never give them a yes or no answer. I just explain the alternatives and what is involved. One course of action may produce one result, and another course may produce a second result. The decision belongs to the boys.

I resent very much that certain roshei yeshiva and certain teachers want to impose their will upon the boys. It is against the law. Both ways are correct, the options are correct, and it is up to the individual to make the decision. I cannot make the decision for him. I am old, he is young. This in itself prevents me from making the decision. I do not like to impose my will upon somebody else. Only the Almighty can do that, but not a human being.

21.07 Our Children's Heroes

Related by Rabbi Bernard Rosensweig, "The Rabbinical Council of America: Retrospect and Prospect,"Tradition, vol. 22, no. 2 (Summer 1986), p. 10.

The Rav once gave me a powerful insight into the changing character of Orthodoxy. We were talking about my son and his grandson, and he said to me: "When you were a student at the Yeshiva, who were your heroes?" and he did not even wait for me to answer. He said: "Rabbis Leo Jung, Joseph Lookstein, Herbert S. Goldstein."[1] And then he said, "Tell me, who are the heroes of your son, and my grandson? Certainly not these people. Their models are the roshei yeshiva, the people who represent learning and scholarship."

1. For an account of these rabbis and their era, see Jenna Weissman Joselit, *New York's Jewish Jews: The Orthodox Community in the Interwar Years* (Bloomington: Indiana University Press, 1990), pp. 54–84.

For a study of the transfer of leadership from the practicing rabbis to the roshei yeshiva, see Aaron Rakeffet-Rothkoff, *The Silver Era: Rabbi Eliezer Silver and His Generation* (Jerusalem: Feldheim Publishers, 1981), pp. 288–300.

21.08 Religious Immaturity

Related by the Rav in a talk to the faculty of the Wurzweiler School of Social Work, Yeshiva University, March 13, 1974.

As a teacher I can transmit my ideas to my pupils on an intellectual level. When it comes to the transmission and passing of experiences I feel so inadequate. Sometimes it drives me to despair. It is very hard. I will tell you frankly, the American *ben torah* or good yeshiva student has achieved great heights on an intellectual level. However, experientially he is simply immature. When it comes to Jewish religious experience, people of thirty and even forty years of age are immature. They act like children and experience religion like children. As a result, Jewish youth is inclined and very disposed to accept extremist views. They do this to such an extent that my own students examine my *zizit* to see whether they are long enough! [Laughter.] The youth is extremely pious, but also very inconsiderate. Sometimes they drive matters to absurdity. Why? Because they have no experience. Their experience is very childish, simply infantile. When it comes to experiencing the emotional component of religion, boys who are really learned simply act like children. This is why they accept all types of fanaticism and superstition. Sometimes, they are even ready to do things which border on the immoral. They lack the experiential component of religion, and simply substitute obscurantism for it. I have never seen such obscurantism as I see among some of my students today. After all, I come from the ghetto. Yet I have never seen so much naive and uncritical commitment to people and to ideas as I see in America. This is the main problem we have today.[1]

I am very helpless in this regard. How can I convey experiences to my students? I simply do not know how. I spoke last night at Moriya in my shiur about the conclusion of last week's sedra (Torah portion). We find that when Moses came down from the mountain the second time that his face radiated light, beaming light. "When Moses descended from Mount Sinai—with the two Tablets of the Testimony in the hand of Moses as he descended from the mountain—Moses did not know that the skin of his face had become radiant when He had spoken to him" (Exodus 34:29). The Torah also tells us: "After that, all the Children of Israel would approach; he (Moses) would command them regarding everything that G-d had spoken to him on Mount Sinai" (Exodus 34:32). This refers to formal teaching. How do you teach formally? By using the medium of the word which is the only medium by which you can teach. Moshe Rabenu was the teacher par excellence. He was an excellent teacher. However, this is not enough. Moses also had to radiate light which represented his teaching at an experiential level. Of course, he could not transmit all of his experiences to the Jews. He was above and beyond them. He was a super-human being. Yet, somehow he tried to transmit to them part of his experience. Here the medium is not the word but silence. Not to say anything and still to transmit and to pass on a great experience.

This is what the verse means when it says "his face was radiant." Experience expresses itself through light . I do not know how to do this. I will tell you frankly, I do not know how to do it.

The so called American modern Orthodoxy consists of middle-aged people by now and their children. We do not have old people, but only middle-aged and children. As far as religious experience is concerned they are very immature. Sometimes they act so clumsily and so awkwardly, and possess a tendency to accept extremist views.

My students are my products as far as lomdus is concerned. They follow my method of learning. However, somehow there is a reservation in their minds regarding my philosophical viewpoint. They consider me excellent in lomdus. However, when it comes to my philosophical experiential viewpoint, I am somehow persona non grata. My ideas are too radical for them. If they could find another one it would be alright. However, the substitutions are completely infantile. This is a tremendous problem in America. This is the main problem we have to cope with, and I do not know how. All extremism, fanaticism and obscurantism come from a lack of security. A person who is secure cannot be an extremist. He uses his mind and his heart in a normal fashion. I am not so interested in finding the cause of this problem but rather in its therapy. What is the proper therapeutic viewpoint? How can we change it? I do not know.

1. By the 1970s, many of the Rav's students espoused viewpoints which were analogous with the then rapidly expanding more right wing American Orthodoxy. (See Charles S. Liebman, "Orthodoxy in American Jewish Life," *American Jewish Yearbook* (1965), ed. Morris Fine and Milton Himmelfarb (Philadelphia: The Jewish Publication Society, 1965), p. 67).

The Rav's disappointment with this trend can be readily understood when contrasted with his own feelings and experiences. Rabbi Yitzchak Twersky declared:

> I want to clarify a bit more the role of philosophy. There is, in my opinion, no justification for debate or equivocation concerning the Rav's relation to general culture—philosophy, science, literature—but it is necessary to put this in a proper perspective. The facts are unmistakable. He achieved sovereign mastery of these fields and used his knowledge selectively, creatively and imaginatively, with great philosophic acumen and originality. He often reminisced with me about his student years and his unquenchable thirst for knowledge, which, he said, was char-

acteristic of many of his contemporaries. He recalled that straitened material circumstances never dampened his enthusiasm for study. The impact of those years on him was great and lasting; his quest for wide-ranging scientific-humanistic knowledge was successful. The record of his dedicated quest for ongoing use of this knowledge is clear and unambiguous. ("The Rov," *Tradition*, Vol. 30, No. 4 (Summer 1996), p 30.)

Rabbi Aharon Lichtenstein related:

> In a moment of striking candor; when my colleague, Rav Yehuda Amital, first visited these shores [U.S.A.] almost twenty years ago, the Rav commented to him: "You know, I have devoted talmidim—very devoted talmidim. If I were to announce a shiur at two o'clock in the morning, they would come en bloc. And yet, deep in their hearts, they think I'm an apikoros." The remark was laced with characteristic humor and confined, presumably, to a select group. Nevertheless, it gave vent to a genuine, if painful, sentiment. ("The Rav at Jubilee: An Appreciation," Ibid., p. 54.)

Rabbi Mosheh Lichtenstein, the Rav's grandson, stated:

> In sum, the Rav's philosophy weaves together the approaches of Scientific Man and Religious Man with that of Halakhic Man to provide existential experience and significance to religious life. Halakhic Man, who is also the man of faith, is nourished by the achievements of others in clarifying and elucidating issues of concern to him, while those others are able to receive satisfaction from the halakhic Torah of our sages. To grasp the scope of this phenomenon within the Rav's writings and to appreciate its breadth and depth, one has to go no further than the footnotes which accompany "Halakhic Man." There, summoned by the author, one can meet, side by side, famous rabbanim and German professors, Rambam and William James, Minhat Hinukh and I. L. Peretz, along with many other such figures. In the Rav's world, it is possible to use such diverse sources and create a single, coherent, Torah-true whole from them. Lest anyone mislead himself and think that this was an intellectual posture detached from the fiber of his soul, I must emphatically state that this was not so. Many a time did he preach to my brothers and myself, from the depths of a grandfather's loving concern, the importance of acquiring general and scientific knowledge. ("For My Grandfather Has Left Me", Ibid., p. 72.)

The author visited with the Rav in his Brookline home on the Sabbath of *Hazon* (August 12th), 1978. The Rav similarly expressed himself to the author regarding the obscurantist trends of many of his best students during that period.

21.09 Student and Teacher

Related by the Rav during a Sheva Berakhot talk in honor of David and Rona Holzer at the home of Rabbi and Mrs. Emanuel Holzer, March 27, 1979.

The relationship of talmid [student] and rebbe [teacher] plays an important role in my life. I have only one son—two daughters and one son. My son is also my talmid, and so are my daughters. The basic relationship between me and my children is that of teacher and student, and not so much of father and child. I was brought up in an environment where the basic relationship—and this is expressed in my ma'amarim [essays]—was not the biologically justified relationship of father and son. Sometimes we have in common nothing else but the genetic code. The Torah respected this relationship, which is the common denominator between people. Science calls this relationship the genetic code. However, there is a higher relationship, and that is the kinship of rebbe and talmid. This relationship has nothing to do with the genetic code because they have two different genetic codes. But there is a certain sense, what shall I say, of identification. When I teach young boys, no matter how complicated the sugya [talmudic topic] is, I try to pass on to them more than just knowledge. I pass on to them not only the knowledge, the abstractions and the concepts of the halakhah, but also something that I experience, something personal, something intimate, a part of myself. I try to pass all this on to my talmidim. Some receive it and some accept it. Some cannot accept it, because the modern American and European Western man has never known what the relationship between talmid and rebbe means. He has never understood Yahadut [Judaism]. Perhaps Plato and Socrates understood it. I do not know. Perhaps they understood the relationship between master and disciple. I do not know. However in Yahadut, this relationship is the foundation of the Torah she-be'al peh [Oral Tradition] and the great mesorah. It is the heart of a great tradition which one generation passes on to the next generation. It is a great message which one generation passes on to the next generation. By passing on this message, the first generation gives itself to the second generation. There is a merger, so to say, an existential merger of the generations throughout the ages and the millennia.

I cannot establish this relationship with every talmid. Some talmidim resist it. They look upon me as they look upon any other teacher, simply as a technician. While they are in class and I am explaining the sugya, they are pretty good students at times. However, once the Gemara is closed and they are outside the classroom, they do not recognize me. It is a world which I do not wish to know. However, some talmidim, who have sensitive hearts as well as sensitive minds, sustain the relationship between talmid and rebbe.

21.10 Students as Pals

Related by the Rav during a Sheva Berakhot talk in honor of Jacob and Cheryl Holzer at the home of Rabbi and Mrs. Solomon B. Shapiro, June 15, 1977.

I have the privilege of teaching two of the children of the father of the groom. My relationship with them can be expressed in the following sentence: They are my pupils and also my pals. Really! We joke together! In the classroom I become young. When I enter the classroom, my youth returns to me. The other day I visited the doctor and he examined me. So finally he asked me: "What is your age?" I told him: "Doctor, it depends where. In your office, one hundred and twenty. In my classroom, twenty."

I like being around young boys, and I become one of the gang. That is the only way to teach. A teacher who does not lose years in the classroom and does not become one of his class cannot teach Torah successfully. You teach pals and friends. You do not teach anything to anyone who is below you! This is my philosophy of teaching Torah!

21.11 The Debt to My Students

Related by the Rav in response to a presentation in his honor at the Yarhei Kallah, Boston, Mass., August 25, 1981.

Whether you are indebted to me as your teacher is a separate question. But I certainly am indebted to you as a teacher more than you are indebted to me as my students. Do you know why? Because a teacher always acquires more from his students than the students from the teacher. Our sages long ago declared: "I have learned much from my teachers, and from my colleagues more than from my teachers, but from my disciples more than from them all" [Ta'anit 7a]. Maimonides explained that just as "a small log can kindle a large one, the young student likewise enables the learned teacher to enhance his wisdom" [Hilkhot Talmud Torah 5:13].

I have a different reason why I owe you a yashar koah [hearty thanks]. My debt to you exceeds your debt to me. Many of my shiurim are organized in the classroom. Quite often, when I prepare the shiur, I cannot find the right approach. I sit with the gemora, but it is a difficult sugya [subject for study]. The basic halakhic foundations upon which the sugya rests are hard to deal with. Sometimes, at night, I am completely in despair. When I come into the classroom and sit down with my students, I slowly begin to analyze the sugya. Suddenly a light goes on, like a light from some mysterious source, and I begin to comprehend exactly what the secret of the sugya is. I begin to understand why it was so difficult for me to prepare the shiur the night before. Somehow, my students always inspire me. Many of my shiurim are products of this consultation with my students. After all, as a rosh yeshiva, I have covered a lot of material. For instance, in Nashim, Nezikin and Moed we covered every tractate. From a quantitative viewpoint, we analyzed all the difficult problems in these sugyot. I needed the help of my students. When I was young, I used to compete with my students. The shiur used to be more of a symposium than a lecture. I let every student express his own understanding of the sugya. Many times I admitted in the classroom that the student was right and I was wrong. All this sharpened my mind and turned the study of Torah into a romance.[1]

Today, when I come into the classroom, I am sometimes in pain. I open up the gemora and ask a student to start reading the text. I am very depressed and dejected. This lasts no more than five or ten minutes. Little by little, the clouds rise. Suddenly, I begin to believe that I am just as young as my students, even though two generations separate us. I begin to compete with them. Sometimes I lose, sometimes I win. Teaching is something I love. I must tell you that I greatly appreciate the devotion that you display vis-à-vis me. Actually, the mere thought that there are hundreds of young men who have studied under my guidance is very gratifying. In particular, the fact that they realize what they acquired in my class is inspiring for me. Your attention is wonderful. I hope that it will be possible for me to continue, and that the Almighty will give me many more years. I should sometimes lose arguments in the classroom, and be able to start all over again the next day.

1. A former student of the Rav's wrote: "Cognizant of this linkage, the Rav organized his shiur as an exercise wherein we, the talmidim, were invited to share in the Rav's experience of 'teaching himself,' as it were, the sugya or halakhic text to be mastered, with the learning and the teaching experience merging as one. Thus, the Rav would force himself to approach a sugya as if for the first time, developing with us the various opinions, problems and possibilities embedded in the text, compelling us to confront with him the difficulties of various approaches, sharing with him in the resolution of these problems." Stanley Boylan, "Learning with the Rav: Learning from the Rav," *Tradition*, vol. 30, no. 4 (Summer 1996), p. 132.

Bibliography of Sources Attributed to the Rav in the Insights

The Rav often cited sources in an undetailed manner, such as "our sages said." Therefore, when necessary, the author provided the exact sources. Accordingly, the sources in this bibliography are attributed to the Rav, although many times they were not actually cited in detail by the Rav.

Details of the Rav's published writings cited in the Insights are listed in the "Selected Chronological Bibliography of the Published Writings of Rabbi Joseph B. Soloveitchik."

The numbers in brackets refer to the location of the sources in the text.

Sources Attributed to the Rav in The Insights

1. Biblical Sources

Genesis

1:31 [12.04]	25:19–28:9 [6.08]
6:4 [21.02]	25:29–25:30 [6.08]
7:23 [13.03]	24:34 [6.08]
11:1 [20.01]	32:14 [15.01]
16:6 [17.13]	32:25 [16.03, 16.07]
17:1 [5.12]	32:29 [16.03]
17:7 [14.02]	37:7 [15.01]
17:10 [14.02]	41:26 [18.02]
18:19 [12.02]	44:18–47:27 [2.04]
21:33 [14.02]	50:1 [5.12]
22:1 [14.07]	50:6 [16.08]

Exodus

15:11 [3.05]	22:3 [5.08]
17:8–16 [17.13, 18.03]	23:17 [14.02]
18:1–20:23 [20.09]	25:22 [19.04]
19:3 [19.13]	26:33 [19.04]
20:14 [20.04]	27:20–30:10 [20.09]
20:21 [20.10]	34:29 [21.08]
21:1–24:18 [20.09]	34:32 [21.08]
21:37 [5.08]	

Leviticus

5:21 [13.02]	19:11 [5.09]
19:1–20:27 [20.09]	19:11–19:12
[14.06]	
19:2 [5.09]	23:15 [2.09]
19:3 [14.06]	23:27 [19.10]
19:5 [5.09]	23:40 [5.17, 8.05]

Numbers

6:1–6:21 [13.04]	11:1 [11.04]
10:35 [11.04]	23:16 [16.05]

Deuteronomy

1:17 [5.10, 14.03]	4:10 [20.10]
4:9 [20.10]	5:1 [20.12]
5:18 [20.04]	25:17–19 [17.13]
11:15 [7.06]	26:11 [5.17]
13:13–19 [21.03]	30:3 [15.05]
16:15 [5.17]	30:14 [12.05]
20:05 [20.13]	

Joshua

16:15 [5.17]	1:8 [14.02, 20.12]

Judges

13:11 [13.02]

1 Samuel

10:24 [5.02]

Isaiah

44:6 [1.04]	63:9 [17.10]

Jeremiah

31:2 [5.12]

Ezekiel

20:41 [17.10]	44:23 [14.05, 14.07]
44:24 [5.10, 14.03]	

Jonah

1:5 [18.01]	1:6 [18.01]
1:9 [18.01]	

Zechariah

9:14 [19.08]

Malachi

3:18 [20.12]

Psalms

8:4–5 [21.01]	104:1 [19.02]
23:1 [2.09]	104:25 [19.02]
23:2 [2.08]	113:4 [2.05]
42:2 [2.05]	116:11 [18.02]
79:6 [10.05]	118:24 [3.05]
90:10 [11.03]	119:126 [1.01]

121:1 [15.01]   145:15 [2.05]   Baba Bathra
145:13 [2.05]   150:6 [18.09]   10:8 [20.09]

Proverbs   Sanhedrin
   1:8 [19.13]   7:5 [17.13]

Song of Songs   Shevuot
   1:1–8:14 [19.04]   6:3 [19.12]   3:8 [17.01]
   7:6 [2.05]
                                 Eduyyot
Ruth   2:9 [20.01]
   1:16 [5.04]
                                 Avot
Ecclesiastes   1:1 [15.01]   3:7 [20.10]
   7:29 [7.03]   1:14 [21.02]   6:9 [17.03]
                                    2:2 [21.02]
Esther
   1:1 [14.06]   4:14 [6.07]   ## 3. Talmud
   2:19 [11.05]   9:29 [15.03]
   4:1 [18.06]   10:2 [15.03]   Berakhot
                                    5a [3.04]   45a [14.08]
2. Mishnah   6a [20.10]   53b [1.02]
                                    6b [20.03]   54b [19.01]
Berakhot   8a [5.04, 10.02]   61a [14.07]
   5:2 [1.01]   9:1 [19.02]   22a [20.10]   63a [4.02]
   9:2 [19.01]   28b [14.07]   64a [20.11]
                                    40a [7.06]
Shabbat
   16:1 [20.09]   Shabbat
                                    88a [3.01]   138b [3.02]
Betzah   116b [20.09]
   1:1 [5.08]
                                 Eruvin
Moed Katan   21b [20.11]
   1:5 [11.08]
                                 Pesahim
Nedarim   3b [17.08]   90a–90b [6.05]
   9:10 [9.07]
                                 Yoma
Baba Kama   19b [15.01]   85b [8.03]
   5:1 [5.08]   29a [20.13]

Baba Metzia   Sukkah
   2:1 [20.13]   6:1 [20.13]   52b [3.04]

Rosh Hashanah
9a [2.08, 2.09]   16b [8.05]

Ta'anit
7a [21.11]   16a [17.10]

Megillah
31a [2.05]

Moed Katan
22b [20.09]

Hagigah
9b [20.12]

Yevamot
22a [1.04]   47b [5.04]

Ketuvot
63a [14.11]   112a [17.05]

Gittin
20a [21.02]   60b [1.01, 20.12]
23a [21.02]   62a [14.03]
60a [1.01]

Kiddushin
29b–30a [6.03]   30b [3.04]

Baba Kama
22a [21.05]   62b–83a [2.03, 20.09]

Baba Metzia
2a–21a [20.09]   83b [5.04]
21a–33b [20.09]   84b [21.02]

Sanhedrin
6b [6.04]   74a–74b [4.01]
44a [16.03]   93a [21.02]
68a [21.02]   105b [16.05]

Shevuot
39a [15.01]

Avodah Zarah
3b [20.02]   4b [17.10]

Zevahim
2b [3.02]

Menahot
99b [14.02]

Keritot
3b [5.02]

Niddah
34a [5.04]

4. Rabbinic Works

Avot de-Rebbe Natan, Version 1, chap. 36 [12.05]
Bereshit Rabbah
    to Genesis 3:9 [12.04]
    to Genesis 82:11 [1.09]
Kallah Rabbathi, chap. 9 [18.02]
Mekhilta
    to be-Shalah, Amalek, chap. 2 (15) [17.10]
    to Exodus 20:1 [13.02]
Shemot Rabbah, chap. 29, div. 4 [1.04]
Shir ha-Shirim Rabbah, chap. 1, div. 8 [20.11]
Tana de-Vei Eliyahu Zuta, chap. 14 [12.05]
Tosefta to Shevuot 3:6 [13.02]

5. Rishonim (Early Rabbinic Authorities)

Ba'alei Tosafot—Tosafot Commentary [20.05]
Maimonides (Rambam)
    Mishneh Torah
Hilkhot Talmud Torah
    3:13 [20.11]
    4:2 [1.06]
    5:9 [20.11]
    5:13 [21.11]
Hilkhot Tefillah
    12:6 [5.15, 5.16]
Hilkhot Terumot
    1:5 [17.04]
Hilkhot Sanhedrin
    1:3 [1.06]
Hilkhot Avel
    1:10 [5.04]
    13:12 [11.09]
Hilkhot Melakhim
    3:10 [5.10]
    4:10 [14.03, 17.10]

Perush ha-Mishnah to Pirkei Avot 1:6 [14.11]
Nahmanides (Ramban)
    Introduction to his glosses of the Rambam's *Sefer ha-Mitzvot* [21.03]
    Milhemet ha-Shem to the Rif on Megillah 3a [7.02]

Rashi
    to Genesis 25:30 [6.08]
    to Numbers 23:16 [16.05]
    to Numbers 24:6 [16.05]
    to Talmud Berakhot 6b [20.03]
Shitah Mekubetzet [5.08]

6. Shulhan Arukh and Its Commentaries

Orah Hayyim

136:1 [13.07]	639:5 [5.01]
292:2 [3.01]	640:4 [5.01]
478:2 [10.05]	

Yoreh Deah

51:1 [4.04]	354:1 [5.10, 6.13, 14.03]

Even ha-Ezer
6:8 [13.11]

Biur ha-Gra to Orah Hayyim 47:4 [1.05]
Magen Avraham to Orah Hayyim 648:21 (23) [8.05]

7. Aharonim (Later Rabbinic Authorities)

Bornstein, Avraham. *Avnei Nezer*. New York: Hozaot Avraham Fried-
    man, n.d.[17.06].
Danzig, Avraham. *Hayyei Adam*. [21.02].
Epstein, Jehiel Michael. *Arukh ha-Shulhan*. [5.09].
Feinstein, Eliyahu. *Halihot Eliyahu*. Vilna: 1932. [7.02].
Ganzfried, Solomon. *Kitzur Shulhan Arukh*. [21.02].
Ha-Kohen, Shabbtai ben Meir. *Siftei Kohen (Shakh)*. [20.05].

Ha-Levi, David ben Samuel. *Turei Zahav* (*Taz*). [20.05].

Heller, Aryeh Leib.*Avnei Milluim* on *Shulhan Arukh*: Even ha-Ezer. [20.09].

Kezot ha-Hoshen on *Shulhan Arukh*: Hoshen Mishpat. [20.05, 20.07, 20.09, 21.03].

Hiddushei Reb Akiva Eiger. [5.08, 20:09].

Lorbeerbaum, Jacob. *Havaat Da'at* on *Shulhan Arukh*: Yoreh Deah. [20.09].

———. *Netivot ha-Mishpat* on *Shulhan Arukh*: Hoshen Mishpat. [20.05, 20.07, 20.09].

Medini, Hayyim Hezekiah. *Sedei Hemed.* [5.02].

Soloveitchik, Chaim. *Hidushei Rabenu Chaim ha-Levi* (al ha-Rambam). [5.08, 20.09, 21.03].

8. Homiletical, Philosophical, and Theological Volumes

Bornstein, Shmuel. *Shem mi-Shmuel.* Jerusalem: Sochotchover Yeshiva, 1987. [17.06].

Flavius, Josephus. *Contra Apionem* (*Against Apion.*) [16.03].

Ibn Pakuda, Bahya. *Hovat ha-Levovot.* [5.08].

Judah ha-Levi. *Kuzari.* [17.05].

Luzzatto, Moshe Chaim. *Mesillat Yesharim.* [5.08, 14.01].

Maimonides, Moses. *Moreh Nevukhim.* [17.09].

Rosenzweig, Franz. *Der Stern der Erloesung.* Frankfurt am Main: Suhrkamp Verlag, 1988. [15.05].

———. *The Star of Redemption.* New York: Holt, Rinehart & Winston, 1971. [15.05].

Shneur Zalman of Lyady. *Likutei Amaraim: Tanya.* [2.03, 2.07, 16.03, 20.12].

———. *Likutei Torah.* [2.07, 16.03, 19.12].

Volozhiner, Chaim. *Nefesh ha-Hayyim.* [3.01].

9. Liturgy

"Benai Heihalah" ("The Dwellers of the Sanctuary"). A mystical Sabbath song composed by R. Yitzhak Luria, known as ha-Ari [2.09].

Daily Prayer Book. Translated by Philip Birnbaum. [1.01, 12.06, 16.03, 17.03, 17.12, 18.04, 18.10].

Daily Prayer Book. Edited by Chief Rabbi Joseph Hertz of the British Empire. [5.08].

High Holiday Prayer Book. Translated by Philip Birnbaum. [1.04, 2.05, 6.05, 19.03, 19.04, 19.05, 19.08, 19.11, 20.12].

Kinot. Translated and published by Abraham Rosenfeld. London, 1965. [1.08, 9.06, 9.07, 16.03].

10. Literature and Memoirs

Bialik, Hayyim Nahman. "Ha-Matmid." In *Kol Kitvei H. N. Bialik*, pp. 73–78. Tel Aviv: Hozaot Dvir, 1956. [21.03].

Peretz, Isaac Leib. "Bontzye Schweig." In *Y.L. Perez Alla Werk*, vol. 2, pp. 412–420. New York: Central Yiddish Culture Organization, 1947. Hebrew Version: "Bontzye Shatik." In *Kol Kitvei Y.L. Perez*, vol. 3, book 2, pp. 167–176. Tel Aviv: Hozaot Dvir, 1948. [15.04].

———. "Zwishen Zwei Berg." In *Y. L. Perez Alla Werk*, vol. 4, pp. 103–117. New York: Central Yiddish Culture Organization, 1947. Hebrew version: "Bein Shenei Harim." In *Kol Kitvei Y. L. Perez*, vol. 2, pp. 11–24. Tel Aviv: Hozaot Dvir, 1948. [19.12].

Shakespeare, William. *The Merchant of Venice.* [16.03].

Weizmann, Chaim. *Trial and Error.* London: Hamish Hamilton, 1949. [17.02].

11. Shiurim and Lectures of the Rav

1. Shiurim at Yeshiva University

Haggadah Shiur, April 11, 1978 [10.05].
Shavuot Shiur, June 2, 1981 [11.03].
Talmudic Shiur, February 6, 1969 [19.01].
Talmudic Shiur, April 23, 1969 [4.05, 12.09].
Talmudic Shiur, November 13, 1975 [6.08].
Talmudic Shiur, December 9, 1976 [20.08].

2. Lectures on Parshiot ha-Torah at Yeshiva University

Parshat va-Yigash [Genesis 44:18–47:27], December 16, 1980 [16.07].

Parshat va-Yekhi [Genesis 47:28–50:26], December 23, 1980 [11.09, 16.08].
Parshat Sh'mot [Exodus 1:1–6:1], December 30, 1980 [18.05, 18.07].
Parshat Mishpatim [Exodus 21:1–24:18], February 3, 1981 [20.09].
Parshat Terumah [Exodus 25:1–27:19], February 10, 1981 [2.02].
Parshat Ki Tissah [Exodus 30:11–34:35], February 24, 1981 [4.03].

3. Hag ha-Semikhah Addresses at Yeshiva University

ca. 1953 [13.03].
April 12, 1970 [21.03].

4. Yahrzeit Shiurim in Memory of Rabbi Moshe Soloveichik at Yeshiva University

January 17, 1945 [12.03]
January 29, 1952 [7.01]
January 15, 1956 [1.09, 3.05]
January 6, 1957 [12.04]
January 11, 1959 [8.04]
January 11, 1970 [1.02, 1.05, 20.11, 20.12]
January 18, 1972 [5.15, 9.03, 20.03]

5. Shiurim and Lectures in Memory of Ha-Rabbanit Tonya Soloveitchik at Yeshiva University

March 10, 1968. Tonya Soloveitchik Memorial Lecture [11.02]
March 11, 1968. Mishnayot Shiur on the Yahrzeit of ha-Rabbanit Tonya Soloveitchik [1.01, 4.04]
March 18, 1970. Tonya Soloveitchik Memorial Lecture entitled: "The Anonymous Man and the Covenantal Community" [15.03]
March 14, 1973. Tonya Soloveitchik Memorial Lecture entitled: "Insights into Megillat Esther" [11.05]
March 4, 1974. Tonya Soloveitchik Memorial Lecture entitled: "Purim Ideas" [18.03]
March 23, 1977. Tonya Soloveitchik Memorial Lecture entitled: "The Nine Aspects of the Haggadah" [21.04]

May 22, 1979. The Benjamin Gottesman Lecture in Jewish Thought and the Tonya Soloveitchik Memorial Lecture entitled: "The Haftorot Between Pesach and Shavuot" [5.10, 13.06]

February 24, 1983. Purim Shiur in memory of ha-Rabbanit Tonya Soloveitchik on her Yahrzeit [13.08]

6. Memorial Shiurim at Yeshiva University

March 27, 1968. Memorial Shiur for Rabbi Eliezer Silver [6.12, 14.09].

January 14, 1974. Shiur in memory of ha-Rabbanit Pesia Feinstein Soloveichik [5.04]

7. Public Talks at Yeshiva University

May 2, 1979. At a convocation honoring Mr. Moshe Krone, head of the Department for Torah Education and Culture of the World Zionist Organization [17.06]

May 17, 1979. At the dedication of the renovated Bet Hamedrash in the Main Academic Center in honor of Mr. Joseph Gruss [15.01]

8. Lectures for Social Workers at Yeshiva University

ca. 1972. Lecture on "The Institution of Marriage" [7.04].

December 24, 1973. Lecture entitled: "Holy Days and Weekdays" [15.02]

March 13, 1974. Lecture to the faculty of the Wurzweiler School of Social Work [21.08]

March 6, 1975. Lecture to the National Association of Traditional Communal Workers [21.06]

9. Lectures at Yeshiva University's Institute of Mental Health Project

February 5, 1959 [15.04].

February 12, 1959 [18.01].

February 26, 1959 [6.10, 13.01, 18.02].

10. Lectures to the Yeshiva University Rabbinic Alumni

February 8, 1955. Lecture at YURA Midwinter Conference [1.03, 6.07].

ca. 1955. Lecture on "Covenants in the Book of Genesis" [12.08, 14.02, 16.01, 17.07, 18.08].

May 18, 1955. Lecture on "The Role of the Rabbi" [14.03, 14.05, 14.07, 14.08, 19.07].

March 1, 1956. Lecture on "The Uniqueness of Yeshiva University" [21.02].

October 20, 1971. Lecture on Parshat Bereshit (Genesis 1:1–6:8) [19.03].

November 12, 1973. Lecture on Parshat Hayei Sarah (Genesis 23:1–25:18) [2.01, 11.01].

June 19, 1975. Lecture on Gerut [13.11, 20.10].

11. Shiurim and Lectures in Boston

March 30, 1957. Lecture on Parshat Tazria (Leviticus 12:1–13:59) [6.05].

May 4, 1968. Lecture on "The Sanctity of the Land" in honor of Israel Independence Day [17.04].

September 14, 1968. Lecture on the Saturday night before the recitation of the first Selihot [1.04].

December 18, 1971. Hanukah Lecture [16.03, 18.04, 18.10].

March 30, 1974. Memorial Lecture for ha-Rabbanit Tonya
Soloveitchik entitled: "The Story of the Exodus" [19.06].

12. Yarhei Kallah Lectures in Boston

August 28, 1974. Lecture on Rosh Hodesh [17.12, 17.13].

August 27, 1975. Lecture on Kriat ha-Torah [5.03, 5.16].

September 1, 1976. Lecture on "The Ramban's Critique on the *Sefer ha-Mitzvot* of the Rambam" [20.07].

August 28, 1979. Lecture on Sukkot [8.05].

August 25, 1981. Response to a presentation in the Rav's honor at the Yarhei Kallah [21.11].

13. Talmudic Shiurim in Boston

March 19, 1972 [12.02, 14.01].
July 18, 1974 [5.02, 7.02].

14. Tishah be-Av Kinot Lectures in Boston

August 13, 1978 [1.08, 9.07].
July 22, 1980 [9.06].
August 9, 1981 [18.09].

15. Teshuvah Drashot under the aegis of the Rabbinical Council of America

September 1968 [11.10].
October 7, 1970 [17.14, 19.08, 20.02].
September 1972 [15.05].
October 3, 1973 [7.03, 20.13].
September 23, 1974 [2.05, 2.08].
September 1975 [19.09].

16. Lectures for the the Rabbinical Council of America

February 7, 1968. Lecture on "The Abridged Havinenu Prayer" at RCA Midwinter Conference [5.08, 12.06, 19.04, 20.05].
June 30, 1970. Lecture on "Rashi on Aseret Hadibrot" at RCA Annual Convention [5.07, 5.09, 13.02, 14.04, 17.08, 19.10].
January 18, 1971. Lecture on "The Duties of the King" at RCA Midwinter Conference [3.03, 14.06, 17.10].
January 29, 1973. Lecture on "Mi-Macharat" at RCA Midwinter Conference [2.09, 6.04].
June 10, 1974. Lecture on Parshat Beha'alotkha (Numbers 8:1– 12:16) at RCA Dinner honoring Rabbi Israel Klavan [11.04].
June 27, 1974. Lecture on Parshat Hukat (Numbers 19:1–22:1) at RCA Annual Convention [13.04, 17.09].
June 4, 1975. Lecture on Parshat Shelakh Lekha (Numbers 13:1–15:41) at RCA Annual Convention [16.04].
June 20, 1977. Lecture on "The Profundity of Jewish Folk Wisdom" at RCA Annual Convention [11.07, 12.07, 18.06].
June 20, 1979. Response to Rabbi Israel Klavan's introduction at RCA Annual Convention [14.11].

ography* 259

17. Shiurim at Congregation Moriya

December 28, 1971 [7.06].
May 20, 1975 [1.07].
December 14, 1976. Eulogy for Rabbi Moshe Dovber Rivkin [2.03, 9.01, 19.02].

18. Special Addresses

November 17, 1955. Address at annual convention of American Mizrachi Organization [12.01].
December 6, 1972. Lecture on "The Synagogue as an Institution and as an Idea" at New York's Congregation Kehilath Jeshurun [14.10].
February 20, 1974. Sheva Berakhot talk in honor of David and Karen Klavan, Queens, N.Y. [13.10].
March 20, 1974. Talk at Pidyon ha-Ben of Zev Karasick at the Windermere Hotel, New York, N.Y. [20.01].
May 28, 1975. Lecture on "The Future of Jewish Education in America" at Lincoln Square Synagogue, New York, N.Y. [2.04, 19.11, 20.04, 20.06].
June 15, 1977. Sheva Berakhot talk in honor of Jacob and Cheryl Holzer, Queens, N.Y. [21.10].
May 27, 1979. Sheva Berakhot talk in honor of David and Rona Holzer, Queens, N.Y. [21.09].

19. Special Publications and Letters

April 11, 1941. Letter to Rabbi Israel Rosenberg [11.08].
May 27, 1960. "Al Ahavat ha-Torah u-Geulat Nefesh ha-Dor."
Ha-Doar, 1 Sivan 5720, pp. 519–523. Later published as 9:6 and 20:20 in Selected Chronological Bibliography of the Published Writings of Rabbi Joseph B. Soloveitchik [19.05].
April 21, 1961."Reb Chaim Heller–Shmuel ha-Katan Shel Doreinu." *Ha-Doar*, 5 Iyar 5721, pp. 400–405. Later published as 9:3 and 12:05 in Selected Chronological Bibliography of the Published Writings of Rabbi Joseph B. Soloveitchik" [5.11].
September 27, 1963. "Mah Dodekh Mi-Dod." *Ha-Doar*, 9 Tishrei 5724, pp. 752–759. Later published as 9:2 and 12:2 in Selected Chro-

nological Bibliography of the Published Writings of Rabbi Joseph B. Soloveitchik [17.03].

November 13, 1963. "Devorim." Address given at annual convention of Religious Zionists of America, 26 Heshvan–1 Kislev 5724, Long Beach, N.Y. Translated from the Yiddish and published by Yitzhak Raphael (Werfel). This address was published in another version as 7:3 in the Selected Chronological Bibliography of the Published Writings of Rabbi Joseph B. Soloveitchik [6.09].

September 5, 1975. Interview with Levi Yitzhak ha-Yerushalmi. Published in *Ma'ariv*, Ellul 29, 5735 [17.11].

February 1994 (date of publication). Talk at Brit Milah of a grandson. Published in *Mesorah* (Kashruth Division, Union of Orthodox Jewish Congregations of America), no. 9, pp. 69–70 [6.03].

Bibliography of Sources Cited by the Author

This Bibliography of Sources details the sources cited by the author in the Insights and their footnotes.

Details of the Rav's published writings cited by the author in the Insights are listed in the "Selected Bibliography of the Published Writings of Rabbi Joseph B. Soloveitchik."

The numbers in brackets refer to the location of the sources in the text.

1. Rabbinic Sources

Braun, Shlomo Zalman. *Sha'arim Metzuyanim be-Halakhah* on the *Kitzur Shulhan Arukh*. New York: Feldheim, 1952. [5.14]

Danzig, Avraham. *Hayyei Adam*. [1.08]

Feinstein, Moshe. *Igrot Moshe*, vol. 4, Even ha-Ezer. [17.08]

Henkin, Yosef Eliyahu. *Kitvei ha-Gaon Reb Yosef Eliyahu Henkin*. New York: Ezras Torah, vol. 1, 1980; vol. 2, 1989. [7.03]

Hoffman, David Zevi. *Melamed Leho'il*, vol. 3. [17.08]

Maimonides. *Mishneh Torah*: Hilkhot Shabbat 2:1–3. [10.06]

———. *Moreh Nevukhim*. [20.11]

Mishnah and Talmud

Avodah Zarah 19b. [9.08]

Hagigah 5b [1.02]

Kidushin 1:1. [13.09]

Megillah 4:6; 24a, and Rashi and Tosafot ad loc. [13.06]

Rosh Hashanah 19a. [5.01]

Sukkah 47a. [5.01]

Schachter, Hershel. *Beikvei ha-Tzohn*. Jerusalem: Hoza'ot Bet ha-Medrash d'Flatbush, 1997. [13.03]

———. *Nefesh ha-Rav*. Jerusalem: Reshit Yerushalayim, 1994. [3.01, 4.01, 4.02, 5.02, 5.14, 7.05, 13.04, 13.05, 13.07]

Shulhan Arukh and Commentaries

Even ha-Ezer

      6:8. [17.08]

      21:1. [4.06]

Mishnah Berurah

  to *Shulhan Arukh*: Orah Hayyim 58:1, (4). [5.04]

  to *Shulhan Arukh*: Orah Hayyim 235:1, (12) and *Biur Halakhah*. [5.04]

  to *Shulhan Arukh*: Orah Hayyim 639:5 (35). [5:01]

Orah Hayyim 294:1 and *Taz, Biur ha-Gra*, and *Mahzit ha-Shekel*, ad loc. [1.01]

————. 554:6 and *Mishnah Berurah* (11). [7.05]

————. 639:2; 640:4. [9.04]

————. 639:5 and 640:4 and *Mishnah Berurah* ad loc. [10.04]

Remah to *Shulhan Arukh*: Orah Hayyim 128:44; *Magen Avraham* (70); *Taz* (38); *Mishnah Berurah* (165–67); and *Arukh ha-Shulhan* 128:63–64. [13.05]

Rema to *Shulhan Arukh*: Orah Hayyim 142:1. [5.15]

Soloveichik, Ahron. *Od Yisrael Yosef Beni Hai.* Jerusalem: Yeshivas Brisk of Chicago, 1993. [13.12]

————. *Sefer Parach Mateh Aharon*, ed. David Applebaum. Jerusalem: Targum Hozaoh Le'or, 1997. [6.10]

Spektor, Yitzhak Elchanan. *Be'er Yitzhak* (1858).

————. *Nahal Yitzhak.* 2 vols. (1872, 1884).

————. *Ein Yitzhak.* 2 vols. (1889, 1895). [6.02]

Talmudic Encyclopedia, vol. 17. [16.01]

Volozhin, Chaim. Introduction to the commentary of the Vilna Gaon on the *Sifra di-Zeniu'ta*, published as an appendix to *Nefesh ha-Hayyim.* Jerusalem, 1973. [1.05]

————. Introduction to Vilna Gaon's *Biur ha-Gra* to *Shulhan Arukh*: Orah Hayyim. [1.05]

2. Hebrew Books

Dembitzer, Hayyim Nathan. *Kelilat Yofi.* New York: Hozaat Yisrael Zev, 1960. [1.01]

Eiger, Avraham, and Shelomo Eiger. *Toledot R. Akiva Eiger.* Berlin, 1862. [1.09]

Eliav, Mordechai, and Esriel Hildesheimer. *Bet ha-Medrash le-Rabanim be-Berlin, 1873–1938.* Jerusalem: Leo Baeck Institute, 1996. [21.02]

Encyclopedia Shel Goliyot: Sidrat Poland. Vol. 2, *Brisk de-Litta*, ed. Eliezer Steinman. Tel Aviv, 1954. [5.12]

Glitzenstein, Avraham Hanoch. *Sefer ha-Toldot: Rebbe Shneur Zalman mi-Ladi.* Kefar Habad: Kehot Publication Society, 1976. [9.01]

Kahane, Yitzchak Zev. *Sefer ha-Agunot.* Jerusalem: Mosad Harav Kook, 1954. [16.01]

Karlinsky, Chaim. *Ha-Rishon le-Sholshelet Brisk: Ha-Gaon Rav Yosef Ber Soloveitchik.* Jerusalem: Machon Yerushalayim, 1984. [4.02]

Katz, Dov. *Pulmus ha-Musar.* Jerusalem, 1972. [3.04]

———. *Tenuat ha-Musar,* vols. 1 and 2. Tel Aviv: Avraham Zioni Publishing House, 1958. [2.08, 8.02]

Klausner, Yisrael. *Korot Bet-ha-Almin ha-Yashan be-Vilna.* Vilna, 1935. [1.04, 15.01]

Lewin, Isaac, ed. *Eleh Ezkarah,* vol. 5. New York: Research Institute of Religious Jewry, 1963. [6.01]

Rabotenu she-ba-Golah. Jerusalem: Agudat Nahliel, 1996. [5.02]

Sefer Yevul Hayovloth. New York: Rabbi Isaac Elchanan Theological Seminary, 1986. [21.04]

Sharett, Moshe. *Mi-shut be-Asia: Yoman Masa.* Tel Aviv: Dvar, 1957. [16.06]

Sperling, Avraham. *Sefer Ta'amei ha-Minhagim u-Mekorei ha-Dinim.* Jerusalem: Eshkol, 1957. [4.05]

Stampfer, Shaul. *Ha-Yeshiva ha-Litait be-Hithavtah.* Jerusalem: Zalman Shazar Center for Jewish History, 1995. [3.01, 5.02]

Verdiger, Yaakov. *Edut le-Yisrael.* Tel Aviv: A. Gitler, n.d. [9.05]

Wertheim, Aaron. *Halakhot ve-Halihot be-Hasidut.* Jerusalem, Mosad Harav Kook, 1960. [2.08, 5.17]

Zevin, Shelomo Yosef. *Ishim ve-Shitot.* Tel Aviv: Bitan ha-Sefer, 1952. [6.01, 6.02, 6.13]

3. English Books

Bernstein, Louis. *Challenge and Mission: The Emergence of the English-Speaking Rabbinate.* New York: Shengold Publishers, 1982. [13.01]

Davis, Moshe. *The Emergence of Conservative Judaism.* Philadelphia: Jewish Publication Society, 1965. [21.04]

Freedman, Shalom. *In the Service of God: Conversations with Teachers of Torah in Jerusalem.* Northvale, N.J.: Jason Aronson., 1995. [2.04]

Gurock, Jeffrey S. *The Men and Women of Yeshiva.* New York: Columbia University Press, 1988. [21.04]

Horowitz, Raichel. *The Bostoner Rebbetzin Remembers.* New York: Mesorah Publications, 1996. [18.07]

Joselit, Jenna Weissman. *New York's Jewish Jews: The Orthodox Community in the Interwar Years.* Bloomington: Indiana University Press, 1990. [21.07]

Klaperman, Gilbert. *The Story of Yeshiva University: The First Jewish University in America.* Toronto: Macmillan Company, 1969. [21.04]

Meiselman, Shulamith Soloveitchik. *The Soloveitchik Heritage: A Daughter's Memoir.* Hoboken, N.J.: KTAV Publishing House, 1995. [1.04, 5.14, 7.04, 7.05, 7.07, 8.05, 9.01]

Rabinowicz, Harry. *A Guide to Hassidism.* London: Thomas Yoseloff, 1960. [2.01]

Rakeffet-Rothkoff, Aaron. *The Silver Era: Rabbi Eliezer Silver and His Generation.* Jerusalem: Feldheim Publishers, 1981. [6.12, 11.08, 18.07, 21.07]

Rosenblum, Yonason. *Reb Yaakov: The Life and Times of ha-Gaon Rabbi Yaakov Kamenetsky.* Brooklyn: Mesorah Publications, 1993. [8.02]

Shimoff, Ephraim. *Rabbi Isaac Elchanan Spektor: Life and Letters.* New York: Yeshiva University, 1959. [6.02]

Shirer, William L. *The Rise and Fall of the Third Reich.* New York: Simon & Schuster, 1960. [5.08, 18.04]

Waxman, Meyer. *A History of Jewish Literature*, vol. 4. New York: Bloch Publishing Co., 1947. [15.04]

4. English Articles

Boylan, Stanley. "Learning With the Rav: Learning From the Rav." *Tradition*, vol. 30, no. 4 (Summer 1996), pp. 131–144. [21.11]

Carmy, Shalom. "On Eagle's Flight and Snail's Pace." *Tradition*, vol. 29, no. 1 (Fall 1994), pp. 21–31. [19.04]

Genack, Menachem. "Walking with Ramban." *Tradition*, vol. 30, no. 4 (Summer 1996), pp. 182–192. [1.06, 19.12]

Lichtenstein, Aharon. "Brother Daniel and the Jewish Fraternity." *Judaism*, vol. 12 no. 3 (Summer 1963), pp. 260–280. [6.11]

———. "The Rav at Jubilee: An Appreciation." *Tradition*, vol. 30, no. 4 (Summer 1996), pp. 45–57. [19.05, 21.08]

Lichtenstein, Mosheh. "For My Grandfather Has Left Me." *Tradition*, vol. 30, no. 4 (Summer 1996), pp. 58–78. [21.08]

Liebman, Charles S. "Orthodoxy in American Jewish Life." *American Jewish Year Book: 1965*, ed. Morris Fine and Milton Himmelfarb. Philadelphia: Jewish Publication Society, 1965, pp. 21–97. [21.08]

Rosensweig, Bernard. "The Rabbinical Council of America: Retrospect and Prospect." *Tradition*, vol. 22, no. 2 (Summer 1986), pp. 2–15. [21.07]

Soloveitchik, Haym. "Rupture and Reconstruction: The Transformation of Contemporary Orthodoxy." *Tradition*, vol. 28, no. 4 (Summer 1994), pp. 64–130. [19.04]

Twersky, Mayer. "A Glimpse of the Rav." *Tradition*, vol. 30, no. 4 (Summer 1996), pp. 79–114. [20.07]

Twersky, Yitzchak. "The Rov." *Tradition*, vol. 30, no. 4 (Summer 1996), pp. 13–44. [21.08]

Wolowelsky, Joel B. "Modern Orthodoxy and Woman's Self-Perception." *Tradition*, vol. 22, no. 1 (Spring 1986), pp. 65–81. [13.12]

Wurzburger, Walter. "Rav Joseph B. Soloveitchik as Posek of Post-Modern Orthodoxy." *Tradition*, vol. 29, no. 1 (Fall 1994), pp. 5–20. [16.01]

5. Hebrew Articles

Horowitz, Rivkah. "Yitzhak Breuer, Franz Rosenzweig and Rabbi A. I. Kook." In *Torah im Derekh Eretz Movement*, ed. Mordechai Breuer. Ramat Gan, Israel: Bar-Ilan University, 1987, pp. 109–131. [15.05]

Lichtenstein, Aharon. "Divrei Hesped al Maran ha-Gaon Rav Josef Dov ha-Levi Soloveitchik." *Mesorah*, no. 9 (February 1994), pp. 8–33. [19.12]

———. "Ha-Tefilah be-Mishnato shel ha-Gaon Rav Josef Dov Soloveitchik." *Shanah be-Shanah: 5759*, vol. 39, pp. 287–301. [5.04].

Mirsky, Samuel K. "Yeshivat Volozhin." *Mosdot Torah be-Europah be-Vinyanam u-be-Hurbanam*. New York: Histadruth Ivrith of America, 1956, pp. 1–86. [1.05]

Schachter, Hershel. "Me-Peninei Rabenu Zal." In *Bet Yitzhak*, ed. Zvi David Romm and Azriel Rosner. New York: Student Organization of Yeshiva, 1995, pp. 1–20. [21.05]

Soloveitchik, Joseph B. "Mitzvat Yeshivat Sukkah," ed. Harold Reichman. In *Bet Yosef Shaul*, New York: Gruss Kollel Elyon of Yeshiva Rabbi Isaac Elchanan Theological Seminary, 1985, vol. 1, pp. 9–21. [10.04]

6. Newspapers and Letters

Commentator (undergraduate newspaper of Yeshiva Collge), April 15, 1970; March 22, 1994. [21.03]

Jerusalem Post, June 17, 1970. [17.08]

Karasick, Joseph. Letter to the author, May 13, 1996.[20.01]

7. Interviews

Derovan, Rabbi David. Interviewed by Joseph Epstein, June 20, 1993. [3.02]

Genack, Rabbi Menachem. Interviewed by Aaron Rakeffet, January 25, 1993. [19.12]

Horowitz, Rabbi Levi Yitzchak (Bostoner Rebbe). Interviewed by Joseph Epstein, April 29, 1993 and April 5, 1994. [4.06, 5.01, 13.09]

Kasdan, Rabbi Menachem. Interviewed by Joseph Epstein, May 13, 1993. [2.06, 9.02]

Lichtenstein, Dr. Tovah. Interviewed by Aaron Rakeffet, February 18, 1994. [9.04, 9.05, 13.09]

Shurkin, Rabbi Michel. Interviewed by Joseph Epstein, March 27, 1993. [17.01]

Soloveichik, Rabbi Yosef. Interviewed by Aaron Rakeffet, February 16, 1992. [5.13]

Soloveitchik, Rabbi Joseph B. Interviewed by Aaron Rakeffet, August 12, 1978. [21.08]

———. Interviewed in *Ma'ariv*, October 28, 1977, p. 25. [2.07]

8. Lectures

Klavan, Rabbi Israel. Introducing the Rav at RCA Annual Convention, June 20, 1979. [9.08]

Schachter, Rabbi Hershel. Lecture in memory of the Rav at Congregation Kehilath Jeshurun, New York, N.Y., January 5, 1994. [10.06]

Supplementary Index to the Insights

The selection of the headings of the "Insights" was based upon considering the main theme of each "Insight". These volumes have been organized upon these main themes as stated in the "Table of Contents".

Nevertheless, many of the Insights contain multiple themes. To facilitate and enable the full utilization of the Insights, the following supplementary index of secondary themes has been compiled. To ease the usage of this supplementary index, each topical area first restates the primary sources which are then supplemented by the listings of the secondary themes.

Supplementary Index

3.03	Amalek	*The Volozhin Yeshiva*
9.01	Khaslavichy's Rabbis	*Khaslavichy*
9.02	Spying for the Czarist Army	*Khaslavichy*
15.05	Franz Rosenzweig	*Jewish Laymen*
17.06	Mizrachi Leaders	*Zionism and Redemption*
19.05	Experiencing the High Holiday Days	*Religious Sensitivity*
19.12	Teaching a Hasidic Text	*Religious Sensitivity*
19.13	Two Traditions; Two Communities	*Religious Sensitivity*
20.12	The Hundred and First Time	*The Study of Torah*
20.13	Relearning is Harder	*The Study of Torah*

The Volozhin Yeshiva

3.01	Constant Torah Study	*The Volozhin Yeshiva*
3.02	Pride and Vanity	*The Volozhin Yeshiva*
3.03	Amalek	*The Volozhin Yeshiva*
3.04	Rejecting Mussar	*The Volozhin Yeshiva*
3.05	Unresolved Questions	*The Volozhin Yeshiva*
5.01	Succot in Volozhin	*Reb Chaim Soloveitchik*
5.02	Intellectual Honesty	*Reb Chaim Soloveitchik*
7.02	Grandfathers in Debate	*Reb Eliyahu Feinstein*

Reb Yosef Baer Soloveitchik

4.01	Modern Clothes	*Reb Yosef Baer Soloveitchik*
4.02	The Slutzk Rabbinate	*Reb Yosef Baer Soloveitchik*
4.03	Twelve Thousand Signatures	*Reb Yosef Baer Soloveitchik*
4.04	The Traefe Chicken	*Reb Yosef Baer Soloveitchik*
4.05	Seudah Shlishit	*Reb Yosef Baer Soloveitchik*
4.06	The Singing Maid	*Reb Yosef Baer Soloveitchik*
4.07	Enmity Between Litigants	*Reb Yosef Baer Soloveitchik*
5.14	A Special Request	*Reb Chaim Soloveitchik*
14.01	What is a Rabbi?	*The American Rabbinate*
19.09	Fear and Joy	*Religious Sensitivity*
19.12	Teaching a Hasidic Text	*Religious Sensitivity*
20.08	The Torah Highway	*The Study of Torah*

Reb Chaim Soloveitchik

5.01	Succot in Volozhin	*Reb Chaim Soloveitchik*
5.02	Intellectual Honesty	*Reb Chaim Soloveitchik*
5.03	The Torah reading in Vilna	*Reb Chaim Soloveitchik*
5.04	Communal Prayer	*Reb Chaim Soloveitchik*
5.05	Justice and Righteousness	*Reb Chaim Soloveitchik*
5.06	Uncircumcised Jewish Infants	*Reb Chaim Soloveitchik*
5.07	The Role of the Rabbi	*Reb Chaim Soloveitchik*
5.08	The Master of Benevolence	*Reb Chaim Soloveitchik*
5.09	Unity in Serving G-d	*Reb Chaim Soloveitchik*
5.10	Courage and Justice	*Reb Chaim Soloveitchik*

Indicies to the Insights[*]

Names

Abaye – 1.02, 12.01, 21.01

[R.] Abba – 17.05

Abraham – 12.02, 14.07, 14.10, 16.05, 17.10, 18.08

[Rav] Aha the son of Rav Ika – 5.02

Ahasuerus – 18.06

[R.] Akiva – 20.01

Alexander [of Macedon] – 18.10

Aloni, Shulamit – 17.13

Altenberg, Peter [Pseudonym of Richard Englaender] – 15.02

Amalek – 17.13, 18.03

Apion – 16.03

Aristotle – 14.01, 15.03, 17.09, 21.04

Aronowitz, Binyamin – 21.04

Ashkenazi, Bezalel – 5.08

Ashkenazi, Yisrael – 9.01, 9.02

Ba'al Halakhot Gedolot [of the Geonic period] – 20.07

Ba'alei Tosafot – 20.05

Bahk [R. Joel Sirkes] – 1.01

Balaam – 16.05

Bar Abbuha – 1.02

Ben Gurion, David – 17.10, 18.02

Beres, Berel – 15.01

Berlin, Chaim – 1.09, 5.02

Berlin [Bar-Ilan], Meir – 5.05, 5.07, 5.17, 21.02

Berlin, Naftali Zvi Yehudah [a.k.a The Netziv of Volozhin and Reb Herschel Leib] – 1.09, 3.01, 3.04, 3.05, 5.02, 7.02, 14.07

Bet Shmuel [authored by R. Shmuel ben Uri Shraga Feibush] – 21.02

Bialik, Hayyim Nahman – 17.04, 21.03

Blaser, Yitzhak – 3.04

Bornstein, Avraham – 17.06

Bornstein, Shmuel – 17.06

Breuer, Yitzhak – 15.05

Brezhnev, Leonid – 13.02, 16.03, 18.03

Buber, Martin – 15.05

Ceausescu, Nicolae – 17.09

Charlemagne – 18.01

Churchill, Winston – 18.08

Danzig, Abraham – 21.02

David [King] – 18.08

David b. Samuel – see Taz

Jacob, the blacksmith [of
  Khaslavichy] – 2.04
James, William – 20.06
Johnson, Lyndon B. – 15.03
Jonah – 18.01, 18.02
Joseph – 14.10, 15.01, 16.08
Joshua – 17.03
Jung, Leo – 21.07
Kant, Immanuel - 14.01
Karo, Yosef [author of the Shulhan
  Arukh and the Bet Yosef] – 14.08,
  15.01
Kennedy. John – 11.09, 15.03
Kennedy, Joseph – 11.09
Kennedy, Robert – 11.09
Kennedy, Rose Fitzgerald – 11.09
Khrushchev, Nikita – 13.02
Kissinger, Henry – 17.09, 17.12,
  17.13, 21.06
Klavan, Israel – 14.11
Kosygin, Aleksei – 13.02
Krakowsky, Menachem – 17.01
Krone, Moshe – 17.06
Lamm, Norman – 17.06
Landau, Shmuel Hayyim – 17.06
Lapidot, Alexander Moses – 8.02
Leibniz, Gottfried Wilhelm – 14.01
Leibowitz, Baruch Baer – 8.02, 12.04
Levi Yitzhak [of Berdichev] – 9.02
Levovitz, Yeruchem – 3.04, 20.11
Lichtenstein, Tovah – 21.09
Lieberman, Saul – 13.04
Lifshitz, Chaim Zalman – 5.10
Lookstein, Joseph – 14.10, 21.07
Lorbeerbaum, Yaakov – 20.05, 20.07,
  20.09
Lublin, Meir – see Maharam Lublin
Luria, Shlomo – see Maharshal
Luria, Yitzhak [[Ha-Ari] – 2.09
Luzzatto, Moshe Chaim – 5.08, 14.01
Luzzatto, Shmuel David – 13.03

Maharam Lublin [R. Meir Lublin] –
  1.01
Maharil [R. Jacob Moellin] - 1.01
Maharshal [R. Shlomo Luria] – 1.01
Maimonides [Rambam] – 5.04, 5.08,
  8.01, 8.02, 14.02, 14.08, 15.01,
  17.02, 17.09, 17.10, 20.01, 20.07,
  20.11, 21.02, 21.03, 21.11
Mao Tse-tung – 18.03
Marx, Karl – 13.02, 16.03
McCarthy, Joseph – 13.01, 14.03
Medini, Chaim Hezekiah – 5.02
Meir [of Rothenberg] – 16.03
Meiselman, Shulamith Soloveitchik –
  11.07
Meislisch, Moshe – 9.01, 9.02
Mittwoch, Eugen – 21.02, 21.03
Moellin, Jacob – see Maharil
Mohammed – 16.05
Montefiore, Moses – 15.01
Mordecai – 11.05, 15.03, 18.06
Moses [Moshe Rabbenu] – 14.10,
  15.01, 18.08, 20.09
Nahmanides [Ramban] – 15.01,
  20.05, 20.07, 21.02, 21.03
Napoleon [Napoleon Bonaparte] –
  9.01, 9.02
Nasser, Gamal Abdel – 13.02
Netziv of Volozhin – see Berlin,
  Naftali Zvi Yehudah
Nicholas I – 3.03, 4.01
Nixon, Richard – 17.09, 21.06
Orenstein, Yaakov Meshullem – 14.01
Orenstein, Zevi Hirsch – 14.01
Padua, Yaakov Meir – 14.01
Pasweiler, Abale – 1.08
Peretz, Isaac Leib – 15.04, 19.12
Pharaoh – 16.08, 18.05
Plato – 15.03, 17.09, 21.09
Plotsky, Moshe – 6.09
Podgorny, Nikolai – 13.02

14.02, 14.03, 14.07, 14.11, 15.03,
17.03, 18.09, 19.03, 19.04, 19.05,
19.13, 20.03, 20.05, 20.11, 20.12,
21.02
Soloveichik, Pesia Feinstein – 5.14,
7.05, 8.01, 11.10, 14.06, 19.13,
20.10, 20.11
Soloveichik, Samuel – 20.10
Soloveitchik, Chaim – 1.10, 1.04,
2.02, 2.03, 3.04, 4.07, 5.01, 5.02,
5.03, 5.04, 5.05, 5.06, 5.07, 5.08,
5.09, 5.10, 5.11, 5.12, 5.13, 5.14,
5.15, 5.16, 5.17, 5.18, 6.01, 6.02,
6.03, 6.04, 6.05, 6.06, 6.07, 6.08,
6.09, 6.10, 6.11, 6.12, 6.13, 7.01,
7.02, 7.03, 7.05, 8.03, 8.04, 10.02,
10.06, 12.04, 13.11, 14.01, 14.02,
14.03, 15.03, 15.04, 17.01, 17.02,
17.11, 19.03, 19.04, 19.06, 19.08,
19.09, 20.01, 20.03, 20.07, 20.09,
20.10, 20.11, 20.12, 21.02, 21.03
Soloveitchik, Haym – 21.09
Soloveitchik, Lipsha Shapiro – 5.01,
5.02
Soloveitchik, Tonya Lewit – 11.02,
11.04, 11.05, 11.06, 11.07, 11.10,
15.01, 20.02, 20.10
Soloveitchik, Yitzhak Zev – 5.08, 9.08,
17.03
Soloveitchik, Yosef Baer – 1.01, 1.04,
4.01, 4.02, 4.03, 4.04, 4.05, 4.06,
4.07, 5.14, 5.17, 6.01, 14.01,
19.09, 19.12, 20.08
Spektor, Yitzhak Elchanan – 5.02,
6.02, 6.05, 14.07
Stalin, Joseph – 18.03
[Rabbenu] Tam – 5.04, 8.01, 14.03,
14.08, 20.01
Taz [R. David b. Samuel] – 1.01,
14.07, 14.08, 20.05
Toynbee, Arnold – 18.08

Truman, Harry – 18.06
Trunk, Isaac Judah – 17.06
Twersky, Atarah – 21.09
Twersky, Isadore – 20.10
Twersky, Mayer – 20.10
Twersky, Moshe – 20.10
Twersky, Rebecca – 19.13
Vastolher, Elya – 9.06, 18.09
Vespasian – 18.08
Vilna Gaon [R. Elijah b. Solomon
Zalman] – 1.04, 1.05, 1.06, 1.07,
2.01, 3.01, 5.08, 5.17, 7.07, 9.01,
9.02, 13.12, 15.01, 15.03, 20.05,
20.11, 21.02
Volozhin, Chaim – 1.01, 1.04, 1.05,
3.01, 3.02, 3.03, 15.01, 17.14
Volozhin, Relka – 17.14
Volozhin, Yitzhak – 3.03, 7.02
Wallace, Henry – 18.07
Weizmann, Chaim – 17.02
Yehudah, Halevi – 17.05
[Rabban] Yohanan ben Zakkai –
14.07, 18.08
[R.] Yose b. Kisma – 17.03
Yosef, Ovadiah – 5.02

Places

Alexandria – 16.03
Algeria – 18.02
Altona – 14.03
America – 2.07, 12.03, 12.04, 12.06,
12.09, 13.01,13.02, 14.02, 14.04,
14.05, 14.06, 14.07, 14.10, 15.04,
16.01, 16.02, 16.03, 16.04, 17.03,
17.07, 17.10, 18.02, 18.04, 18.06,
18.07, 19.03, 19.04, 19.08, 19.11,
20.05, 21.02, 21.03, 21.08, 21.09.
Asia – 16.06
Auschwitz – 18.05, 18.07
Australia – 16.01
Babylonia – 21.01

Glossary

afikoman — the final *matzah* eaten at the *seder*

aggadah — non-halakhic rabbinic teachings

agunah (pl. agunot) — a woman who cannot clearly establish that her missing husband is dead

aharon (pl. aharonim) — later rabbinic scholar

Al Het — Yom Kippur confessional prayer

aliyah — 1. being called up to the reading of the Torah
2. emigrating to the Land of Israel

am ha-aretz (pl. amei ha-aretz) — an unlearned Jew

am ha-aretz mideoraita — a most unlearned Jew

am yisrael — the Jewish nation

Amidah — the standing prayer consisting of nineteen blessings. Also known as the "*Shemonah Esreh*"

amkha-yisrael — Thy people Israel

aninut — the period of grief between death and burial of a close relative

apikores — a Jew who does not believe in the Torah

Aron ha-Kodesh — the Holy Ark

Aseret ha-Dibrot — the Ten Commandments

asher lo yada et yosef — that did not know Joseph

ashkenaz — a Jew or tradition of German or East European origins

av zaken — aged father

avelut — mourning

avi rabi u-mori — my father, rabbi and teacher

avodah — sacrificial ritual of the High Priest in the Temple on Yom Kippur

avodah she-be-lev — heartfelt worship

avodat hashem — worship of the Almighty

291

ba'al habayit — layman (lit. one who owns a house)

ba'al ha-Tanya — the author of the Tanya, Reb Shneur Zalman of Ladi (1745-1813)

ba'al hesed — a person constantly doing acts of benevolence

ba'al koreh — the reader of the Torah scroll

ba'al shaharit — leader of the morning prayers

ba'alei batim — laymen

ba'alei teresim — warriors (lit. shield bearers)

ba'alei teshuvah — returnees to Torah observance

ba'alei tosafot — authors of the *Tosafot* (lit. additions) commentaries on the Talmud

ba'alei zedakah — charitable people

baki — a knowledgeable person in all aspects of rabbinic literature

bannai (pl. bannaim) — Torah scholars (lit. builder)

be-hesed elyon — par excellence

ben Torah — devotee of Torah

Bet ha-Mikdash — The Holy temple

Bet Medrash — study hall

bimah — the elevated platform on which the Torah scroll is read

binyon ha-Aretz — building of the Land of Israel

birkhat ha-Torah — blessings recited before the study of the Torah

birkhat Kohanim — the Priestly benedictions

blat — a Talmudic folio

brit (pl. britot) — circumcision ceremony

Chabad — see Habad

chavruta — Torah study mate

chesed (hesed) — acts of kindness

Chinuch Atzmai — the independent school system of Agudath Israel in the State of Israel

chupah — the marriage canopy

chutzpah — impudence

daas Torah — the concept of the supreme authority of Torah sages associated with Agudath Israel

daven — pray

dayyan — rabbinical judge

din Torah (pl. dinei Torah) — litigation before a rabbinical court

dinei mamonot — civil laws

drashah (pl. drashot, derashot) — lecture or sermon

drush — homiletics

dukhan — to recite the Priestly benedictions
ehrlicher yid — an honest and pious Jew
Eicah — Lamentations
emunah — faith
Eretz Yisrael — the Land of Israel
eretz yisroeldicker ma'aseh — an exaggerated story (lit. a story from *Eretz Yisrael*)
erev — the day before the Sabbath or a festival
eruv (pl. eruvim) — a symbolic partition which permits carrying on the Sabbath
eshkol (pl. eshkolot) — outstanding rabbinic scholar (lit. grape cluster)
esrog (ethrog) — a citron for use with the *lulav* during the *Sukkot* festival
Ezra ha-Sofer — Ezra the scribe

farbrengen — hasidic festive gathering
frum — pious

gabbai (pl. gabbaim) — manager or director of the synagogue ritual
gaon — an eminent rabbinic scholar
gaon olam — universally respected rabbinic scholar
gedolei yisrael — rabbinic scholars and leaders
Gemara (Gemora) — the Talmud
gemilat hasadim — acts of loving-kindness
ger zedek — a male righteous convert
gerut — conversion
get — divorce document
gevalt — outcry
giyores ha-zedek — a female righteous convert
gut yom tov — the festival greeting (lit. a good festival)

ha ahavah ha-tivit — the basic commitment of a Jew to Judaism (lit. natural love)
Habad — the philosophy of the Lubavitch hasidic movement (lit. acronym of *hokhmah, binah, da'as*— "wisdom, understanding and knowledge")
hag ha-semikhah — the celebration of the rabbinic ordination ceremony
haggadah — the liturgy of the seder service on the night of Passover
hakafot — procession of the Torah scrolls around the synagogue
hakhmat ha-Torah —Torah wisdom
hakhmei yisrael — great rabbinical scholars
halakhah — Jewish law

hallah — bread eaten on the Sabbath and Festivals
Hashem — the Almighty
hasid — a follower of the hasidic sect (lit. pious)
hasidei elyon — true saints
hasidishe ma'aseh — a hasidic story
havdalah — the blessing recited at the conclusion of the Sabbath (lit. differentiation)
haver le-deah — a friend of similar views
hazal — the Talmudic sages (lit. the Hebrew acronym for our "sages, may their memory be for a blessing")
hazzan — the leader of prayers
heder — esp. in Europe, a Jewish elementary school
hefker — ownerless
hesed — see *chesed*
hevrah kadishah — burial society
hevrah shas —Talmudic study group
hiddush — new intellectual insight
hiddushei Torah — original Torah insights
hokhmat yisrael — scientific Jewish scholarship
hol ha-moed — intermediate days of the festival
humash — the Five Books of Moses

Ichud ha-Yeshivos — council of Yeshivot
imi morati — my mother, my teacher
inyana de-yoma — the unique sanctity of each holy day
ir ha-nidahat — the wayward city [Deuteronomy 13:13-19]
ish hasid — a pious individual
ispravnic — Chief of Police [Russian]

Kabalah — tradition. Also a system of esoteric Jewish theology
kabalat panim — a reception or collation
Kaddish — prayer recited in memory of the departed
kadosh — a holy person
kapote — a long coat worn especially by male Jews of Eastern Europe
kaved — heavy
kavod — honor
kedushah — sanctity
kedushat ha-yom — the sanctity of the holy days
kehunah — the priesthood
kelapei hutz — external affairs
keria — tearing ones garment as an act of mourning

ke-she-amedah — to oppose (lit. when she rose up)

ketav rabbanut — rabbinical appointment

ketuvah — marriage document

kiddush — the blessings recited over a cup of wine at the start of the Sabbath or a festival

kiddush ha-levanah — the blessing recited over the new moon

kiddush Hashem — the act of sanctifying the Almighty's name

kinah (pl. kinot) — elegies recited on the Ninth of *Av*

kinus teshuvah — a gathering to hear a lecture on repentance

kittel — a white garment worn by pious men on the High Holidays and at the Passover *Seder*

klal — the entire community

Kodashim — sacrificial ritual division of the Talmud (lit. hallowed things)

kohen (pl kohanim) — priest descended from Aaron *ha-Kohen*

kohen ha-gadol — the High Priest

Kol Nidre — the prayer that begins the Yom Kippur eve service (lit. all our vows)

kulot — lenient halakhic rulings

la'asok be-divrei Torah — the blessing for the study of Torah (lit. to be involved with the study of Torah)

lamdan (pl. lamdanim, lomdim) — learned Jewish scholars

lamed vav nistarim — the thirty-six hidden saints

Levi — descendant of the tribe of Levi

litveshe — following the Lithuanian tradition. Generally in contradistinction to the Hasidic tradition

lomdut — unique method of advanced Torah study

lulav — a palm branch for use with the *etrog* during the *Sukkot* festival

ma'amarim — essays

ma'ariv — the evening prayer service

ma'aseh — story

Mafdal — the Hebrew acronym for the Israeli Religious Zionist political party

maftir — the final portion of the torah reading on the Sabbath and Festivals which is followed by the Haftorah (prophetic reading)

maftir Yonah — the reading of the Book of Jonah during the afternoon service on Yom Kippur

maggid shiur — Talmudic lecturer

mahshavah — philosophical thought

mahzor — the High Holiday Prayer book

makor — origin

malkhut — kingship or royalty

malkhuyot (malkiyot) — the kingship prayers recited on Rosh Hashanah as part of the Musaf service

malkot — punishment of lashes

mamzerut — a child born of certain forbidden marriages

mashgiach — 1. supervisor of kashruth
     2. supervisor of the spiritual atmosphere of a yeshiva

mashpiah — one who influences others

matanah — gift

matmid — diligent rabbinical scholar

megillah — the scroll of Esther read on Purim

meikel — to be lenient

mehalkhim — those who enter the outside world (lit. walkers)

mehudar — beautiful (*etrog*)

mekabbel — recipient

melamed — teacher, especially of young children

melihah — salting of meat as part of the *kashering* process

mesader kiddushin — the officiant at a wedding ceremony

mesekhet — a tractate of the Talmud

meshumad — an apostate

meshuganer — crazy person

mesorah — tradition

me'un — a minor bride's rejection of her husband

mezorah — a person afflicted by leprosy

middah megunah — a deplorable trait

mide-oraita — from the Torah

midrash (pl. midrashim) — exegetical rabbinic interpretations of the Bible

mikveh — ritualarium for immersion in water

minhag — custom

minhah — the afternoon prayer

minyan — quorum of ten males required for public worship

mishnah (pl. mishnayot) — the basic text of the Oral tradition

mispar ha-dorot — the number of generations

mitnaged (pl. mitnagdim) — those opposed to the Hasidic innovations

mitnagdishe (misnagdishe) — in the fashion of the *mitnagdim*

mitzvah (pl. Mitzvot) — Divine commandment

Moed — the division of the Talmud devoted to the laws of the Festivals (lit. "Festival")

mofes (pl. mofsim) — miracle

Moshe Rabenu — Moses our teacher

moshiach — messiah
motzai shabbat (motzoay shabbat) — Saturday night
murkav — an *etrog* which is a hybrid
Musaf — the additional prayer on the Sabbath and the Festivals
musar — moral instruction
musar avikha — the instruction of your father
musmach — one who has received rabbinical ordination

narishkeit — foolishness
nasi — head of the *Sanhedrin*
Nashim — the division of the Talmud devoted to the laws of marriage, divorce, and vows (lit. "Women")
nazir — a person who vows abstinence (see Numbers 6:2)
Neilah — the service concluding Yom Kippur
Nephilim — giants who fell (see Genesis 6:4)
Nezikin — the division of the Talmud devoted to the laws of damages
nisah — lofty

oved hashem — a servant of the Almighty

parshah — the section of the Torah read on the Sabbath
Pesach — the Passover festival
pesak halakhah — a decision rendered on a question of Jewish law
pesharah — compromise
Pesukei de-zimra — verses of praise recited as part of the Morning Prayers
pidyon ha-ben — redeeming the first born
pikuach nefesh — saving a life or danger to life
pittum — tip of the *etrog*
podrabin — assistant to the rabbi [Russian]
porush — an ascetic individual
posek (pl. posekim) — rabbinic scholar who decides questions of Jewish law
posek shealot — deciding questions of Jewish law

rabbanut — rabbinate
rabossai — gentlemen
ram — high
rav ha-hesed — the master of benevolence
rebbe — teacher
rebbe muvhak — a student's main teacher

rebbetzin — the wife of a rabbi
refuah shlemah min ha-shamayim — May the Almighty grant a speedy recovery
resh — the 20th letter of the Hebrew alphabet
ribono-shel-Olam — The Master of the Universe, i.e. the Almighty
rishon (pl. rishonim) — early rabbinic authority
rosh ha-medabrim — prime spokesman
Rosh Hashanah — the Jewish New Year
rosh yeshiva — a teacher of Talmud in an advanced Yeshiva
Rosh ha-Yeshiva — the head of a yeshiva
sandek — the person who holds the child on his lap during the circumcision ceremony
seder — the Passover eve family ritual
sedra (sidra) — the weekly Torah portion
sefer Torah — the Torah Scroll
sefirah — the counting of the forty-nine days between Passover and Shavuot
segulah — unique trait
semikhah — rabbinical ordination
sephardic — Jews of Spain and Portugal and their descendants
seudah shlishit — the third meal eaten on the Sabbath
shabbat ha-gadol — the great Sabbath before Passover
Shabbat — Sabbath
shabbat teshuvah — the Sabbath of repentance before Yom Kippur
shaharit — the morning prayer service
shaliakh tzibbur — cantor (lit. the messenger of the community)
shas — the entire Talmud
Shavuot — Feast of Weeks, seven weeks after Passover
she'aleh — see *sheilah*
Shehehiyanu blessing — the blessing recited upon achieving a new milestone in life
sheilah (pl. sheilot) — question of Jewish law
shekatzim — hoodlums
Shekhinah — the Divine Presence
shelishi — the third aliyah to the Torah
Shema — The "Hear, O Israel" prayer
Shemonah Esreh — the standing prayer originally consisting of eighteen blessings (also known as *Amidah*)
sheretz — the contaminating carcass of a creeping animal
Shir ha-Shirim — Song of Songs
shiur — class, lecture

shivah — the seven days of mourning

shmad — apostasy

Shmini Atzeret — the holiday of the Eighth Day appended to the Holiday of Sukkot

shofar — the ram's horn blown on Rosh Hashanah and at the conclusion of Yom Kippur

shohet (pl. shohatim) — ritual slaughterer

shomer mitzvot — an observant Jew (lit. one who observes *mitzvot*)

shlishi — the third *aliyah* to the Torah

shtat — city or town

shtiebel (pl. shtiblach) — small synagogue, generally hasidic

shul — synagogue

sidra — the Torah portion for the week

sihas hullin — mundane speech

siyyum (pl. siyyumim) — conclusion of a tractate of rabbinic literature

sonei yisrael — haters of the Jewish people

sugya — a Talmudic theme

sukkah — booth built for the celebration of *Sukkot*

Sukkot — the festival of Tabernacles

tahnun (tahanun) — supplication prayer recited on weekdays

talmid (pl. talmidim) — student

talmid hakham — rabbinic scholar

tanna bathra — the last opinion in the Mishnah

tanna kamah — the first opinion in the *Mishnah*

tanu rabbanan — the rabbis taught

tefillin — phylacteries

Tehillim — Psalms

teku — an unresolved Talmudic question

teshuvah — repentance

teshuvah drasha — sermon on repentance

Tisha be-Av — Ninth of *Av* fast day on the anniversary of the destruction of the Temple

Tohorot — Division of the Talmud devoted to the laws of purity (lit. cleanliness)

torah li-shemah — Torah studied for its own sake

Torah shebe'al peh — The oral tradition

Torah she-bikhtav — The written Torah

torat imekha — the teachings of the mother

tosefet shabbat — the additional time added before and after the Sabbath

treif — non kosher

trop — the cantillation traditionally ascribed to the Torah text
tumah (tumot) — impurity
tumat ha-met — defilement engendered by the dead
tzedakah — charity
tzimtzum — withdrawal, limitation

vaad hair — the city council or governing body
vaad hayeshivas — the joint governing body of various yeshivot
ve-ha-lomdah — those who study the Torah
ve-hu ha-ketz — the appointed time i.e. the redemption
ve-hu rahum — the prayer requesting the Almighty's mercy

ya'aleh ve-yavoh — prayer added to the *Amidah* on New Moons and Festivals (lit. ascend and come)
Yahadut — Judaism
yahrzeit — anniversary of the day of death
yarchei kallah — public study sessions
yarmulka — skullcap
yasher koach — thanks (lit. more strength to you)
Yekum Purkan — Aramaic prayer recited on the Sabbath (lit. may salvation arise)
yeled zekunim — young child of an aged father
Yisrael — Israel
yishuv — the Jewish community of *Eretz Yisrael*
yizkor — memorial prayer
Yom Kippur — Day of Atonement
yom tov — festival
yomim noraim — High Holy Days (lit. Days of Awe)
yomom velailah — day and night, i.e. constant
yoshvim — those who withdraw from the outside world (lit. sitters)

zady — grandfather
zav — a person contaminated with venereal disease
Zeraim — the Division of the Talmud dealing with agricultural laws (lit. seeds)
zikhronot — sentences of remembrances recited on Rosh Hashanah as part of the Musaf service
zizit — fringes
z"l — Hebrew abbreviation recalling the memory of the departed for a blessing (zikhrono li'vracha)
zocheh — privileged

ABOUT THE AUTHOR

Dr. Aaron Rakeffet-Rothkoff, Professor of Rabbinic Literature at Yeshiva University's Caroline and Joseph S. Gruss Institute in Jerusalem, is a noted scholar, author and teacher.

Born in New York City in 1937, in 1969 Rabbi Rakeffet moved with his wife, Malkah, and his family to Israel. This followed seven years as a *rosh yeshiva* at Yeshiva University and as the spiritual leader of the first Orthodox synagogue in suburban Essex County, Congregation Beth Ephraim of Maplewood and South Orange, New Jersey. A 1959 *summa cum laude* graduate of Yeshiva college, he earned three degrees from Yeshiva University's Bernard Revel Graduate School, including his doctorate in 1967. Rabbi Rakeffet was ordained by the University's affiliate Rabbi Isaac Elchanan Theological Seminary (RIETS) in 1961. He was also ordained by the mashgiach of RIETS, Rabbi Jacob Lessin.

Rabbi Rakeffet was a pioneer in Torah education for diaspora students in Israel. He was a member of the initial faculty of Jerusalem's Torah College for Men (B.M.T.) in 1969, and taught there for twenty years. He also taught at Machon Gold and Michlalah. He is currently a founding faculty member at Midreshet Moriah, an advanced Torah study program for women.

Rabbi Rakeffet's primary association is with Yeshiva University's Caroline and Joseph S. Gruss Institute in Jerusalem. He has been a *rosh yeshiva* in this program since its inception in 1978. Among his teachings at the Gruss Kollel is a five year course on the world of his mentor Rabbi Joseph B. Soloveitchik.

Rabbi Rakeffet wrote numerous entries for the Encyclopaedia Judaica in his capacity as a staff editor. He is the author of *Bernard Revel: Builder of American Jewish Orthodoxy*, the biography of Rabbi Bernard Revel, the first president of Yeshiva and Yeshiva college. Dr. Rakeffet also authored *The Silver Era: Rabbi Eliezer Silver and His Generation* about the life and times of Rabbi Eliezer Silver. Both these volumes have gone through two editions. In 1997, he published two volumes of *Rakafot Aharon,* a collection of published scholarship in the realms of Halakhah and Jewish history.

Rabbi Rakeffet was very active in the teaching of Torah behind the Iron Curtain during the last decade of the Soviet Union. He was also a founding board member of the Jerusalem-based Shvut Ami International Center for Russian Jews.